AMOLE
One More Time

Rocky Mountain News columnist Gene Amole reads the *News* on the front steps of his childhood home in Denver. His grandfather taught him to read with the newspaper and a magnifying glass. "Glenn Asakawa/*Rocky Mountain News*"

AMOLE
One More Time

Gene Amole

Johnson Books
BOULDER

Published in the United States by Johnson Books, a division of Johnson Publishing Company, 1880 South 57th Court, Boulder, Colorado 80301.

9   8   7   6   5   4   3   2

Cover design by Debra B. Topping
Cover photograph, courtesy of the Oxford Hotel

Library of Congress Cataloging-in-Publication Data
Amole, Gene, 1923–
    Amole one more time / Gene Amole.
        p.   cm.
    ISBN 1-55566-217-X (paper)
    1. Denver Region (Colo.)—Social life and customs.   2. Rocky
Mountains Region—Social life and customs.   3. United States—Social life
and customs.   4. Denver Region (Colo.)—Social conditions.
5. Rocky Mountains Region—Social conditions.   6. United States—Social
conditions—1980–   7. Amole, Gene, 1923– .   I. Title.
F784.D445A45   1998
978.8'83—dc21   98-3203
                                                                                                    CIP

Printed in the United States by
Johnson Printing
1880 South 57th Court
Boulder, Colorado 80301

♻ Printed on recycled paper with soy ink

For my daughters, Muffy and Susan
my sons, Brett and Jon
and for my grandson, Jacob

Contents

Introduction

The guy at the service station looked at my credit card and said, "Are you the Gene Amole who writes for the *Rocky Mountain News*?"

"Yes," I answered tentatively, feeling some apprehension at what was coming next.

"There's one thing I don't understand," he continued. "Does the *News* pay you, or do you pay the *News*?"

Let me tell you, it's a humbling experience when a reader can't tell the difference between an advertisement and your personal commentary. I suppose, though, that not everyone understands the relationship between the columnist and the newspaper where he works.

I can't speak for all columnists, only for myself. But my opinions are my own and are not controlled in any way by the *Rocky Mountain News*. That was the deal when Michael Balfe Howard hired me 20 years ago. Three editors later—Ralph Looney, Jay Ambrose and Bob Burdick—that's still the deal.

There have been issues, like Denver International Airport, upon which the *News* and I have had opposite views. I rarely agree with its choice for president. I cherish this freedom, even though there have been times when I have regretted some of the things I have written.

This is the third book and probably the last collection of my columns to be published in book form. The first was *Morning*, in 1983. The second was *Amole Again*, in 1985. Frankly, I had not planned on publishing another. I am 75 now and my work as a columnist will end one of these days.

But then Steve Topping of Johnson Books approached me and *News* managing editor John Temple about putting together a new collection. That's how *Amole One More Time* was born.

It was a daunting task to go back and read the approximately 2,500 columns I had written since *Amole Again*. I pulled out about 500 I thought might work. John Temple cut the list down to about 150. He, Topping and I decided on the final 120 or so appearing in this book.

I welcomed their participation because I am not always the best judge of my work. Some things I have written that I really like were generally ignored by the readers. Others that I have "blown out my nose," as we say in this game, have proved to be popular.

I am indebted to John and Steve for their assistance and editorial judgment, to Zoe Lappin for her proofreading, and to *Rocky Mountain News* librarians Janet Boss, Carol Kasel and Leslie Parsley for their invaluable and time-consuming work in locating these columns from our clipping files and our electronic Vu-Text database.

Gene Amole
May 1998

News *and I grew up together*

I was only three when Scripps Howard purchased the *Rocky Mountain News* in 1926. You can understand, then, why I can't recall a time when the *News* and Scripps Howard were not part of my life.

In my dimmest childhood memory, I can still see myself sitting on Grandpa Will Amole's lap in the dining room of his house at 64 W. Maple Ave. We are at the head of the old dark-oak dinner table. The *News* is spread out before us under the frosted glass Tiffany shade of a heavy brass table lamp.

Grandpa had only a grammar school education, but he had great respect for learning. Long before I went to Alameda School, where my father had gone before me, Grandpa wanted me to know about the things in life he loved. We would listen together to RCA Red Seal recorded arias of Enrico Caruso and Amelita Galli-Curci played on the windup console Victrola in the corner of the sitting room. We would watch together from the third-base line bleachers of old Merchants Park while he explained squeeze-bunt baseball strategy.

The *News* figured in all of this because Grandpa used it to teach me how to read. After he had been depot master at Denver Union Station, Grandpa became the all-night switchman. He worked from 11 P.M. to 7 A.M., arriving back home on the No. 3 street car about 8 o'clock in the morning. After his breakfast of shredded wheat and Postum, he'd read the *News* at the kitchen sideboard. Then, we'd go in the dining room to look at it together.

Holding a magnifying glass in his big calloused hand, Grandpa would find the letters that spelled my name. "That's an 'A,' Bub," he would say. "Remember it looks like the roof on a house. 'A' is the first letter in our name, Amole." We'd go through the paper finding different letters until he went to bed about 9:30 or so. He would say, "Some day, Bub, you'll be able to read about Thomas Paine and Eugene Debs. Eugene is your name, too." Grandpa was a Socialist and an atheist. I never knew for sure, but I have always thought my father and I were named after Eugene Debs.

After Grandpa went to bed, Grandma Nora would let me play with empty Clark O.N.T. spools and with the wondrous button collection she kept in an ornate old tin box. When Grandpa got up in the late afternoon, sometimes we would walk up Broadway to get a strawberry ice cream cone at the creamery. After supper of boiled potatoes, pork spare ribs and sauerkraut, Grandpa would go back to work with his lunch packed in a black, metal "pie can," the laboring man's term for a lunch box. Because my mother was a teacher and my father a traveling salesman, I spent many days like that with my grandparents. They were good days.

I have often thought that Grandpa was drawn to the *News* because of its long record of concern for the little guy. He had been a working man all of his life, running away from home in Ohio when he was just 15 and coming West with a herd of breeder cattle. Like so many others of that era, he searched in vain for the mother lode in the gold fields around Victor and Cripple Creek, finally coming up empty-handed and settling down to work for the railroads for 50 years.

A newspaper's relationship with its readers is a personal one. The contact is both tactile and intellectual. There is an elusive quality about being able to touch the thing that brings you information. To see something in print seems to validate its meaning. "There it is, in black and white," is what we say when we believe something we see to be true.

Growing up, and growing old, with the *Rocky Mountain News* has been a great adventure for me. I have always cherished its fierce independence. I loved it when the *News* occasionally was irreverent, unafraid to deflate the pompous and the powerful, unable to swallow the big lie, unwilling sometimes even to take itself too seriously.

When I entered the journalism trade 50 years ago as a broadcaster, I was attracted to the *News* because it was the feisty underdog in the never-ending newspaper war. The *Denver Post* then was the influential, self-proclaimed voice of what it arrogantly designated as the Rocky Mountain Empire. The *News* was doing more than just nipping at the heels of the mighty *Denver Post*, however. With a much smaller staff of reporters and photographers, it was kicking butt on its share of big stories.

There was humanity in News stories, too. Readers felt they knew its reporters, and the people about whom they crafted their sharply written stories. What a wonderful columnist Lee Taylor Casey was! Molly Mayfield, a.k.a. Frankie Foster, the wife of editor Jack Foster, turned the town on its ear with her advice-to-the-lovelorn column. Pocky Maranzino was everyone's bon vivant man-about-town.

Bob Perkin's "One Man's Pegasus" was one of the best literary columns in the nation. We laughed at Bob Stapp's and Jack Mohler's satire. When British long-distance walker Dr. Barbara Moore walked across the United States, Foster sent Leo "Blindy" Zuckerman to accompany her when she crossed the Utah border. After a few days on the road, Leo telephoned the city desk, "You better bring me in. She is beginning to look good to me." And when she finally arrived in Denver, Max Greedy wrote an eye-popping Page-1 headline that proclaimed, "SHE'S HERE!" Max, by the way, was also the editor who pepped up a slow news day with the banner headline, "NO WAR," and another that said "WORLD IN TURMOIL."

The *News* always had a stable of scrappy reporters including Sam Lusky, Al Nakkula, Tom Gavin, Jack Gaskie, Frances Melrose, Ken Pearce, Chuck Roach, Bob Whearley, Dusty Saunders, Bill Logan, Bill Brennaman, Dave Stolberg, Betty Caldwell, Barbara Browne, Bill Miller, Ed Oschmann, Al DeCredico, Jimmy Briggs, Hank Still, Wes French, Mort Margolin, Danny Cronin, Warren Lowe and Darlene Wycoff, and sportswriters Chet Nelson, Leonard Cahn, Bob Collins, Clair Jordan, Harley Key and Manuel Boody.

The photographers were Morey Engle, Bob Talkin, Dick Davis, Bill Peery, Mel Schieltz and good old Harry Rhoads. Bob Chase was associate editor and columnist, and Vince Dwyer was managing editor. The artists were Dan Gibson and Jack Shannon. Among the copy editors were Leonard Tangney, Gene "Moon" Mullins, Paul Lilly, Hal Heffron and Greg Pearson. There were others who passed this way who deserved to be remembered but who somehow got lost in what is left of my memory.

The *News* has since evolved from a plucky little underdog to the dominant newspaper in what *The Denver Post* used to call its Rocky

Mountain Empire. We are the big dog now, but I hope we always remember how we got here. We must continue to be aggressive and fiercely independent. We must never take ourselves too seriously. We must never forget that there is no fun in the world quite like putting out a daily newspaper. I worry sometimes that our younger people forget that.

In my small contribution to our editorial product, I remind myself of those virtues every day. I am less interested in the powerful than I am in the powerless. You can have the movers and the shakers. Give me instead the people in the supermarket checkout line, or the gang in the barbershop, or the neighborhood tavern crowd, or the folks in the church, or at the PTA meeting. They are my people. I suppose in some ways I am writing my column for them and for Grandpa. I would like to think that somewhere right now is another grandpa with a little kid on his lap learning how to spell his or her name by looking through a magnifying glass at the *Rocky Mountain News*.

June 7, 1992

REASONS FOR SEASONS

Spring is comforting reminder of Mother

FUSSY.

Falling blossom petals from our crab apple trees were like pink snowflakes last Sunday. Errant breezes swirled them into the bright blue sky and then down across the grass. It was a picture-perfect day, just right for the annual planting ritual at our house.

As I nudged my cart through the aisles at Sato's Garden Center, I thought of my mother and how we always shopped together for bedding stock the week before Mother's Day. She knew precisely how many petunia plants she needed, and what kind of tomato and bell pepper plants she would put along the back fence of her old home in north Denver. Sometimes we would add a rose to her garden to replace one that didn't survive the winter. The ancient red peony plant my great-grandmother, Lizzie Fiedler, brought from Iowa to Denver at the turn of the century is still alive to remind us she passed this way. It will bloom next month.

Mom was fussy about her petunias, as was the older woman wearing a red coat I saw at Sato's Sunday. A young clerk listened respectfully as she explained that she didn't want "scraggly, stringy" petunias, but petunias that were "full, and bushy, and hardy."

Shopping for bedding stock in the spring elevates the spirit. We seem to draw warmth and friendliness from our communion with the plants. Maybe it's because we come together for a common purpose of celebrating life. My mother died several years ago, and I always feel so close to her in the spring when it is time to plant the petunias.

But my pushcart was filling with other things, too. Fantastic tomato plants, of course. There were flats of alyssum, verbena, marigolds, coleus, portulaca, ageratum, geraniums, impatiens, and about five varieties of petunias. I also had some ivy, spike grass, springer and a bunch of other stuff I can't pronounce.

I was a little early this year with my planting, but decided to go ahead after I saw Carole Harrison putting in her bedding stock in the old memorial horse trough in front of the Rocky at the triangular intersection of West Colfax, Tremont Place and 13th Street. It's on city property, but Carole maintains it at her own expense because City Hall won't. She does the same thing with the plants in front of the Denver Press Club on Glenarm Place, and the old Firehouse Museum on Tremont Place.

Kris Vogts has barrels of plants and trees at the corner of West 12th Avenue and Cherokee Street, the location of her Cherokee Bar & Grill. Kris even painted the city trash container green. It's wonderful what a few plants, a splash of paint and some imagination will do.

I finished all my planting the middle of the week after Wednesday's frost. Now, the lilacs are blooming. I am never quite sure of what finally goes in our hanging baskets, and so we are always surprised at how they turn out.

Spring is so comforting for those of us whose mothers have passed away. It is almost as though they stopped by to leave us a reminder among the flowers that they will always be with us in springtime. Every red petunia I will ever see will remind me of my mother.

The Haggerty family next door lost their lovely Jan in 1988. But for me, she is still there in those bright red, orange, white and yellow tulips in their front yard. I am sure that Pat, Kelly and Chip feel her presence there, too.

And so, for all the mothers here now, and for those forever with us in springtime among the flowers, thank you for the life and the love you have shared with us.

May 13, 1990

For sheer joy, seize the moment

ILLUMINATES.

It's nice to smell rain in the air again, to see the hint of green in the grass, to hear the first meadowlark, to watch puppies frisk along a fence, to listen for the thwop! of a baseball in a glove, to see little teal ducks fly along Bear Creek, to watch lollygagging lovers in the park, to feel young again.

Maybe it's because I am in the longer shadows of life that I cherish the coming of spring so much. It's not that winter doesn't have its charms. Naked cottonwood limbs against a somber sky are like old Brittany lace. When the foothills on the horizon are frosted with fresh snow, they seem close enough to reach out and touch.

But that is all past. It is time now for grape locusts, yellow crocuses and the first tulips to push into sunlight from the the moist, black earth. Golden forsythia will be next. Shocking pink blossoms of flowering crabapple trees will burst into life, and then it won't be long until the fragrance of April lilacs fills the air.

One of my favorite passages from the Bible is Matthew 6:28 and 6:29: "Consider the lilies of the field, how they grow; they toil not, neither do they spin. ... Even Solomon in all his glory was not arrayed like one of these."

There is loveliness in the simplest of nature's gifts. I have forgotten who said it, but it is true that there is an entire universe in a single drop of dew. Look closely at life in all its forms and you will find joy and beauty.

How sad not everyone will be aware of the subtle changes around them. The young will live forever, they believe, and are in such a hurry that they have no time to savor the moment. How many springs did I miss this way? I can't remember, but I am sorry I let so many slip away, unnoticed, unloved.

Is there a great orgiastic crescendo to life, an experience of complete joy and fulfillment as a reward for just living? I don't think so. In maturity, most of us learn to relish moments of happiness where and when we find them and to live the rest of our times as best we can.

As no two snowflakes are alike, neither are sunrises. That the sun comes up at all is enough for some, but not for me. I cherish the dawn when great streaks of gold touch downtown buildings and shimmer against their glass curtain walls.

A sunrise is something to carry through the day. Regardless of what goes wrong, or what challenges lie ahead, the memory of those first precious minutes of daylight can sustain us.

Of course the sunrise doesn't care if we watch it or not. It will keep on being beautiful even if no one bothers to look. It is not like the tree that falls silently in the forest because there is no ear to hear it. The sunrise makes no demands on us. It illuminates and blesses our lives, expecting nothing in return.

It is a time to take pleasure in small things: a single blade of grass fighting its way through a crack in the concrete, a kitten scratching at the door, the fragrance of coffee brewing in the morning, the reedy voices of children Easter morning singing "Jesus Wants Me for a Sunbeam," the soft bud of leaves on the twig of a tree branch, folks wondering if it's too early for petunias and geraniums.

And so it is spring. Let us not waste a moment of it. Look to the sky for little house finches roller-coastering from tree to tree. Revel in nature's ethereal changes. Why squander our lives waiting for what might be, or regretting what never was?

None of us knows whether this will be our last spring. Should it be, let us make the most and the best of it.

April 7, 1996

Wintry reflections on bygone Denver

SHOOTING THE DUCK.

This may not be our "winter of discontent," as Shakespeare put it in *Richard the Third*, but folks are sure crabby about it. First, it was too hot, then too cold. We didn't have enough snow, and then we had too much. Like Goldilocks, we wanted a winter that is just right. Forget it.

In the grand scheme of things, if you prepare for the worst, it probably won't happen. Last year Trish's old Buick and my old Saab wore out. Weary of digging out of driveway snowdrifts, she bought a Chevy Blazer, and I opted for a little Jeep Cherokee Sport.

Since then, the snow hasn't been deep enough to use four-wheel drive. Sometimes, though, I shift into four-wheel just to see the little light on the dash turn on.

Riding to Boulder one day with Ben Blackburn in his Blazer, he quoted fishing writer John Gierach who said: "Four-wheel drive doesn't mean you can go anywhere. It just means you get stuck in worse places."

Those of us who have been hanging around here for a long time know there is no such thing as a typical Colorado winter. It wasn't until all those newspaper editors migrated from Florida that we started taking our blizzards so seriously.

It has been unseasonably warm. The TV weather guys have been gamely predicting pleasant weather from StormCenter4. Maybe they should have a NiceWeatherCenter4.

Winter was fun when there were just us folks around. The cops would rope off streets with hills so kids could go sledding on their Flexible Flyers. Now, the politicians sand the streets just as the flakes begin to fall, fearing angry citizens will throw them out of office and they will have to get honest work.

When we still lived in Bear Valley, I had a couple of old Flexies hanging in the garage. On cold nights before the sand trucks came in the morning, I'd go whizzing alone down South Depew from Yale to Amherst. Ever watch an old man go bellywhopping?

Another fun thing you can't do anymore is ice skate on city lakes. Insurance liability rates are too high. When we lived on South Corona Street, the Wash Park lake was a couple of blocks away. Ask kids today what it's like to crack-the-whip or shoot-the-duck, and they don't have a clue.

On cold nights, there'd be a fire by the boat house so kids could warm up after cracking the whip and shooting the duck, and maybe even waltzing on rink skates with Lila Lee Butcher.

Winter is easier now that we have natural gas for heat. Denver homes were heated by coal furnaces for years. Anthracite coal went for about $5 a ton, delivered to your front yard. Bituminous was cheaper but smokier.

We'd have to wheelbarrow it back to the coal chute in back. Denver had a black cloud instead of Dick Lamm's brown cloud. There was air pollution long before Lamm was a gleam in his daddy's eye.

We thought we had died and gone to heaven when coal stokers came on the market. They automatically fed ground coal into the furnace. We didn't have to bank the fire at night so it would still be burning in the morning.

Stoker coal was more efficient. It left only clinkers instead of the ashes we dumped in ash pits by the alley in our back yards. We also used ash pits to burn our trash. Garbage? We had no disposers then. The city actually made money on our garbage by selling it to hog growers for feed. You didn't know that?

Quote: "Sometimes it snows in Denver, and sometimes it doesn't."—Bill Gallo.   *February 19, 1995*

The good old summertime

LISTEN TO THE ECHOES.

"Here's that band again! Good evening, ladies and gentlemen, this is Starr Yelland. From the Trocadero Ballroom of beautiful Elitch Gardens, the summer home of America's big-name bands, it's the music of Dick Jurgens! To get our dance party under way, the ensemble joins the inimitable Harry Cool for the toe-tapping 'One Dozen Roses.'"

That was a summer night 50 years ago on KOA. Over at KLZ, it went something like this: "From out of the night, it's the music of Ted Weems and his orchestra with vocal stylings of Perry Como! Good evening, ladies and gentlemen, this is Mack Switzer speaking to you from El Patio Ballroom at Lakeside Amusement Park, overlooking beautiful Lake Rhoda. Ted gives the downbeat, and here is whistler Elmo Tanner and 'Heartaches.'"

But if you were downtown, you could hear C.C. Rider at Benny Hooper's place and Fine and Mellow at the Rossonian Lounge in Five Points. At the old La Bonita, "Manana Me Voy, Manana Me Voy de Aqui" was served up with the menudo. If you lived in Globeville, Swansea or Elyria, you might have been kicking up your heels to "Whoopee" John Wilfhart's polka music.

Other sounds from the deep past would be the "clop clop" of an ancient horse pulling a vegetable wagon through Denver alleys. An old Italian man would rein the horse to a halt, climb from the seat of the wagon, and would holler through cupped hands, "Veg-a-ta-BULES! Veg-a-ta-BULES!"

You could hear backdoor screens slamming as women walked

out of kitchens and into the alley to see what was fresh that day. The old man rolled up the canvas sides to the wagon to display rows of sweet corn, bunches of radishes, green onions, small cucumbers for pickling, thin-skinned tomatoes and leafy Swiss chard that would be steamed in bacon grease and served with chopped raw onions at dinner that night. The women gossiped some, then filled their aprons with the produce and went back inside to listen to Vic and Sade and Mary Marlin on the radio.

People from all over town took the No. 5 streetcar to Wash Park to swim in the lake. There were always a few kids on the bank of the lily pond, using bits of fresh beef liver to catch crawdaddies. Out on the neighborhood sidewalks little girls were skipping rope and chanting, "Down by the ocean, down by the sea, Johnny broke a bottle and blamed it on me."

Old men stopped by the Broadway Creamery for all the buttermilk they could drink for a nickel. Old women picked choke cherries and wild plums along the banks of Cherry Creek and carried them home in brown paper grocery sacks.

Circle Drive ladies wearing fussy hats had lemonade and watercress sandwiches at Daniels & Fisher's tearoom. Blue-collar guys were hanging out at "George the Chinaman's" at 19th and Champa streets. On bawdy Curtis Street were the Empress, Rialto, Isis, Tabor and Victory theaters. The Denham was over on 18th, and the Orpheum was on Welton. And of course the Denver was across 16th Street from the Paramount.

Baur's on Curtis Street was serving ice cream sodas and chocolate tortes. Soft chimes signaled floor walkers in the Denver Dry. On a summer afternoon, 16th Street pedestrians could smell expensive perfume just by walking past Neusteters' open doors. There was the strong odor of medicine in the lobby of the Republic Building. And there was the pleasing aroma of freshly polished mahogany inside the dark and cool showrooms of the original American Furniture Co.

At dusk, teen-age lovers necked in Model-A Ford rumble seats on Inspiration Point. Little boys would go to the park to chuck donies at the bats zig-zagging across the sky. If the day's heat had shimmered into the night, sometimes Dad would take the family to a drive-in for root beer floats, or maybe to that place that served Cream Port, a dark, sweet, carbonated beverage that was supposed to taste just like port wine.

11

Back home, you knew it was almost bedtime when Amos and Andy came on the radio and a small voice cried out in the darkness, "Ollie, Ollie oxen free!" The kids would lie back on the front lawn for a few minutes and fill their eyes with the Milky Way, a great splash of starry light across the summer sky that would disappear from urban view in the next 50 years. The night birds became quiet, and then crickets began to rasp away at the night.

We slept.

September 2, 1990

If it's October, I'm in the mood for love

REJOICING.

There is no month so welcome as October. Its magic heightens awareness. Maybe it's the chill in the air that draws us closer together.

Hard to put into words. The October sky is brighter, bluer. The foothills seem closer, almost like scenery for a stage play. In the distance, Canada geese honk and wheel into great formations along ancient flyways.

Frost edges into the city, turning locust trees along Cherry Creek golden and touching sumacs with crimson in old north Denver. Yellow leaves on giant cottonwoods clatter in the slightest breeze. Bohemian waxwings can't wait for fruit to dry on ornamental crabapple trees. Cottontails hunch low in the shelter of long grass.

Watch kaleidoscoping clouds race along the horizon. A wisp of wood smoke briefly scents the air. Clusters of children with day packs wait for Blue Bird school buses. From open church windows on warm Sundays, reedy-voiced choirs "come rejoicing, bringing in the sheaves."

I love October.

I love an autumn morning because it is the innocent time of day. I love crisp, red Jonathan apples, cold pumpkin pie, tiny bedsheet ghosts at my door, pot roast simmering in the kitchen, slipping into a favorite old sweater, the moon close enough to touch, that first cup of hot cocoa, cattails and pussy willows in the marsh, lopsided pumpkin faces, crayon witches and goblins on refrigerator doors.

I love bronze sunsets, whirlpools of swirling leaves, memories of our dog Oreo frisking along the fence, a Tony Hillerman mystery by the fireplace, the tiny hand of a child in mine, the whistle of a rooster pheasant exploding from tumbleweeds, pulling a familiar old comforter under my chin at night.

I love downtown people scurrying from the 5 o'clock chill, the boathouse reflection in Wash Park's Smith Lake, jumping-jack high school football players, soldiers going home on furlough, the Colorado Symphony playing Dvorak, fruit cellars with put-up chili sauce and bread-and-butter pickles.

I love a mug of hot cider, grilled ham steak with fried hominy, laughing long distance with old soldiers about how we survived, wishing we could still burn leaves in the front yard, not worrying about the Broncos anymore, waiting to be a grandpa, feeling lucky I have such a wonderful wife and family.

I love watching our cat Jim sleeping in the rocking chair, listening to a compact disc of Ellyn Rucker, reading again Tom Ferril's *My Strange Encounter With Lily Bull Domingo*, showing up each day in the newsroom, remembering Mom and Pop when they were young and full of fun, walking along a frosted stubble field, watching hawks soar in updrafts, Edith Piaf's "Feuilles Mortes."

I love hand-knit afghans, afternoon naps on the couch, Charlie Parker with strings, kids selling candy bars for their schools, old guys having coffee at McDonald's, melting butter on a slice of fresh-baked banana bread, the Marston Slopes owl, Ravel's *Daphnis et Chloe*, Billie Holiday singing "My Man."

I love King Soopers checkers, Halloween candy corn, my ancient plaid Pendleton jacket, having lunch with old KVOD pals, Cole Porter's "Easy To Love," City Park at dusk, Red Mountain Pass when aspens turn, remembering those who sleep at Fort Logan, Tom Gavin's old newspaper columns, "A little song, a little dance, a little seltzer in the pants."

I love it all.   *October 15, 1995*

When Halloween was up my alley

MISCHIEF.

I can't wait until Halloween is over. It's not the little squirts coming to the door I dislike. They are fun. It's all the horror movies that have been drenching the television channels in faux blood I don't like. Each year, Halloween decor gets gorier and gorier.

Pardon me if I seem like a priss, but I don't find replicas of body parts or disemboweled torsos amusing. A cardboard skeleton or an imitation ghost isn't in bad taste, but most of the other contemporary Halloween decor is disgusting.

All of which reminds me of how much Halloween has changed. Little kids have always gone from door to door for treats. When you answer the door, they routinely chant, "Trick or treat," which I suppose originally meant that if you didn't come up with a treat, the kids would play a trick on you.

That's not the way it was back in the 1930s. We'd knock on the door and when it was opened, we'd say, "Handout!" The reason was that during the Depression, the great army of the unemployed fanned out across the country and would go to residential areas and ask for "handouts."

When they came to our door, we weren't much better off than they were. But my mother would always come up with something, even if it was only a bread-and-jelly sandwich. It was only natural that we would ask for a handout on Halloween when we went door to door.

Oh, it was always a time for mischief. About the dirtiest trick we would play would be to upset the garbage can on top of the ash pit in the alley at the rear of the house. World War II and technology ended all that.

It must have been about 1950 or so that garbage disposers went on the market. Until then, the city made money out of garbage. Bids were called each year to see which company would pay the most to pick up the garbage. The garbage was really sold to the hog growers for feed. You didn't know that?

Eventually, ordinances were passed that made the installation of garbage disposers mandatory. Soon, there were no more garbage cans to upset on Halloween. They became as obsolete as outdoor privies that kids a generation earlier would upend on Halloween.

Oh, yes, the garbage cans sat on the ashpits in the alley. Folks heated with coal in those days and the ashes and "clinkers" from the furnace were put in the ashpits. But then heating with natural gas or electricity replaced coal because of air pollution. And so the ash pit became obsolete, too.

World War II also meant the end of the residential alley. Developers found they could jam more houses on land and make more money selling them to veterans by eliminating alleys. When the alley disappeared, so did separate garages at the rear of homes.

Now the garages are in the front of homes. This made them look, as I heard once on National Public Radio, like places were automobiles live and keep people as their pets. Now, we put our trash in front of the house because there are no more alleys.

Pity. I always liked alleys. When I was a little kid on West Maple Avenue, we had two alleys in our block, one running east and west and the other north and south.

The only other Halloween mischief I can remember was soaping windows with scraps of hand soap. No real harm was done. It just made people wash their windows and the soap was already on them.

Boo! *October 31, 1996*

One holiday that's still just a holiday

DOORBUSTERS.

Let's hear it for Sarah Josepha Hale, author of "Mary Had a Little Lamb" and the journalist who persuaded Abraham Lincoln to make Thanksgiving Day a national holiday. She wrote articles promoting it in America's first publication for women, *Woman's Magazine.*

I suspect, however, that there are some women right this minute trying to get a 23-pound turkey into a 20-pound pan who wish Sarah had minded her own business.

On balance, though, most of us cherish the day. We do at our house.

It's my favorite holiday. I like it because it's simple. The idea is to celebrate our blessings by getting the family together for a big turkey dinner. No gifts. No guilt trips. No fireworks. It has remained relatively free of commercial influence.

President Franklin Roosevelt did cave in to retailers in 1939, when he pushed Thanksgiving Day back one week to extend the Christmas shopping season.

Since then, the annual shopping frenzy begins the day after Thanksgiving, as it will tomorrow. But for today, there is the rich aroma of turkey in the oven and the sound of football from the family room TV.

Thanksgiving is probably the only holiday that has retained its meaning.

Presidents Day, Martin Luther King Day, Independence Day, Memorial Day, Christmas, Easter, Labor Day and all the rest have simply become excuses not to work.

We jimmy around with their exact dates so we can have three-day weekends.

In February, citizens reflect on the accomplishments of George Washington and Abraham Lincoln by heading to the ski slopes. The contemporary meaning of Easter is to shop for a new spring wardrobe.

Christopher Columbus rates a three-day weekend, at least for government workers. We know he was born in in 1451 and died in 1506. We don't know the exact dates, so we honor (or condemn) him on the second Monday in October.

I have always thought it interesting that when Christmas falls on Sunday, we can't celebrate it then because Sunday is set aside for worship. Not being able to celebrate a religious holiday on a religious day, we take the day off Monday.

Memorial Day, or Decoration Day as we used to call it, is no longer necessarily on May 30. We move it to the nearest weekend to give us three days away from work so we can go camping while we honor those who served in the War Between the States.

We luck out in 1994 because Memorial Day will actually fall on May 30, which, incidentally, is also Tom Gavin's birthday.

Depending on which calendar you use, there are about 98 holidays or observances we celebrate every year. We keep adding more all the time.

16

Just glancing at that, one would think that our national preoccupation is to find excuses for not going to work.

Maybe we ought to have an annual All Sloth's Day to honor the habitually lazy among us.

But good old Thanksgiving Day remains on Thursday, like a rock. There are very few red-tag sales, doorbusters, sell-a-brations or inventory clearances on Thanksgiving Day.

Somehow its meaning hasn't been distorted by the almighty dollar. It really is a day to be thankful.

At the top of my list is our family. I can't imagine my life without Trish, or my sons and daughters. Later today, we'll do justice to the 23-pound bird in the oven and be grateful for the bounty in our lives. *November 25, 1993*

Hold that sweet cologne and stuff those gloves

DEAR SANTA:

Understand, I hate to be picky, but I was wondering if I could give you my list of things I don't want for Christmas. Look at it as something I can do to lighten your burden.

I get stuff I don't want, don't need and won't use. These kinds of gifts are usually purchased during the last-minute shopping frenzy when folks literally throw money at clerks for gimmicky crud that no one really wants.

Topping my list again this year is men's cologne. Even Eddie Bauer has a new scent he is promoting, and I notice the Brut people are pushing the smelly stuff this year, too. "Men are back!" Brut proclaims. What does that mean? I didn't know we had been away.

The woman in the English Leather TV commercials says her man wears English Leather or "nothing at all." I don't know what that means, either, but she seems to be sending some kind of erotic message that she wants her guy to wear English Leather or get naked, or both.

What I secretly do with a cologne gift is dribble a little of the sissy stuff down the drain each morning when I shave until the bottle is empty. Lord knows I certainly don't want to come into the newsroom smelling like a bleeping gardenia.

Women don't understand shaving lotion. They believe we use it because we like the way it smells. But you and I know that good shaving lotion, like bay rum or Pinaud's Lilac Vegetal and Clubman, has therapeutic value. I was introduced to Lilac Vegetal when I got my first barber shave years ago in Walt Miller's shop in the old Oxford Hotel.

And Santa, hold off again this year on Isotoner gloves. I don't care what Miami Dolphins quarterback Dan Marino says about them; they may look nice, but I don't like them. The only time you see Isotoner gloves advertised or on display is during the last few shopping days before Christmas.

Oh, yes, thanks again for not bringing me a cellular telephone last year for Christmas. I have never heard any good news on a conventional telephone, and I suspect I wouldn't get any on a cellular phone, either.

Some companies are giving away cellular telephones when you purchase something else. That's sneaky. Once they hook you with a cellular phone, you'll use the fool thing and your phone bill will get outrageous. Carry around a cellular phone and you will lose your privacy.

Please don't give me red socks this year. Right after Trish and I were married, she gave me a pair. I don't know why. Maybe it was because movie star Van Johnson always wears red socks. Maybe she thought I would look like Van Johnson if I wore red socks, but it didn't work. I resembled Van Johnson only from the ankles down.

You can add soap-on-a-rope to my list of unwanted gifts. Put anything that requires a rechargeable battery on my list, too.

Ties. Boy, oh, boy, you have to be very careful when you give a man a tie. Women select ties that they would wear themselves. It's awful to get a chintzy floral tie as a gift and then be forced to wear it to work.

"Why is it you never wear the tie I gave you for Christmas?" she asks. "You don't like it? You said you liked it. I told you you could exchange it if you didn't like it."

That's my list, Santa. If any of this stuff shows up in my stocking, there'll be no cookies and milk for you, big guy.

December 12, 1993

18

THINGS AIN'T WHAT THEY USED TO BE

Note to boomers: Try saving string

GOALS.

We certainly meant no harm. Those of us who were parenting the baby boom thought we were "just doin' what comes naturally," as the old song went. But if you have been reading the newspapers, you are aware of how frustrated our progenies have become. That's quite a problem since my generation cranked out 78 million boomers, or one baby every 7 seconds, from 1946 to 1964.

"The great American reproduction frenzy," as Steve Chawkins called it in our *Rocky Mountain News* baby-boom series, had less to do with passion than it did with keeping up with the Joneses. That's the way it was in University Hills where a significant number of local boomers were conceived.

My generation seemed to be responding to some kind of unwritten rule that we produce 3.2 kids per family. I have no explanation for this except to suggest that maybe we were unconsciously trying to replace the millions of people we had killed during World War II.

In any event, our children have reached maturity, and many of them are depressed that they have not been able to accomplish either what my generation did or those goals they have set for themselves. Poor babies!

Strike, that. I do not wish to be an old fuddy about this. I am the first to admit there were distinct advantages to being born when I was. Two of the most important were the GI Bill and FHA loans. In fairness, it should be added that some of us had to go to hell and back to get them.

However, millions of us were educated and housed because of these programs, both of which were developed and passed into law by the Democratic Party. The great irony is that the chief beneficiaries of those programs were enriched to the point that they could move to the suburbs where they became Republicans. I leave the explanation of this phenomenon to others.

The two events that shaped my life were the Great Depression and World War II. It was because of them I embraced what I have come to call "my three negative goals." When I got home from the war with all my arms, legs, fingers and toes, I solemnly promised myself I would never again be cold, hungry or frightened. I did not concern myself with a membership in a country club.

As children of the Depression years, my generation is offended by today's disposable society. It seems terribly wrong to us to throw away a no-deposit-no-return bottle. I came from people who saved string, tinfoil, buttons, rubber bands and coat hangers. The only people who care about those things now are the refugee Vietnamese. Keep your eye on them. While some worry about a lack of material fulfillment, the Viets will find a way to get ahead.

One generation cannot really be compared to another. But I do feel there are no guarantees and that life's goodies are not entitlements. There are still rewards in the good old U.S. of A. for those who know how to use the intangibles of thrift, determination, imagination and hard work.   *January 23, 1986*

Name dropping stirs memories

REMEMBER:

Cream Port; Marcus Motors; El Patio Ballroom; Edelweiss; Pell's Oyster House; Pick-A-Rib; Red and White Stores; Larry Robar; Cosmopolitan Hotel; Lake Russian Baths; *South Side Monitor*; The Golden Lantern; Murphy's Chili Parlor; Lantz Laundry; Orpheum Theater; Blue Parrot Inn; Beacon Supper Club; Telenews Theater; Yacht Club; Windsor Hotel; Band Box; Benny's Basement; *Meet the Boys in the Band*; Milt Shrednik; *The Denver Post* operas; Saliman's Deli; Shaner's Bar; Blackie Mazza; Boys' Market; PenCol Drug; Wade's Keg; Berg's Candies; George Begole; Merchants Park; Chez Paree; Miss Helen; Albany Hotel; Abe Pollock; Rossonian Lounge; Inspiration Point; Robin's Next; Men of the West; John Gilbert Graham; Red Wing Cafe; Hop Alley; Piedmont Hotel; Queen Theater; Tivoli Terrace; The

Golden Eagle; Otto Floto; West Side Court; Assembly Bar and Grill; *Cervi's Journal*; Rialto Theater; Ringside Lounge; Manhattan Restaurant; *Empire Magazine*; Citizen's Mission; Sam's Numbers 2, 3, 4 and 5; Ellie Weckbaugh.

Or, the Shirley Savoy Hotel; Rockin' with Leroy; Jack Carberry; National AAU Basketball Tournament; the Tabor Grand; Save-A-Nickel stores; Urit Jory's Drug Store; Dan Thornton; Denham Theater; Elmer Slater's Barber Shop; Roosevelt Bar and Grill; Goodheart Laundry; Molly Mayfield; Neusteters; Lazy Lloyd Knight; Miller Super Markets; Clark's Drug Store; George Kolowich; Capitol College of Pharmacy; Carlson Frink Dairy; Murphy Mahoney Chevrolet; *Johnny Timberline*; Swayne-Marsh-Wimbush; Basil Swank; Republic Building; Victory Theater; Pearl O'Laughlin; *Roundup*; The Trocadero; Mizpah Arch; Aeroplane Ballroom; Eddie Ott's Sherman Plaza; Coors malted milk; Boggios; Highlander Boys; Eat-A-Pig; Dawn Patrol; Weber Theater; Edith Eudora Kohl; Broadway Theater; Baur's; Larry Tajiri; Purity Creamery; Colorado Women's College; Holiday Drive-Ins; Frosted Scotchman; Werner's Delicatessen; Pioneer Village; the old Denver Club building; *Ching Chow*; Isis Theater; Denver Drumstick restaurants; Denver Dry Goods Co.; the Navarre; the Rev. Harvey Springer; Arcade Pool Hall; Taylor's Supper Club; Broadway Creamery; Green's Drive-In; Wolhurst Country Club; Ray Perkins; Red Owl Stores; Henritze's; Windsor Players; Manhattan Beach; Empress Theater; Progress Plunge; Boettcher kidnapping.

How about the Rainbow Ballroom; Alameda Theater; Zang's Ice Cream; Rockybilt hamburgers; Tivoli bock beer; Jack Gilmore; Kiowa and Navajo Studios of KFEL; Park Lane Hotel; Lou Coffee's Steak House; Piggly Wiggly Stores; *Treasure Trails of Melody*; Harry Bramer's Bar; Lee Casey; The Loop; Marvene; Interocean Hotel; Lund's Pancake House; Keables' Sandwich Shops; Pelican Bar; *Yampa Valley Mail*; Art Bazata; Pistol Pete; Silver Glade Room; Loretto Heights College; Spiderman; Rush to the Rockies; Fred 'n Fae; Matt Skorey Packard; Mozart Cafe; Bruce Gustin; Morey Mercantile Co.; Brecht candies; Walters beer; Doug and Willie; Blue Lake; Jack Guinn; *Uncle Gene and Holly*; Donnelly James; Lande's; Westminster Law School; El Paso del Norte; or the Denver Bears?

April 21, 1988

21

Old, lonely need our help to bloom

ISOLATED.

Now that it is spring, old folks venture from the shadows into the warm sunlight. It is a special time because it may be their last April. Some sit and listen, and look and recall other Aprils when colors were brighter, sounds were clearer and images were sharper.

Time may have blurred their senses, but it has left precious memories intact. Behind their eyes are lifetimes. Families and friends are gone. They sit alone and unnoticed on 16th Street Mall benches. They walk carefully along park pathways.

They are invisible because we refuse to see them. Are we so absorbed with ourselves that we don't have time for people who have worked their way through the last of life's illusions? Do we ignore them because they are our future, and we don't like what we see?

When I was 14, a friend and I would ride our bikes to visit his grandmother, who lived alone in a little house on Eliot Street. It became a sort of Saturday ritual, instituted by my friend's mother.

We didn't mind going, though, because the old woman would let us back her Model-A Ford out of the garage and run the motor for a while to keep the battery charged. It hadn't been driven since her husband died.

The one thing about our visits I remember most clearly was that my friend would always bring cigarette butts to her that his father had discarded. He carried them in a little brown paper sack.

The first time I went to her house, I thought she was going to smoke them, but my friend whispered that she didn't smoke. She took us into the kitchen and gave us some sugar cookies. She fixed a cup of Postum for herself.

The floor was covered by green linoleum that was worn and cracked. We sat at a white metal sideboard beside the sink. It was one of those mail-order kind that had drawers, a flour bin, cabinets underneath and a top that slides out.

There was an old-fashioned coal stove on the other side of the kitchen. Hanging on the wall in a dime-store frame was a rotogravure newspaper photograph of Charles Lindbergh. The caption under it said "Lucky Lindy." He was seated with his helmet and goggles in his lap. The boyish aviator was looking into the distance as though he were contemplating another adventure in the clouds.

After we had put the Model-A in the garage, we went back inside to say goodbye. She had taken a couple of the cigarette butts and placed them on the edge of the stove where they were smoldering.

As my friend and I pedaled back across Federal Boulevard for home, he explained that she burned the cigarettes on her stove because the smell of the tobacco made it seem to her as though her husband was still alive and was having a smoke in the kitchen.

When I see old people alone and isolated all these years later, I think of my friend's grandmother. I will always remember her in her rocking chair and the cigarette smoke curling up from the stove in front of Lucky Lindy.

Why does wisdom have to come so late? Two kids were about her only contact with the outside world. We didn't know exactly what to say to her when we were there. We spent more time sitting in that old Model-A than we did with Lucky Lindy and her in the kitchen.

She didn't last many more Aprils. My friend's father inherited the Model-A. I don't know what happened to the picture of Lucky Lindy.

April 2, 1991

Looking back: A quiet moment opens curtain on a magical past

One of my favorite noon-time diversions is to sit alone on one of the 16th Street Mall benches. I close my eyes and try to remember the way downtown was 50 years ago. I can still hear streetcars clanging their way from one intersection to the next.

The traffic cop at 16th Street and Champa was Dominic Crow. His brother, Silver Crow, whistled the cars along at the California Street intersection, and big Mike Carroll was calling the shots at 16th and Stout streets. They were gregarious men, calling many people by name, as traffic would ebb and flow.

The strollers were the window shoppers. The people who walked briskly were downtown workers who didn't have time to look in the concave display windows of Gano Downs on Stout Street, or at the mannequins stiffly posed in the May Co. windows on Champa Street.

There was a medicinal smell in the lobby of the Republic Building where elevators whooshed patients to doctors' and dentists' offices in the floors above. The seductive aroma of expensive perfume came though the open doors of Neusteter's. Inside, stylish clerks dressed in black maintained a special dignity as they coolly advised their customers on the business of beauty.

In the Denver Dry, soft chimes signaled secret messages to floor walkers and department heads. And on the top floor Tea Room, shoppers paused to lunch on chicken croquettes and deviled crab.

Across 15th Street, on California, was the wonderful Home Public Market. Inside, the senses were seduced by the smells of fresh bread, roasting coffee and smoked herring.

It was a sad day when the old market closed to make way for *The Denver Post*, which moved from its old "Bucket of Blood" plant between 15th and 16th on Champa Street. The building is empty now, hollowly waiting to be the site of a 1,000-room convention hotel. On the front of the building are the words, "O Justice, when expelled from other habitations, make this thy dwelling place." You can look through the dirty windows, but you won't see any justice inside.

The other downtown market was the Loop Market at 15th and Arapahoe Streets where all the downtown streetcars turned around. It was right across the street from the Central Bank and Trust Co., enabling working people to do their banking and their grocery shopping on a tramway transfer.

Joe "Awful" Coffee, owner of the Ringside Lounge on lower 17th Street, would shadow box with you as he escorted you to a booth for dinner. A former bantam-weight boxer, Coffee had a terrible voice but insisted on jumping up on tables and singing operatic arias.

The real opera singers were working at Mario's on Tremont Place. On any given night, you could hear the sextet from *Lucia* or the quartet from *Rigoletto* while you swirled your pasta. Around the corner at Shaner's on 17th Street young crew-cut bucks played kneesies with classy Van Schaack stenos while Johnny Smith played "Moonlight in Vermont" on the guitar. Timmy Shaner stirred a very arid martini.

If you were ordering flowers, Ardelt's, next to the Cosmopolitan Hotel, had lovely carnations, giant purple orchids and long-stem American

Beauty red roses. Inside the hotel, when bell captain Robert Stapp snapped his fingers, a "front boy" was there to carry your luggage.

When Pete Smythe snapped his fingers in the Silver Galde Room, his society band began to play "Oh Johnny, Oh Johnny, How You Can Love." In the Pioneer Room, maitre d' Max Hummle commanded a corps of immaculate waiters and busmen. Across Broadway at the Brown Palace Hotel, manager Harry Anholt traveled all of Europe to obtain art objects to decorate the beautiful Palace Arms Room.

At 16th and Broadway, the Shirley Savoy Hotel was the "official" headquarters of both political parties. The Shirley Tavern was where free-spending lobbyists plied legislators with Dewars White Label to have their way with them. At the Albany Hotel bar, it didn't matter what you ordered, Johnny Megill would pour you a double.

Clark's Drug Store in the Albany poured the richest, thickest chocolate shakes in Denver. The "Mayor of 17th Street" was Danny Abeyta, whose shine parlor was right next door. Every morning, bookies, horse players, stock brokers and other gamblers lined up for a Kiwi luster on their Florsheims while Danny's wife blocked Stetsons at the rear of the store.

I was a member of the Dawn Patrol, an irreverent band of sports writers and broadcasters who had the center table late every night at Charles Suchnotzki's Edelweiss restaurant on Glenarm Place. Over pork chops and eggs, we'd second guess Denver Bears manager Andy Cohen's pitching strategy, sometimes until 3 A.M.

During the early 1930s, we escaped blistering summer heat by attending the air-conditioned matinees at the Denver, Paramount, Broadway, Orpheum and Denham theaters. There was no air conditioning on bawdy Curtis Street, but there was plenty of glitter on marquees of the Empress, Isis, Rialto and Victory theaters. You could smell Coney Islands and fried onions passing by Sam's No. 3, the place where George Armatas invented his famous Curtis Street chili.

"George the Chinaman" owned the diner at 19th and Champa, across the street from the old Post Office garage. Truck drivers were the clientele of the Milwaukee Tavern at 18th and Curtis and also at the Paris Inn at 19th and Lawrence.

Like a faded bag lady from another century, the old Tabor theater survived on a diet of "B" movies. Stripped away was the grandeur Horace had invested in his "opera house" during the silver boom.

Across the street was the Old Customs House, where thousands of us were inducted into wartime military service.

Lower downtown was anchored by the Windsor Hotel, a replica of Windsor Castle in London. The grand staircase to the second-floor ballroom was spectacular. In later years it became a flop house, just one step above the Rev. Earnest Baber's Citizen's Mission where railroad Gandy dancers sang "Bringing in the Sheaves" for slumgullion stew and day-old bread.

The old downtown may be gone from view, but it is still a magical mosaic of memory. *September 29, 1991*

Across the alley from memories

ICE CHIPS.

It must have been right after World War II that some numbskull decided Denver wasn't going to have alleys anymore. The reason was probably economic. Developers put a slide rule to the problem and figured that by eliminating alleys they could shoehorn more houses onto their land.

The genesis of my thoughts about alleys came the other day while I was walking over to the Press Club for lunch. There was a rock on the sidewalk, and without thinking, I started to kick it forward as I walked. Why was I doing that? You know why. I was regressing to my childhood and I was kicking a Campbell soup can down an alley.

We always kicked cans coming home from school. Sometimes if we could find two condensed-milk cans, we'd stomp down on them so the bent cans would hook on our heels. That way we could really make a lot of clatter in the alley. Crunch! Crunch! Crunch!

When we lived at 64 W. Maple Ave., there were actually two alleys in our block. One of them ran north and south between Maple and Cedar. The other ran west to Acoma. Every now and then, I drive through those alleys just to see what unexpected memories rise to the surface.

Grandpa Amole used to charm a squirrel out of the backyard tree and feed him. "Jim!" Grandpa would holler. "I got something for you, Jim." In a flash, the little guy would scramble down to the ground and over to Grandpa and would nibble nuts out of his hand. Do you suppose Jim's descendants are still frisking around in the West Maple Avenue trees?

By the way, Tom Gavin lived only a few blocks away on Lincoln Street. Elitist that he is, Gavin never fails to remind me that because his house was east of Broadway, he lived in south Denver, and that because our house was west of Broadway we were poor railroad folks who lived in west Denver.

Is it possible that the dissolution of the American family began when we lost our alleys? Neighbors knew each other then because the women would meet in the alley to buy fresh produce from horse-drawn wagons owned by old Italian men. Monday was wash day and there was a lot of gossip while the mothers were hanging the laundry on the clothesline.

People planted hollyhocks and pink cosmos along back fences. Garbage cans were kept on top of the ash pits. Before the garbage disposer was invented, the city actually made money on garbage. It was privatization before its time. Hog raisers would bid on the right to pick the garbage to feed their pigs.

The icemen also used the alley. You'd leave a card in the back porch window with the number 25 or 50 on it. That way the iceman would know how much ice you needed for your ice box. He was always a big guy. He'd grab the block of ice with iron tongs and then flip it up on his shoulder where there was a heavy canvas pad. While he was in the house, kids would scramble up into the back of the truck to pick up ice chips to suck on.

Milkmen also delivered from the alley. That's when milk came in glass bottles and the cream would rise to the top. You could homogenize it yourself by just shaking the bottle. Most folks poured off the cream to use in their coffee or Postum.

You knew it was dinnertime when your ma would come out of the kitchen and onto the back porch and sing out into the alley, "Jim-ee! Din-ner! Right now! Jim-ee!"   *November 17, 1991*

Naked lovers go to a new window

THE KISS.

Have you been wondering what happened to the erotic marble statue of *Cupid and Psyche* that used to stop traffic at 920 Speer Blvd.?

Psyche was lounging back in Cupid's arms. He is kneeling behind her with his left arm cradling her bosom. Her arms are extended above her with her hands on his head as he is about to kiss her. Both are naked as jaybirds. The figures are about half life-size.

For years it was displayed in the front window of Erickson Monuments and was illuminated at night. It was the subject of columns in the *Rocky Mountain News* by Molly Mayfield and Lee Casey. One man and woman even thought of using it as a grave marker when they died but decided it might be inappropriate.

The original *Cupid and Psyche* by Antonio Canova belongs to the Louvre Museum in Paris. Like the original, the Denver version is sculpted from Carrara marble, the same marble Michelangelo used in his sculpture. The models were Napoleon's sister, Pauline Bonaparte, and a friend. "A rather close friend," Molly Mayfield observed in her column.

The copy was donated to the Denver Art Museum by the Phipps family. It was sold in 1939 to Erickson Monuments "just for cartage costs," according to Julie Hendee, the daughter of Roy Erickson, who with his brother, Milton, inherited the company from their father, Carl Erickson. Hendee now operates Erickson's Monuments with her husband, David.

Otto Karl Bach, then director of the Denver Art Museum, snorted, "Degenerate Hellenism! … Canova rated pretty high at the beginning of the 19th century and during the era that enjoyed iron deer on front lawns, but he was a weak classicist."

But was he? Robert Hughes, reviewing the Antonio Canova exhibit at the Museo Correr in Venice for the current edition of Time magazine, writes, "Long out of fashion and hard to love, Canova was nevertheless a spectacularly gifted sculptor.

"*Amor and Psyche* is the masterpiece of Canova's 'graceful' style— and by any standards, one of the most spectacular technical tours of force in the history of stone carving. … Here, the empty spaces, the holes in the white love knot of figures are as interesting as the limbs, bodies and heads."

The Metropolitan Museum of Art in New York makes do with a plaster model for its collection. The Denver marble statue is almost identical with the original except, "the draping on Psyche's thigh is a bit more revealing on the original," Hendee said.

According to Greek mythology, Venus was jealous of Psyche's beauty and ordered her son, Cupid, to kill her. But he fell in love with Psyche instead. They were separated, and when Cupid finally found her asleep beside a road, he gave her the kiss Canova immortalized in stone.

In 1983, Erickson's moved from Speer Boulevard to 1245 Quivas St., off West 13th Avenue. You can see *Cupid and Psyche* in their famous embrace there. Milton Erickson designed the Cranmer Park sundial. The company is one of only 50 members in North America of the American Institute of Commemorative Art.

Roy Erickson, who died in 1986, was a friend of mine. When the statue was displayed on Speer Boulevard, he rigged up a hidden microphone in the bushes so he could hear comments of pedestrians. His favorite was from two little boys who stopped to look. After awhile, one lad observed, "He don't have any pants on." The other boy was silent for a moment and finally said, "She don't either."

June 16, 1992

Throwaway society values fabric of old

WILD PLUM.

Running the tips of my fingers over the intricate stitching of my mother's old "Bouquet" quilt was like revisiting my childhood. Its pattern has 30 separate floral arrangements, each with 21 pieces. Examining it closely, I could remember old house dresses, aprons, curtains and cotton remnants I had seen around our house as a boy.

Trish got it out the other day and put it on our bed. I hadn't seen it since Mom died in 1985. There were four or five of her quilts in an ancient steamer trunk in the basement of our family's old north Denver home. Among them were "Wedding Ring" and "Flower Garden" quilts. We brought them home and put them away in a closet.

Seeing the quilt again made me feel close to my parents. Pop died in 1976. He figured in those quilts, too. He was selling tires for the B.F. Goodrich "tower" store at 14th Street and Glenarm Place back in the 1930s. He noticed new tires were spiral-wrapped with white fabric that had been heavily sized with a lacquer substance. When the tires were sold, the wrap was discarded. He brought some of it home one day, and Mom scrubbed out the sizing on a wash board.

Washed clean, it was a tight-weave cotton, almost like linen. She took the tire wrap and bits and pieces of cotton remnants from worn-out and discarded clothing and crafted them into beautiful quilts. Back in the Depression years, she was very good at making something useful out of practically nothing.

Pop caught the spirit, too. He invented a little device made of wood scraps and single-edge Gem razor blades to cut a number of pieces of fabric at the same time to exact measurements.

In those days we didn't think of quilts so much as heirlooms to be kept in a Lane cedar chest or used in bedrooms only when company came. We slept under them. When they wore out, Mom would just make more. Today, quilts are thought to be very special. At our house, they were just bedding.

I don't know how Mom found time to do all the things she did. She was a teacher in the Denver Public Schools. In the summer, she "put up" tomatoes and peaches, jams, jellies and bread-and-butter pickles. In a special corner of my memory is the seductive aroma of her chili sauce being canned.

She and Grandma would ride the streetcar down to Cherry Creek and pick wild plums and chokecherries from the bushes along the bank. They'd come back with big brown paper sacks filled to the tops.

If you know anything about wild plums and chokecherries, you know they are almost all seed. But boy, oh boy, when made into wild plum butter and chokecherry jelly, you'd better bake plenty of biscuits.

Mom and Grandma picked chokecherries and wild plums as routinely as folks shop at the supermarket now. It was the same thing with canning Concord grape conserve, making Siberian crab apple jelly, quilting and darning socks. No one thought much about it.

When Mom died, we found stashed away little boxes of assorted buttons, bits of fabric, rubber bands, paper sacks, balls of string and a lot of other stuff most folks throw away.

We have become a throw-away society, Mom often said. We have deluded ourselves into thinking that convenience justifies waste. We are lazy. We live in a here-today, gone-tomorrow world. Maybe that's why memories are so important.   *July 9, 1992*

Melting pot isn't melting anymore

HYPHENATED.

Have you noticed that society has lost its enthusiasm for integration? Maybe people never really wanted to be integrated in the first place. Certainly not many these days seem to share in Martin Luther King's dream "that one day this nation will rise up and live out the true meaning of its creed: 'We hold these truths to be self-evident; that all men are created equal.'"

That "one day" seems more distant now than it was when King disavowed "separatism" and challenged Americans to learn to live peacefully with each other. We don't call it separatism anymore. "Tribalism" better describes the ethnic confrontations raging as far away as the Balkan states in Europe and as close as the Columbus Day Parade in Denver.

We have become hyphenated Americans. We are African-Americans, Native-Americans, Hispanic-Americans, Irish-Americans, Italian-Americans, German-Americans and as many other kinds of Americans as there are ethnic and national origins. What we have put in the melting pot doesn't seem to be melting anymore.

It's not just here in this country. Ethnic and racial strife has spread across Europe. It was one of the unanticipated consequences of the end of the Cold War.

Once the lid came off the old USSR monolith, ancient religious and national conflicts festered anew. Ethnic cleansing is a new term for genocide.

Black Africans battle each other at the same time they are trying to expel white Africans. Sometimes it seems as though the Catholic Irish have been battling the Protestant Irish since the beginning of time.

The Arab tribes can agree on only one thing, that they hate the Jews. All Asians may look alike to Occidentals, but ask the Koreans about the Japanese, or the Cambodians about the Vietnamese. There are primordial hatreds buried in the psyches of all of them.

It is too bad that we can't have ethnic pride without ethnic hatred. There was a measure of that in Denver when I was a kid. The Bohemian people lived in Globeville, the Italians in north Denver, German Jews in east Denver, Russian and Polish Jews in northwest Denver, the Negroes (the politically correct term at the time) in northeast

Denver and the Spanish-Americans (also politically correct then) on the west side.

"We didn't know we were living in a ghetto when we were kids," a Jewish friend told me. "We just thought it was a wonderful old neighborhood where everyone knew everyone else."

Mayor Wellington Webb once told me that when he went to Manual High School, "it was mostly black, and we were proud of our school. I don't see anything wrong with that."

The recent confrontation between Italian-Americans and Native Americans was sad. Both have had identity problems. In motion pictures, the Indians, until recently, have been represented as bloodthirsty savages. The Italians have been, and still are, represented— mostly by Italian-American directors and actors—as gangsters.

I suppose this will one day run its course and we will all finally learn that we have more in common as people than the differences that divide us racially and ethnically. If Martin Luther King could enunciate his dream for us today, I don't believe it would change much. He would again disavow the separatism that now seems to hyphenate our lives.

November 1, 1992

The old Navarre warmed the bones

SPITTING.

I was walking along Tremont Place the other day when I thought I heard Peanuts Hucko playing "A Closer Walk with Thee." But my mind was playing tricks, and I was just wishing I could hear him play it again.

My little fantasy was prompted by passing the Western Art Museum at 1727 Tremont Place, formerly the Navarre, the restaurant where Peanuts entertained each night in the garden-level bar. He was on clarinet, of course. Morey Feld was playing drums, Fran Feese was on piano and either Bill Bastien or Dick Patterson was playing bass. Fran, by the way, was the musical genius behind all those wonderful Fred Arthur radio commercials a few years back.

Peanuts had been around the block several times, playing with the Will Bradley, Jack Jenny, Ray McKinley and Charlie Spivak big bands before World War II. He was drafted and assigned to the Glenn Miller Army Air Forces band. After the war, Peanuts played tenor sax briefly with Benny Goodman and jobbed around the East with the Eddie Condon and Jack Teagarden two-beat combos. He settled down in Denver as a part owner of the Navarre and married Louise Tobin, a former thrush with the Goodman band. (In the language of *Downbeat* magazine during that innocent period of political incorrectness, a "thrush" was a girl singer.)

Anyhow, the old Navarre had many incarnations. In early Denver history, the building had been used as a proper girls' school, a gambling hall and a whorehouse, in that order. Legend has it that there was a tunnel under Tremont Place linking the Navarre and the Brown Palace hotel, giving male guests easy and discreet access to pleasures of the flesh.

Johnny Ott took over the Navarre in 1946. I had forgotten what a culinary treasure it was until I stumbled across an old menu. It had 16 fresh fish entrees every day, including broiled Maine lobster for $2.75. Broiled fresh red snapper was $1.75, and broiled Columbia River salmon was also $1.75.

Ott featured cut-to-measure filet mignon or sirloins that would feed two for $5.50, which was larger than the double-size at $4.65. Prime rib was $2.25. A double cut was $3.80. A thick, pan-fried ham steak was $1.90. Either broiled or fried chicken was $1.90, as was the roast turkey dinner with stuffing.

If you wanted Chateau Lafite Rothschild to accompany your meal, it was only $10 a bottle. Mumm's Cordon Rouge or Piper Heidsieck champagne were $14. Cutty Sark, Ballantine or Martin's V.V.O. Scotch whisky were all 70 cents a pop. Coon Range, Old Overholt and Guckenheimer bourbon were 60 cents.

But what attracted me to the Navarre was the oyster stew. Lordy, when raw winter winds were whipping through downtown canyons, and the snow was spitting little white BBs in your face, how wonderful it was to slip into the old Navarre for a hot, steaming bowl of oyster stew with a pool of melted butter and a sprinkle of pepper right on top. At 70 cents, it was a complete meal with the basket of oyster crackers served with it.

I'll tell you something, pal, that oyster stew would stick to your ribs and was enough to carry you through the rest of the day. You could throw down a buck and the waiter would get a 30 cents rap and everyone was happy.

Listen! Do you hear something? It's music, and it sounds for all the world like old Peanuts Hucko and he's woodshedding "You're Nobody's Sweetheart Now."

December 10, 1992

A rolly-coaster ride down memory lane

INDELICATE.

I suppose I ought to make a ritual visit to Elitch Gardens before it closes for the year. The 105-year-old amusement park is finally moving next year from West 38th Avenue and Tennyson Street to the Central Platte Valley.

I have vivid memories of my last visit, July 27, 1978. It was that joyous day when Susan, the youngest of my four kids, was finally tall enough to ride the Twister alone. I hate roller coasters.

Sure, I pretended to like them as a kid. I would dance around my folks, pleading with them: "Please let me ride on the rolly-coaster. Pleeez, Pop, just one more time."

Secretly, they scared the daylights out of me. I put on that little charade only because I had seen other kids do it. I wanted people to think I was a thrill-seeker, but underneath all that phony bravado, I was then, and remain to this today, chicken.

Going to sleep in our old house on the north side in the summer, I could hear the roller coaster at Elitch's and its passengers shrieking their excitement into the distant night. I would close my eyes and thank the good Lord I wasn't on the damn thing.

I hated amusement park rides in general. Also etched in my memory is the senior class party at Elitch's, when classmates goaded me into taking my date on the Loop-O-Plane. You sit there, swinging in increasingly wide arcs until the contraption goes all the way around.

Then, the little cab is stopped at the top of the circle, suspending you upside down. My date fainted, hanging limply over the restraining bar like a Raggedy Ann doll.

The keys to my 1933 Chevy and my money fell out of my pockets, and I lost my glasses. A salty taste in my mouth presaged nausea.

34

When we finally got out, my date regained consciousness just in time to watch me pitch my cookies into Arnold Gurtler's petunia patch.

There are good memories, too, of crowding around the bandstand when KOA announcer Gil Verba stepped to the microphone, holding his script in one hand and cupping his ear with the other hand. "Here's that band again! Good evening, ladies and gentlemen. From the Trocadero ballroom at beautiful Elitch Gardens, it's the music of Dick Jurgens and his orchestra, with vocal stylings by Harry Cool."

My father worked as a stagehand at Elitch's summer-stock theater when he was 14. He loved to tell the story of how he and another kid worked behind the scenes in a play starring Lewis Stone. He was the actor who gained fame late in life as Judge Hardy in the Andy Hardy movies with Mickey Rooney.

Part of the play took place on a beach. To try to make the ocean look realistic, a canvas was painted blue with whitecaps. Pop and the other kid were lying on the floor under the canvas, pushing it up and down with their hands and feet to simulate waves.

You can imagine how close and hot it was under the canvas. Just as the scene was starting, either Pop or the other boy began to suffer the flatulent consequences of eating beans.

We all know how 14-year-old boys can sometimes be indelicate. So it was that hot summer afternoon. Pop and his pal became competitive, each attempting to outperform the other with even louder flatus.

Stone tried to ignore the noise and the giggling, gamely attempting to carry on as the waves became increasingly erratic. Then, the ocean suddenly becalmed as the lads stopped kicking and surrendered to the inevitable, gasping and laughing helplessly.

There's no business like show business.

August 2, 1994

Lower downtown pours on the perfume

GHOSTS.

Much of LoDo looks the same but doesn't smell the same as I remember from another time. The fancy word for historic preservation is gentrification, the influx of upper- and middle-class people into an older urban area that's being renovated.

We didn't call it LoDo until recently. I like the new name, and I certainly admire the restoration of old buildings near Coors Field.

Of course, the buildings are not being used for their original industrial purposes. That's where the smells come in. The old Morey Mercantile Co. had the aroma of roasting coffee and spices. When the Seattle Fish Co. was on Market Street, it smelled like mackerel.

Inside the Citizen's Mission on Larimer Street, you could smell boiled cabbage and disinfectant. The Rev. Ernest Baber tried to save down-and-outers. Up the street, the Gin Mill stank of old sweat, cheap booze and smoke from Bull Durham cigarette fixins.

Dana Crawford rescued part of Larimer Street from self-destruction as Denver's skid row. Still, some of the street's hockshop past remains between 20th and 23rd streets. We are also indebted to her for the restoration of the Oxford Hotel. I love that old building. Harry Truman stayed there when he came to town.

Walt Miller gave me my first haircut in the Oxford barbershop. Walt and the shop are long gone, but those heroic urinals in the basement men's room are still there.

My father worked across cobblestone 17th Street at Hendrie & Bolthoff Manufacturing and Supply Co. Grandpa Will Amole was depot master at Denver Union Station a half-block away through the Mizpah Arch. My heart still beats faster when I think of the time he lifted me to the cab of a giant steam locomotive. I could feel its power thundering under my feet.

Hobos during the Depression rode the rods into Denver. They shambled up 17th Street to look through the steamed window of McVitties restaurant and watch folks eat tenderloin steak dinners for a buck.

The really great porterhouse steaks were a specialty of the old Manhattan on Larimer Street, where French-fried onions rings were invented. Too bad Dana didn't come to town in time to save the Manhattan, the Tabor Grand Opera House and the old Windsor Hotel.

The Windsor was an imitation of Windsor Castle in England. What a magnificent lobby and grand staircase to the second-floor ballroom it had! It was embarrassing for President William Howard Taft when he got stuck in the Windsor's presidential-suite bathtub. He hollered for help until the fire department pulled him out.

LoDo is strictly white-collar and Chantilly perfume now, but it was blue-collar when I was young. Gandy dancers drifted in and out of town. They were the section hands who laid and maintained railroad tracks across the nation. They worked with tools manufactured by the old Gandy Manufacturing Co.

In the winter, the dancers flopped at the old Interocean Hotel, on 16th Street, and lived off $65 a month in "rocking chair money" from the federal government. Most of it went for "muskatoo," bottles of cheap muscatel wine in brown paper bags.

If the ghosts of those old guys are still haunting Blake, Market, Wazee, Lawrence, Arapahoe and Larimer streets, they must be surprised at how upscale and snooty lower downtown is now.

Quote: "Gimme a steak smothered with pork chops."—Frank Amole to a waitress at the Oxford Hotel coffee shop.

April 18, 1995

It's a pity manners are so out of style

QUAINT.

Mama didn't tell me life was like a box of choc-o-lates, but she did tell me how to be a gentleman. She showed me how to help a woman on with her coat, how to hold a chair for her when she sits down and how to ask her to dance. She told me that when walking with a woman on a sidewalk, I should always walk nearest the street. She explained that this was to protect her from mud splashes by passing vehicles. She said I should never interrupt someone who is speaking. She told me I should always excuse myself when leaving a room if others are present.

She told me always to open a door and permit the woman either to enter or depart first. She said never let a woman open a car door but do it for her. The man, she said, should always walk around the front of the car so she can see you at all times. Never walk around the back of the car after she has been seated.

My father instructed me on hat etiquette. When riding on an elevator and a woman gets on, step to the rear and remove your hat. When the American flag goes by in a parade, remove your hat and hold it over your heart. Always remove your hat when entering a restaurant or someone's home, he said.

I still do all that stuff, even though such manners are now considered quaint. It must have been back in the 1960s when men started

37

pushing women aside and going through doors first. At the same time some women resented having men help them with their coats.

Who was it who explained his success with women was to treat scullery maids like queens and queens like scullery maids? My generation didn't see it that way. We treated them all like queens.

A girl (they were girls then, not young women) I was dating saw a movie in which Humphrey Bogart put two cigarettes in his mouth and lighted them both. Then he gave one to Lauren Bacall. My girl thought that was cool so that's what I did when we were together.

We would factor a couple of martinis into this romantic setting. And there we were, sitting flank-to-flank in the shadows at Shaner's on 17th Street, listening to Johnny Smith play "Moonlight in Vermont" on his guitar.

I don't smoke cigarettes or drink martinis anymore. I have no idea what happened to her. She probably has blue hair and varicose veins and plays bingo on Friday nights. I am no Bogart, either, what with thinning hair, one eye and bad lungs, but I suspect we both cherish the memory of when we were young.

As is often the case, I had no idea where I was going with this column when I started writing it. Sometimes columns like this take unexpected turns, as my friend Tom Gavin used to say. Geez, I miss his stuff in the other newspaper.

Anyhow, when I am with young women at work, or in public, they always seem surprised and pleased at my archaic deportment and by the respect for them I demonstrate in courteous little ways.

I am left to wonder what life would be like for today's young men if they had mamas like mine who drilled them on the proper way to behave in the presence of the opposite sex. I suspect they would fare much better than the loudmouth who wears a baseball cap in singles bars and hopes to meet the girl of his dreams by saying, "Want a beer?"

Quote: "Pennies in a stream, ski trails on a mountainside. Moonlight in Vermont. Telegraph cables sing along the highway ..."

May 23, 1995

Reliance on phone a modern hang-up

PRATTLING.

It isn't my fault the original North American Dialing Plan for the United States and Canada is overloaded and has been exhausted of available phone numbers. I use my phone only for emergencies, like calling Domino's for a pizza. Otherwise, I could get along just fine without it.

Have you ever had good news over the telephone? Probably not. It's usually some jerk at a Time/Life phone bank waking you up and trying to sell you a set of books on the occult.

One of my kids, who shall remain nameless, calls me and begins the conversation with, "Dad, you're not going to like this, but … " or, "I hate to tell you this, Dad, but … "

There was a time when all my kids lived out of town and I would talk to them occasionally on the phone. But one Sunday I put on a pot roast with oven-browned potatoes and dark gravy, and they all moved back to Denver. Pot roast aroma is very seductive.

I remember when Grandpa and Grandma Amole got their first telephone. I was told never to touch it, but I did one day when they weren't looking. A little lady inside the phone said, "Number puh-leez."

I said, "What?"

She said, "This is central. Number puh-leez." I hung up right away even though I thought it was strange that the little lady's name was Central. What was Central's last name, I wondered.

I remember clearly our first long-distance call. Grandpa answered the phone. "WHAT?" he hollered. "THIS IS LONG DISTANCE? IS THAT YOU, MINNIE? NORA, COME TO THE TELEPHONE. IT'S YOUR SISTER MINNIE CALLING LONG DISTANCE FROM PASADENA. WHAT THE HELL DOES SHE WANT? DID SOMEBODY DIE?"

Grandpa believed the farther away the long-distance call, the louder you had to holler. Long-distance calls were rare in those days, used only for a family crisis like death, serious injury or some other event that couldn't wait for the U.S. Mail, which cost only 3 cents a stamp.

But now, if you believe television advertising, folks are prattling away at each other long distance around the clock. The breakup of AT&T has resulted in several companies bidding for your long-distance business. I can't keep them straight.

I know Murphy Brown represents one company, maybe the one that drops a pin. Then there is the outfit that will make a special deal if you sign up your friends and relatives. No friend or relative of mine had better sic some pushy phone company into my life.

I don't remember which phone company Whitney Houston sings for, but she sure does a nice job on the TV commercial. She is sexier than Murphy Brown. I find it interesting, though, that Murphy Brown has outlasted Dan Quayle.

I predicted years ago when the phone company abandoned user-friendly exchanges like TAbor, MAin, PEarl and SPruce that sooner or later we would be overwhelmed with creeping numeralism. It has happened.

I guess we could blame it on cellular phones, computer modems and dedicated FAX lines or the misguided souls who use them. There is hardly elbow room on the information superhighway anymore. I suspect, though, that much of the information is not really necessary and is just blather like the jerk who calls me in the middle of the night from Time/Life books.

In the meantime, don't call me. I'll call you.

June 4, 1995

Eternal memories of first day of school

PINCH IN.

Have you enjoyed watching little kids shop for school supplies? Sometimes they just sit down in the aisles to look at stuff, oblivious of folks stepping over them. What a wonderful selection of spiral tablets, notebooks, Crayolas, staplers, graph paper, calculators, computer accessories and hundreds of other items.

When I was in the first grade, the little school-supply, penny-candy and notions store at West Byers and South Bannock carried penny pencils and Big Chief tablets for a nickel. Alameda School was right across the street. It's not a school anymore but has been converted to condominiums—nice ones, too.

Alameda School wasn't on West Alameda Avenue but was just a half-block away. When my father attended the same school it was called Byers School after William Byers, founder of the Rocky Mountain News in 1859.

The name was changed to Alameda when Byers Junior High was built at 150 S. Pearl St., the location of Byers' old family home. It's now called Byers Contemporary Learning Academy. His St. Bernard dog is buried somewhere under those beautiful old trees.

There is something special about old school buildings. The first day of school you could smell the fresh varnish on desks, the woodwork and banisters along the iron staircases.

Kids felt safe and secure. I sat next to the window, and in winter I could hear snow pellets peppering against the glass. There was the comforting clank of steam radiators and the squeak of chalk on blackboards.

Later, I attended Steele School, at South Marion and East Alameda, another great old building. It had a first-rate reputation, probably because of Julia White, the principal. She called all the little boys by their last names. We loved it. It made us feel grown-up.

Miss White ran a tight ship. She was particularly concerned with keeping the lavatories immaculate and monitored the little boys during recess to be sure they aimed straight. She'd never get by with that today. She'd be hauled up on child abuse charges.

Let me tell you, though, we were scared when we went to Byers as seventh grade scrubs. We'd heard about Dolly McGlone, the gym teacher. Tough guy. No nonsense with Dolly. It was our first experience taking showers, stepping in the foot bath and snapping each other's butts with wet towels.

"Pinch in and tuck under!" he'd holler—Dolly's way of telling us to stand up straight. That first day in our new gym clothes was hilarious. It was our first experience with an athletic supporter. Some kids didn't know how to put it on. Did it go over the head? Backwards? You mean down there?

I also went to Lake Junior High at 1820 Lowell Boulevard, overlooking Sloan's Lake. A beautiful building! I notice it's celebrating its

75th birthday Sept. 8 and will be given Historic Landmark Designation then.

Anna Laura Force was principal and lived only a few blocks away at West 23rd and Lowell, just a couple of blocks from where I lived. Let me tell you, there was no fooling around in her school. We were there to learn and learn we did. Half the kids were Jewish, the other half, gentiles.

Later I attended both North and South high schools, also in solid, secure old buildings. But this time of year I think mainly of the little ones going to school for the first time in their new clothes. I can almost feel their anxieties, their wonder, their excitement. Their memories will last a lifetime. Mine have.

August 27, 1996

Riding through Denver memories

ABOVE THE DIN.

I have been riding around on the sunny side of the street. You know what a Pollyanna I am, always looking for the dark cloud's silver lining. Pardon my metaphors, but it is spring and I saw my first lilacs this morning.

I've been paying much closer attention to old Denver lately. Because of my recent illness, I have been unable to drive to work. The family has pitched in to help, but my son, Brett, has been doing most of the driving.

What a treat to be a passenger for a change! You know how it is when you do the driving. Your focus is mostly on the car in front of you or the little kid chasing a ball across the street. But as a passenger, you can sit back and watch the neighborhoods flow by.

Because I grew up in different parts of Denver, I can identify easily with most neighborhoods. When Brett drives me through south Denver, the memories seem to emerge from every brick bungalow and every old Denver Square house.

Wash Park? Gosh, yes. I know precisely where I got my first kiss. It was right along Downing Street, near the Martha Washington garden. I think I may have told her I loved her.

Uncle Tom taught me how to swim by throwing me off the end of the pier in the big lake. In the winter, I learned to ice skate on the same lake. Broke through the ice once, and my corduroy pants froze solid.

The old Temple of Youth, at 300 Logan St., was headquarters for the Highlander Boys where I learned "to be kind, to live pure, to speak truth, to right wrong, to defend the weak and to play the game square."

The Highlanders were founded by George W. Olinger who had done well in the mortuary business and wanted to give something back to the community. He was a great man. Until he died in 1954, I received a letter from him on my birthday wherever I was. It was an honor for me to deliver the eulogy at his funeral. Our friendship meant a great deal to me.

Before Speer Boulevard was a reciprocal, one-way street, the south side of Cherry Creek was called Forest Drive because of the ponderosa pines. It was beautiful in the winter, almost like a real forest. There used to be wild plum bushes alongside the creek.

Grandma Amole would take the No. 5 streetcar from West Maple Avenue to Forest Drive to pick the plums. She'd bring them home in brown grocery bags and made plum butter, which was a rare treat when spread on warm biscuits right out of the coal stove oven.

I was just 11 when the Cherry Creek flood roared through town in 1933 and into what we now call LoDo. Grandpa Amole was trapped in a switching tower at Denver Union Station for two days by the flood.

Years later, high school kids from West and South would gather at the Pik-A-Rib at Speer and Broadway for malts, greasy beef ribs and Gene Krupa on the juke box. Above the din, Anita O'Day's voice soared into "Drumboogie."

I would have sold my soul to the devil for a Model-A Ford roadster then. I couldn't afford it, though. Instead, I bought a 1933 Chevy black four-door sedan for 125 bucks. I paid it off at 10 bucks a month to the Jim Furlong Finance Co. Noisy tappets, but snazzy looking with yellow wire wheels, fender wells on both sides and a luggage rack on the back.

Think I'll go downstairs now and wait for Brett to take me home.

May 11, 1997

PHILOSOPHY

Little miracles are all around us

AWARENESS.

I was pleased to hear from a Denver psychiatrist, who wrote that he enjoyed the sunrise last Tuesday. It is reassuring that some people in the head-shrinking game take time to look at the way each day begins. I have always said that the memory of a pretty sunrise at the innocent time of day will help you get over the rough spots later.

For me, a new day is a cause for celebration, if for no other reason than just to be alive. In another letter, C. T. Simkins, a former rifleman from the 88th Blue Devil Infantry Division in World War II, reminded me: "As you can well remember, you used to wonder how you made it through each day and each battle, and then pinch yourself in the morning to see if you were still alive."

The battle between good and evil is in focus here because the Rev. Billy Graham is conducting his 10-day Rocky Mountain Crusade. I suppose it is fair to say that the skirmishing begins anew each day, and that all of us in one way or another are confronted with good-vs.-evil choices.

The problem is that good and evil are rarely presented in sharp, black-and-white terms. When it's decision time, everything appears in subtle shades of gray. No one ever said life is supposed to be easy.

It certainly isn't easy for the lonely. That is why I am glad Graham is addressing this problem in his sermons. Isn't it ironic that people in crowded cities feel so lonely? One would think the reverse would be true. Not so. The more we crowd our cities, the more lonely people become.

You can see it in their faces as they walk through shopping center malls or on crowded downtown streets. They seem to hunger for companionship, yet they are afraid to reach out to others in the throng, and are fearful others will reach out to them.

I feel that way sometimes. I don't look to others for solace, though. I often find it in nature. A little weed that struggles to survive in a crack along a concrete freeway is a big boost to my morale. I love to hear the giant cottonwoods creak in the slow, hot afternoon wind. I never feel alone when magpies nag at me when I walk too close to their nests along Bear Creek.

Graham told *News* reporter Laura Misch that he is directing some of his sermons to young singles. Good. I suspect many of them are having problems keeping their complex lives in perspective. I believe this because I have been around the track several times myself, and like an old boarding house dinner plate, I am a little chipped around the edges.

When it's my time to "rage, rage against the dying of the light," as Dylan Thomas wrote, my regrets will be of flowers I didn't pause to enjoy, the squeal of playing children I didn't hear, the puppies' ears I didn't scratch, and the starlight that was wasted on me because I didn't bother to look up.

Sure, material gain is seductive, but let me tell you something: The relentless pursuit of success isn't always what it's cracked up to be. There are greater rewards for those who simply take time to be aware of the thousands of tiny miracles everywhere around them.

July 19, 1987

Too much church ruins the kneecaps

HALLELUJAH!

I knew from the beginning I wouldn't do well as an Episcopalian. The faith is too intimidating. Actually, I was born a Methodist and wasn't subjected to Episcopalianism until much later in life. About the only thing I can remember about being a Methodist is the first line to "Jesus Wants Me for a Sunbeam."

It seemed important at the time to memorize the names of books of the Bible. I never got past Deuteronomy. I guess I was too preoccupied at the time memorizing the multiplication tables. Coloring with crayons was also involved in Sunday school, and maybe some graham crackers and milk. It was a long time ago.

The Episcopalians are very ritzy people. They have deep, rumbling voices and use words like "propitious." My parents became Episcopalians late in life because they enjoyed the sermons of the late Rev. Robert Russell, rector of Epiphany Episcopal Church. He was not exactly mainstream Episcopalian, but had a rumbling Episcopalian voice anyhow. Episcopal priests want you to think they are just some of the guys. They encourage their parishoners to call them Father Bill, or Father Sam or Father Bob, and maybe even Father Biff. This is a sort of a compromise between familiarity and respect. The clergy usually want it both ways.

One of my problems with orthodox religions is that you have to get up and get down so often. I was always standing up when I was supposed to be kneeling. At my age, my knees snap, crackle and pop going down. Getting up isn't so easy, either. Why can't people just sit still and worship?

Ritual has always baffled me. Everyone seems to know it better than I do. I always sit next to a show-off who knows the prayer book backward. He bellows out the Nicene Creed from memory, and he is always a syllable or two ahead of the rest of the congregation.

I can never keep track of where we are in the service. Following the instructions in the little poop sheet the usher passes out at the door, I try to flip back and forth through the pages in the prayer book. Rarely do I ever find the right page in time. Usually I just mumble my responses along with the congregation. I fake it by whispering, "My Uncle Jake died this morning in the bathtub. Hallelujah!" Have you noticed there are so many more funerals now than there used to be? I am averaging two or three a month. There has been some improvement in funerals over the years, but I still catch a long one every now and then where all 12 of the joyful mysteries are explored. They shouldn't do the joyful mysteries in the summer when it is so hot inside the church and the ventilation is poor.

Hymn singing can get to be pretty boring. Do they have to do all four stanzas? I keep looking ahead to see if there is any chance we may bail out of it early.

I like the way churches for black people sing hymns. They really get into it and have a great time. They enjoy their religion, whereas many white churches lay a big guilt trip on people by telling them they are sinners.

The bottom line in many religions is whether you go to heaven or to hell. I know there is a hell because I have already been there. As for heaven, I don't really know. Everyone seems to want to go to heaven, but no one wants to die to get there.

Quote: "On the whole, human beings want to be good, but not too good and not quite all of the time."—George Orwell.

July 10, 1990

Money's the butter for political bread

DISCREET.

People who believe that there are no strings attached to political campaign contributions also believe in the tooth fairy. Money is the grease that makes the political machine go. Campaign contributions enable members of Congress to stay in power for the rest of their lives.

I will never understand how politicians can keep a straight face and say that their contributors are interested only in "good government." While they may not say so directly, contributors are really trying to buy votes.

Maybe the word "buy" is a little strong. Perhaps the word "influence" is a bit more discreet. The more you pay, the more influence you have. If you don't have any money, chances are you don't have any influence.

Shortly before Democratic Rep. David Skaggs was elected to his first term as a Colorado congressman from the 2nd District, I talked to him about campaign contributions from political action committees. He defended taking the money because he said it was necessary to getting out his campaign message.

I asked him what the contributors got for their money. He denied that they were buying his vote. "What do they get?" I persisted.

"They get in to see me," he answered.

People shouldn't have to pay admission to see their elected officials. All constituents are entitled to equal access whether they make campaign contributions or not.

Former Gov. Richard Lamm considered running for his last term without accepting any campaign contributions. "I wanted to do a 'Proxmire,'" Lamm told me. Until he retired, Sen. William Proxmire, D-Wis., was repeatedly elected to office without accepting PAC money. Lamm said he got right to the point of rejecting PAC money, but decided against it. I think he could have pulled it off. Now, we'll never know.

I raise this issue because we are right at the edge of several local investigations into campaign financing. One of them involves the giant home builder, M.D.C. Holdings Inc. Arapahoe County District Attorney Bob Gallagher was named a special prosecutor to look into charges that M.D.C. had laundered money through its subcontractors to make political contributions.

M.D.C. and Silverado Banking, Savings and Loan were major contributors to both airport election campaigns. They had a direct financial interest in the airport because they owned a key, 877-acre tract of land along the main airport access road. Their donations were funneled through the Greater Denver Corp., an arm of the Greater Denver Chamber of Commerce that made political contributions.

When it comes to making campaign donations to political candidates, the big-money guys play both ends against the middle by making contributions to both sides. They are not just buying candidates. They are buying issues.

Voters suspect that there are strong connections between major banking scandals and campaign contributions. This is why all political candidates are trying to distance themselves from the Silverado collapse.

In the Colorado Voter Poll conducted by Ciruli Associates for 9News and the *Rocky Mountain News*, 84 percent of those who were asked believed that, "Every politician that took money from the people responsible for S&L problems should give back all the money to the taxpayers to help pay for the mess."

Quote: "Money is the mother's milk of politics."—Jesse Unruh.

August 21, 1990

Profit sharing's the missing spark

BETTER IDEA.

There has been a lot of soul searching about the nation's economic decline. Japanese politicians blame American workers. American industrialists blame Japanese politicians. Congress blames the president, and he blames Congress.

Could it be that our present application of the free, competitive enterprise system isn't working because it lacks enough incentive? Now that the dust is settling over what was the Soviet Union, it is clear that the socialist system failed for the same reason. Where there is no incentive, there is no growth.

Incentive is essential to any form of capitalism. It is the fuel that makes the engine go. Improved product quality, increased sales volume, expanded distribution and reduced prices are dependent to some extent on incentive. Another term for incentive is profit motive.

Fewer and fewer of us are being given the opportunity to share in the benefits of the system. Even given the choice, we are less inclined to take risks for higher pay than we are to accept lower pay in exchange for what we believe to be a guarantee of personal security.

If you don't believe that, talk to anyone in human resources, a.k.a. personnel. Job applicants right away want to know about retirement benefits. They are usually not interested in taking risks for greater gain.

Workers have reason to be suspicious of many corporate employers. How many corporations can you name today that you really trust? The way big money is being made today is not by manufacturing and selling products but by making a capital-gains windfall by selling the company to someone else. The new owner will try to inflate the cash flow and dump the company on yet another sucker. These transactions are often leveraged by junk bonds.

Workers' wages are a part of overhead. They do not share in capital-gains benefits when the company is sold. They are at the mercy of the new owners. In order to service the debt, the new owners will cut overhead by reducing the labor force.

George Bush wants to lower capital-gains taxes to encourage investment in business. Paul Tsongas has a better idea. He also would reduce capital-gains taxes, but there would be an established length of time the owner would have to operate the business in order to qualify for the tax break. This would create jobs and force the company to operate at a profit.

My partner and I operated a small, successful business in a very competitive market for years by sharing profits with the employees. It was in their interest, as well as ours, to maintain solid profit margins. They also shared our concern for product quality and for lower overhead.

We worked with our employees. We did not attempt to manage them by fear or intimidation. The profit-share idea is heresy to many corporations because philosophically they believe they are entitled to all the profits. They refuse to believe that their profits will increase by sharing some of them with workers.

If we are going to get back in the business of building better mousetraps, or automobiles, or computers, or whatever, we are going to have to include some kind of incentive in our game plan. When profits are shared with workers, pride of craftsmanship will return. Overhead will be reduced, and everyone will make more money.

Sure, it's risky, but this country became what it is because its citizens were willing to work hard and to take prudent risks.

March 8, 1992

Sexual politics in the military

NOTWITHSTANDING.

The Pentagon would have us believe that if gays are permitted to join the armed forces, there would be homosexual orgies in the latrines, and drag queens would become platoon sergeants.

This is ridiculous. There are homosexuals in the armed services now and none of those has occurred. Sexual orientation has become a public policy issue because more homosexuals are coming out of the closet, and constitutional amendments banning anti-discrimination laws for homosexuals are being passed, as was Amendment 2 in Colorado.

These issues are sometimes attached to unrelated public policy debates. This has happened with abortion. Opinions on both have become tests for true believers. One of the reasons the anti-abortion Republicans were defeated in the election was because they shut out other Republicans who favored abortion rights.

Now, the Democrats will have to come to grips with reversing the conventional wisdom that homosexuals have no business in the armed services. President-elect Clinton has said this will be one of his administration's priorities. Homosexuality could become as divisive for the Democrats as abortion has been for the Republicans.

Because most heterosexuals simply can't relate personally to homosexual behavior, they fear it. I suspect that some are also fearful that they might have repressed homosexual instincts themselves.

As the debate rages over homosexuals in the armed services, I remembered a soldier with whom I served in World War II. There was no question about his sexual orientation. He was quite effeminate and was the only known gay in our battalion.

When we went into combat, he did more than carry his load. By the time the war ended, he had been decorated for bravery twice, had been wounded in action and was awarded the Purple Heart. An impartial observer would have to say that his contribution to the war effort was of much greater significance than was the service of most of the straight troopers behind the lines.

I don't know of a single instance of his trying to seduce or force his attention on anyone. The men with whom he served respected and liked him for what he was—a good soldier.

In later life, I have hired homosexuals in business operations and found them to be good workers and valued employees. And like the gay soldier, none ever created any problems in the workplace because of sexual preference.

In all the 69-plus years I have been kicking around this town, I have sometimes worked for and with gays and lesbians. In all that time, their private sexual preferences were never discussed and were never an issue that interfered with their work. No one ever blew in my ear or pinched my butt, that's for sure.

What we must learn is to accept homosexuals as human beings, who in most respects, are no different from the rest of us. The issue of homosexuals in the armed services can be resolved instantly with enforcement of a regulation that would apply to all.

It should state clearly that any overt sexual activity, either homosexual or heterosexual, on any military installation would be cause for dismissal from the service.

Madonna notwithstanding, let's put sex back in the bedroom where it is a private matter, and get on with our lives.

November 17, 1992

We're here to keep man's hopes alive

MILLIMETER.

Do you suppose the world has been condemned to remain in the Dark Ages for an eternity? Has Judgment Day occurred and this is the last, final dwelling place of the damned?

Just asking.

In looking back over the seven decades of my life, I can't see that we have moved a single millimeter toward peace and enlightenment. We tolerate violence because we have been desensitized to it. There was momentary shock while we watched the immolation of the Branch Davidians, but it will be off Page 1 before long.

You don't believe that? A story about the 6 million Jews and other death camp prisoners exterminated by the Nazis in World War II wound up on Page 37 the other day. It was about public opinion polls that indicated a third of Americans are open to the possibility that there was no Holocaust at all.

This will come as a shocking surprise to the thousands of American soldiers, of which I was one, who actually saw the death camps during the final weeks of the war. This was no dream, no nightmare. It was an experience so horrific that it can never be excised from the memories of those who witnessed or experienced it.

But as my generation retreats into history, public recollection of the event dies with us. There was a brief moment of hope when the war ended. It was a monstrous event with an estimated 60 million killed. Genocide was a crime so terrible that we thought it never could happen again.

But it has. Stalin killed millions of his own countrymen during the Cold War. There was genocide in Cambodia. It's going on now in what is left of Yugoslavia under the sanitized term of "ethnic cleansing." Bands of Nazi thugs are on the march again in Germany. And I suppose that 50 years from now, someone will conduct a poll and find that 30 percent of Americans are open to the idea that none of it happened.

Other ethnic strife is raging at a dozen other places in Europe and Asia. Irish Catholics and Protestants are killing each other in the name of Jesus. Does anyone seriously believe that peace in the Middle East is remotely possible?

A resurgence of tribalism is also sweeping America. We have given up on integration and are now in a process of resegregating ourselves into ethnic fiefdoms that fear each other. We have become tolerant of street gangs, drive-by shootings and assault weapons in the hands of children. Adolescents kill, maul and rape just for the hell of it. We have legitimate reasons for being concerned about our safety.

Is it naive anymore to believe that we will ever do any better than just break even against our dark side? Each generation ultimately learns the lesson that violence begets violence, but by then it has become so old and impotent that it is unable to break the deadly cycle. The younger generation won't listen, and the beat goes on.

If all this is true, what is the meaning of life? I suppose we are here to keep trying. We are here to nurture our aspirations for a world at peace. We are here to reject vengeance as a solution to our conflicts. We are here to at least try to move ourselves even that single millimeter toward sanity.

I don't believe we'll ever get there, but there is some satisfaction in trying. Like all journeys, it is not the destination that gives us satisfaction, but the journey itself that is worthwhile.

April 22, 1993

Supreme killer not a flimsy title

NOTHING PERSONAL.

It's pointless to debate the death penalty. Like gun control, motorcycle helmets and abortion, folks just holler at each other. I am one of those limp-wristed, lily-livered wimps opposed to it. Why? Because I am against killing people.

But mine is the minority view, and I don't try to impose it on others. What's the use? People have already made up their minds and aren't about to budge.

President Clinton finally got his crime bill passed. It adds 60 federal crimes for which death may be the penalty. We know where he stands on capital punishment.

There is also no disagreement on that issue between Gov. Roy Romer and his challenger, Bruce Benson. Their pro-death-penalty position is popular. To hear folks talk these days, were it not for the courts, we'd hang the crooks first and ask questions later.

My problem with this is philosophical. I don't like it that the guys in charge never get their hands dirty. It's that way in war. Congress declares war but goes home to warm beds at night and never gets shot at and never has to shoot, stab, bomb or strangle anyone.

With this in mind, I propose a law that the president administer the death penalty to those convicted of federal capital crimes, and the governor would be obligated to perform the same duty to those guilty of state capital crimes. The buck should stop at the top.

The way that has been done in the past is to hire someone for $500 to do the job. I suppose there is a politically correct term for executioner, but I don't know what it is. Maybe "termination specialist" or "euthanasia technician" or simply "euthatech."

In a democracy, our leaders should not ask us to do anything they wouldn't do themselves. And so Bill Clinton would become the President and Supreme Killer of the United States of America. Similarly, either Roy Romer or Bruce Benson would be designated the Governor and Supreme Killer of the State of Colorado.

The supreme killer ought to arrive at the prison in time to spend 15 minutes alone with the convict, or "client" if you prefer, before the execution. It would be a sort of an informal get-acquainted session.

This would give the president or governor an opportunity to tell the client face-to-face not to take his execution personally. The supreme killer would explain that while he would do the actual killing, he would be acting on behalf of all of us. Then he would assist the guards in strapping down the client. When everything was set, the supreme killer would look the condemned man in the eye and then kill him.

There aren't that many executions, and so it shouldn't intrude upon too much of the president's time. His staff could coordinate his supreme killer duties with other events, perhaps a political fund-raising dinner.

If Romer is elected Colorado's supreme killer, he could wear his bomber jacket and assume his populist mode. You get the picture: There he goes, smiling and waving to the other clients on death row and pausing to shake hands with guards and prison officials. Before the execution, Romer could have a final bowl of oatmeal with the condemned man.

Should Benson be elected, he could explain to the client that he really doesn't want to kill him, but is doing so for a friend. It would be sort of like the way he explained his $500 donation to the pro-airport referendum campaign even though he now says he opposed it.

September 1, 1994

Accept old age for what it is

GRACEFULLY.

After reading "In Step with Time" by Becky Jones in the Spotlight section of Monday's *Rocky Mountain News*, I tried to remember what my midlife crisis was like, but it was so long ago I can't remember. Becky was reviewing Gail Sheehy's new book, *New Passages: Mapping Your Life Across Time*.

The author made up the word "middlescence" to describe the period in life that begins at age 45. Sheehy believes that's when folks begin living their "second childhood."

Don't you just love the way pop sociologists invent words to validate their opinions? If middlescence describes life after 45, I guess that makes me an elderescent, now entering my third childhood. Yippee!

A young preacher from Nebraska was on a tour through the *News* the other day. He asked about my job, and I told him I am a columnist. "What are you trying to do," he demanded, "educate people, and for what purpose?"

"I'm not trying to educate anyone," I told him. "I'm just trying to get through the day." He seemed surprised at the answer, and we started talking about goals in life. I said I am not goal-oriented and that I take life one day at a time. And then I told him I think there is too much emphasis these days on goals.

Some folks, I told him, are so narrowly focused on their goals that they fail to perceive the rich texture of life around them. But who am I to tell a preacher how to live? It's supposed to be the other way around, isn't it?

The thrust of Sheehy's book seems to be how to grow old gracefully. But how graceful can you be if you have arthritis, knees that snap, crackle and pop like a bowl of Rice Krispies and your belly gets big?

56

This is not to say that many people don't make a fight of it, opting for liposuction, Grecian Formula, penile implants and cosmetic surgery. It is possible to have one face lift too many, though. I wonder if Nancy Reagan is able to close her eyes at night. Cosmetic surgery has left her with a perpetual look of surprise on her face. Peggy Lee looks strangely Oriental.

I suspect Dick Cavett has had a tuck or two. There was a period when lines of wisdom were beginning to form on his forehead. And then, bingo, they were gone.

You've got to hand it to Robert Redford. I read not long ago that a film was being made of Jack Finney's wonderful book, *Time and Again*, and Redford would be the star. The role calls for a young man. Redford said the part would have to be rewritten because he can't pretend he is 27 anymore.

As wrinkled as Redford's face has become, he still has that thick shock of hair. Hair loss is a staggering blow to male ego. No price is too great to avoid that telltale horseshoe at the back of the noggin. Some guys say to themselves, "I'll raise a beard so people won't notice my head."

There is even a spray on the market to paint your bald spot. And of course there is the toupee. Every time I see a guy wearing a really expensive hair piece, I am tempted to go up to him and say, "Nice toupee!" I suppose, though, that really defeats its purpose.

I don't remember exactly when in my second childhood I decided to accept being old and not continue to wage a hopeless battle against the inevitable. My advice is relax, sit back and listen to your stomach rumble.

Prune juice, anyone?

Quote: "I'm not bald. My hair has prematurely turned to skin."
—Carl Akers.   *August 24, 1995*

Life and death decision not easy

POTBELLIED.

Just a guess, but I suspect most people who favor capital punishment have never actually killed anyone themselves or even have watched someone get killed.

Wanting to execute criminals puts the killing into the abstract. It's certainly not looking someone in the eye, face to face and then killing him. Bam! Just like that.

Colorado has not executed anyone for many years even though opinion polls indicate citizens favor it by a large majority. One of the litmus tests of the true conservative is support of capital punishment. Even so, Colorado jurors rarely invoke it, compared to jurors in Texas or Florida.

The death penalty is obviously on the minds of both prosecuting and defense attorneys in the Oklahoma City bombing trial. Sometimes it seems as though Timothy McVeigh has already been convicted, and all that is left is to select a jury that will determine whether he will be executed or imprisoned for the rest of his life.

Talking-head lawyers on cable TV believe that chief defense lawyer Stephen Jones is adopting a strategy of just keeping McVeigh from getting the death penalty.

I don't think so. I think Jones will mount a strong defense focused on reasonable doubt.

It is easy enough to sit back and watch 12 other people call the shots, but if you are one of the 12 who will decide whether McVeigh lives or dies, it brings killing up close and personal. You can try to tell yourself that society made the decision and that you were only doing what society wants you to do.

During the war, if soldiers were a little squeamish about killing they were told they were only the guys pulling the triggers. It was the whole country that did the killing. If the soldier still couldn't cleanse the guilt from his conscience, he'd tell himself that he was only following orders.

Where have we heard that before? One thing the soldier learns early in the killing game is never look back at those he kills. Their faces will haunt him forever.

The way to get soldiers to kill is to convince them the enemy are not humans. Surely the prosecution in the bombing trial will use the same strategy of convincing the jury that McVeigh is a monster in human clothing.

Obviously the death penalty doesn't deter people from killing other people. It's not even cost-effective. With the appeals system we have, it actually costs more to execute a criminal than to lock him up for life.

So what do we want from Tim McVeigh?

We want revenge. We want him to pay in the currency of his own life.

If we agree that he is to receive the harshest possible sentence, we must ask ourselves which is worst, a painless injection of a lethal fluid or spending the rest of his life alone in a cell with years to dwell on the tragedy he's accused of instigating.

If they have their way, I would bet that the nutty patriot movement gunslingers in this country would like McVeigh to be executed. His death would give them a martyr that would help them recruit other potbellied warriors.

His name would forever be linked with the shootout at Ruby Ridge, and the burning alive of the Branch Davidians at Waco, Texas.

Sitting alone in a jail for the rest of his life he would become just another forgotten old man.

April 6, 1997

THE CITY, DIA AND OTHER FOOLISHNESS

P. T. Barnum was right once more

SEND IN THE CLOWNS.

That's a crackerjack idea to put the new airport terminal under a tent. I like it "big top" symbolism. You can almost hear the circus band playing "Entrance of the Gladiators" and see the parade of trapeze artists, tumblers and wild animals.

Silverado International Airport may not be "the greatest show on Earth," but it is certainly nip-and-tuck with the brothers Ringling. For sheer excitement, you can't beat its high-wire financing, its masterful political juggling and its death-defying connection with the savings-and-loan scandal.

As the whole world knows, Silverado and M.D.C. Holdings Inc. were major contributors to the airport referendum campaigns. Silverado kicked in $95,000 even though its collapse is expected to cost taxpayers $1 billion. M.D.C. donated $131,521.

The reason Silverado and M.D.C. were so enthusiastic about the new airport was because they owned a key 877-acre tract of land on the main access road. Enter developer Bill Walters with another $50,000 donation before he defaulted on $100 million in loans to Silverado. At one time, he was one of Silverado's largest stockholders. The money was funneled through the Greater Denver Corp., an arm of the Greater Denver Chamber of Commerce. One of the reasons it was established, according to an administrative law judge, was "to support the successful outcome of the annexation election and to otherwise promote the airport."

The whole thing gets pretty incestuous at this point, with Walters, who was chairman of the board of the Greater Denver Chamber of Commerce, named co-chairman of the Greater Denver Corp.'s Advance Division. Michael Wise, who was chairman of Silverado, became chairman of the Greater Denver Corp.'s Pacesetter Division. Also on the board was Steve Farber of the law firm of Brownstein, Hyatt, Farber and Madden. Norman Brownstein, one of the partners in the firm, was on the board of M.D.C.

You get the idea. It was a very cozy arrangement for these guys who were in line to make big bucks out of the airport. You might look at it as a relationship that was as close as one hand washing the other. Now, there is more. Just as M.D.C. was trying to distance itself from the Silverado scandal, there are new charges that it made improper campaign contributions to political candidates. The money was allegedly laundered through its subcontractors.

Some of the money supposedly went to 1987 mayoral candidates Federico Peña and Don Bain. The contributions were made at a time when M.D.C. and Silverado were also funneling campaign money into the airport elections. Both Peña and Bain supported the new airport. M.D.C. is conducting an internal investigation of the charges.

When asked last week if the Greater Denver Corp. would return tainted Silverado donations as have a number of political candidates, Greater Denver Corp. Chairman Jim Smith said it would not.

Where would the money go, anyhow? Probably into that black hole known as the Federal Deposit Insurance Corp., which succeeded the Federal Savings and Loan Insurance Corp. Silverado went belly up before the Resolution Trust Corp. was created to clean up after the elephants.

Quote: "You can fool most of the people most of the time." —P. T. Barnum. *August 7, 1990*

It's time to eat Grand Prix crow

HE GUSHED.

Why don't you come over here and sit by me. You'll want to be close to the front when the show begins. As soon as the house lights dim, all those people who talked us into the Denver Grand Prix Indy-car race are going to step up to the microphone to apologize. Make yourself comfortable because there is a whole gang of them.

Let me take you back to June 5, 1989. Maybe you were watching on cable TV, or were jammed into Denver City Council chambers. The usual suspects had been rounded up to testify on behalf of civic progress, which in this case involved subsidizing a downtown auto street race to the tune of $3.3 million of taxpayer money.

Gluttons for punishment that they are, Denver City Council members voted to approve the contract. They had somehow forgotten their previous investment of $1.7 million of taxpayer money in a hockey rink. The hockey team went bankrupt. Anybody want to buy a hockey rink?

But let us not digress. It is the Denver Grand Prix that concerns us here today. I have a clear memory of Denver Revenue Manager Alan Charnes telling the packed council chambers that the race would turn a profit on the city's investment.

Actually, the race lost its promoters almost $5 million the first year. Grand Prix officials now want to cancel their contract with the city because it will lose more than $5 million the next four years. The Grand Prix wants to move to Arapahoe County after the second race, still scheduled for this August. Where in Arapahoe County, I cannot say, although the Greenwood Village Grand Prix has a nice ring to it.

Do you remember all those men in suits and dressed-for-success women who lined up to support the race? I do. For one, there was Richard C.D. Fleming, president of the Greater Denver Chamber of Commerce. For another, there was Diana Boulter, then president of the Denver Partnership.

And the Rotarians! I lost count of the Rotarians who were there. You could almost hear them singing, "R—O—T—A—R—Y, That spells Ro-ta-ree!"

Many of them invoked the name of Sidney Shlenker, owner of the Denver Nuggets. They praised his contributions to the community. Shortly after the council approved the Grand Prix contract, however, Shlenker sold the Nuggets and moved to Memphis. Andrew, son of Sidney, was left to run the race.

Andy, as we came to know him, painted a rosy picture of the event. "It's like the Olympics," he gushed. "It comes along only once and you can't turn it down. We have to tell the rest of the world that we're going to play ball."

One after another, the guys in the suits endorsed the Grand Prix. They were all wearing lapel badges promoting the race. There were bankers, developers, Realtors and other movers and shakers. They stood up to say something like this: "We have to send out the message that Denver is open for business!"

As I watched them thumping the podium, it occurred to me that these were the same wonderful people who are bringing us Denver's Incredible Shrinking Airport. It was just a passing thought.

OK, we're all in place now. Who will be first to publicly beg for community forgiveness? No groveling, please. A nice, dignified apology will do just fine. Oh yes, one other thing on your way out, please sign an affidavit promising you will never screw up this town again.

February 5, 1991

Engineer's marvel or concrete tomb?

HAM HOCKS.

When Daniel entered the lions den, he had only a few of the big cats to contend with. When I toured Denver's new airport last week, the lions outnumbered me 9,000 to one. But they were friendly lions.

I didn't meet all the 9,000 construction workers on the job, but those I talked to were nice guys. I hadn't expected such a warm reception in light of my monotonously frequent criticisms of the giant project. After all, there are a lot of paychecks out there.

These are proud, talented people. They work hard and are devoted to the project. Coordinating all the elements of construction and bringing them together on time is indeed a formidable task. I don't know how they do it.

Mayor Wellington Webb's office called with an invitation to accompany him on the tour. I was puzzled. Surely he didn't think that after I had seen the airport I would slap my forehead with the heel of my hand and say: "Gee whiz, this is wonderful! Golly, now that I have seen it, I can understand why we are building it. Wow, was I ever wrong about this!"

I'll have to say, though: DIA is one big sucker. The bridge to Concourse A is billed as "the longest free-standing bridge" in the U.S.

Looking down from the FAA tower, the highest in North America, monster earth-moving machines with 7-foot tires look like Tonka toys.

Denver International Airport is indeed awesome. It is the Aswan Dam, the great pyramids and the Panama Canal all rolled into one. It was difficult for me to absorb its size. The amount of money involved is impossible to comprehend. Just during the two hours I was there, $1.6 million was spent on construction.

I did feel a little out of place because I wasn't carrying a cellular telephone like everyone else. Webb and the others seemed to be using theirs all the time. I should have borrowed one and telephoned Holger Jensen for a briefing on the fighting in Bosnia-Herzegovina, or called Patty Gutierrez at the Press Club to save me some ham hocks, beans and corn pone for lunch, which she did anyhow.

While there, I was able to confirm that United Airlines has contingency plans to take over Concourse A if Continental doesn't survive. I also learned that the airport has been contacted by a major hotel chain about building an airport hotel. Aviation director Jim DeLong declined to identify the chain for publication.

I still believe the airport is a mistake, and I take no pleasure, as some do, at the increasing body of evidence that suggests that it is fraught with problems. I do not look forward to being vindicated should it fail.

No one should envy Webb, who is really a nice man. "Someone else rolled the dice, and now I've got to play the game," he told me. He is not starry-eyed about the project as was Mayor Federico Peña. Webb is a realist and he knows that when DIA opens, people will be furious when it finally sinks in that air travel from Denver will be more expensive and much less convenient than it is now from Stapleton.

Of course the big gamble is whether DIA can generate enough new passenger traffic to pay off the bonds that were sold to finance it. The shakeout in the troubled airline industry will have a profound effect on DIA. Webb knows this is a factor over which he has no control. And he also knows that a bond default would be a devastating blow to Denver.

And so I saw DIA. Is it an engineering marvel from which we shall prosper into the next century? Or is it a giant concrete tomb into which a beautiful city will be buried? I hope it is the former but still believe it is the latter.   *April 25, 1993*

Webb erred, but Peña created the monster

ROTTEN EGG.

The timing was perfect. Just three weeks before the June 6 runoff election, Transportation Secretary Federico Peña is blaming Mayor Wellington Webb for what went wrong at Denver International Airport. So is George Doughty, aviation director when Peña was Denver mayor.

Peña didn't mention Webb's name in testimony last week before a congressional subcommittee. Instead, he invoked the classic excuse bureaucrats use to evade responsibility: "Mistakes were made." It was clear he was accusing Webb of making those mistakes. In a written statement to the subcommittee, Doughty blamed Webb for being "outmaneuvered" by United Airlines.

Sure, Webb has made mistakes in the management of DIA construction. The whoppers, though, were made by Peña when he was mayor. Now, he is trying to rewrite history.

It was Peña who hatched this rotten egg. DIA was his idea. He sweet-talked us into believing we needed a less convenient and more expensive airport than the one we had. Folks swallowed it hook, line and sinker.

Then he established a construction schedule that would be impossible to meet. He did this in the first bond prospectus by setting the date when the first interest payments on the bonds were to begin. They couldn't be paid until the revenue stream began with the opening of the airport. Then there was delay, after delay, after delay, increasing bonded indebtedness and inflating the cost of the project.

Peña was not outmaneuvered by the airlines. He outmaneuvered himself by proceeding with airport construction without agreements with United and Continental airlines. Redesign of the airport to meet their needs further delayed the project and increased its cost.

Peña used a sweetheart deal he cut with Continental Airlines to force United into an agreement. Because of the size of the project,

66

United required an automated baggage system or it couldn't use the airport.

His agreement with Park Hill and Adams County to close Stapleton to all flights once DIA opened was responsible for the loss of Continental's maintenance base here. This set in motion a series of developments that resulted in Continental's abandonment of its Denver hub and most of its Denver passenger service.

United now has a virtual monopoly of origination and destination passenger traffic in Denver. This will mean increased landing fees and passenger fares.

We were told United would spread the higher landing fees over its entire system. Didn't happen. Local passengers are picking up the tab. We are paying through the nose every time we use Peña's airport.

"It's working, and it's working well," Peña told congressional investigators. But for whom? It sure isn't working well for us poor fools who are forced to use it.

Did you naively believe airports were for the convenience of citizens who use them? It didn't work out that way. DIA was built to make money for the investment bankers, the developers, the real estate tycoons, the construction industry and others who feed at the public trough.

Now we are trying to pick up the pieces and make DIA work. And where are Peña and Doughty now? Gone. They dumped the whole mess in Webb's lap and bugged out before the job was done. They left us with a monster debt and the very real possibility of a bankrupt airport. You know what they are? They are a couple of quitters. That's right, quitters.   *May 16, 1995*

Shackle thyselves to big-money sports

BUZZ OFF.

I have returned from the top of the mountain. I traveled there to seek the truth from an ancient wise man. Here in the longer shadows of my life, I am troubled by the blurred lines between fact and fiction, good and evil.

67

The old man was sitting in the lotus position, his eyes fixed on the distant horizon. Seeing me, he smiled enigmatically and said, "Sit here, next to me, and rest, my son. You look tired."

After I caught my breath, I said to him: "Thank you, Master. The journey has been long and perilous, and I am weary. Immoderate storms had left I-70 almost impassable because of jackknifed trucks and tourists from Kansas who know not the the secrets of mountain driving in snow.

"I postponed my pilgrimage until after the ski season, hoping my way would be blessed by sunshine. Having been born in Colorado, I am mystified by this thing called skiing. Those of us who are natives have special knowledge that visitors do not."

"And what is that, my son?"

"It is cold up there, Master, and besides, had the great God wanted man to ski, man would have been born with boards on his feet. To ascend a mountain only to slide back down is pointless," I told him.

"Ah, so, but you have climbed my mountain, my son. What is the purpose of your visit?"

"I was coming to that, but first, please grant me dispensation from sitting in the lotus position. My legs are arthritic and my knees snap, crackle and pop like a bowl of Rice Krispies."

"Granted, my son, but let's get on with it. Other pilgrims are waiting," he said.

"I have anguished long and hard over this question, and I have no answer. That's why I have come to you. What, oh revered one, is the meaning of life in Denver?"

The old man's eyes fluttered briefly and then closed. His lips parted as he whispered something to himself, perhaps his mantra. He sat serenely for several moments and then took a deep breath. Suddenly he eyes opened wide and he said, "The meaning of life in Denver is professional sports."

I was unable to speak at first, and then I said, "But Master, what about education, the environment, health care, the problems of senior citizens, unwed mothers, gangs, dirty politics, fade-away fathers, potholes, the homeless and Denver International Airport?"

"Unimportant," he said. "The people of Denver crave the limelight and will sacrifice anything to get it. Major league sports give them this recognition, and they are willing to endow team owners with tax breaks. The new National Hockey League team will mean that Denver will be only one of 10 cities to offer all four major sports. The new team will be a great economic generator for the city."

I thought about this for a minute, and then I said, "But Master, many restaurants and even sports bars have suffered a 10 percent to 15 percent decline in their business since the Colorado Rockies came to town. They may not be able to afford any more economic generators."

"No pain, no gain, my son," he said. "No one promised the pathway to professional jock Nirvana would be easy. Denver fans will just have to dig down deeper to subsidize millionaire athletes so they can continue to enjoy the life to which they have become accustomed."

"But Master … "

"Buzz off, old-timer. Don't forget to feed the kitty on your way out. No change. Just unmarked bills."

May 30, 1995

Schools can arise from busing's ashes

INSPIRATIONAL.

Trish and I were understandably apprehensive. It was the first day of school and our Susan was getting on a Blue Bird school bus to enter the first grade on the other side of town. We lived in Bear Valley, and Greenlee Elementary School was at West 11th Avenue and Lipan Street.

It was 1974, and Susan was in the first grade of the first class to be bused under court-ordered desegregation of Denver Public Schools. Even though busing triggered the great white flight to the suburbs, Trish and I never considered moving from Denver. We decided instead to make personal commitments to our city and to its public school system.

Susan? She was fine. She went on to graduate from Kennedy High School and then to graduate from Whittier College in California. I'll never forget the night at her high school graduation at Red Rocks Amphitheater. Some of the student speakers took pride in having been in that first class. They spoke warmly of their teachers and classmates who devoted themselves to trying to make desegregation work.

A column I wrote about that night was the only mention in the media of what I thought was really a significant event in Denver history. In my column I reflected on how Trish and I became involved in every way we could to support Greenlee's administrators and faculty.

We got to know and respect Fred Manzanares, Greenlee's principal. He was an inspirational leader, not just of the students and faculty, but of the entire neighborhood. Greenlee was more than a school. It was a community resource center.

Busing changed all that. Hispanic parents were not comfortable participating in school events at Traylor Elementary School in Bear Valley. Housing-project kids didn't profit from busing. They became intimidated and uncommunicative in a middle-class school and neighborhood environment.

Make no mistake, though, there was de facto segregation of Denver Public Schools before busing. Black and Hispanic kids in poor neighborhoods were denied educational resources available to well-off kids.

I know that to be a fact. Manzanares had tried unsuccessfully for years to get Greenlee's library and playground equipment upgraded. Almost overnight, when Susan and the other Bear Valley Anglo kids were bused to Greenlee, it got its new playground equipment and library supplies.

Back in 1974 none of us realized the profound changes school busing would cause to the way we live. The malignant bloat of the suburbs was unexpected. We didn't know Denver would be a dumping ground for indigent families. We didn't anticipate that the Poundstone Amendment would curtail the growth of Denver's tax base.

Sure, some kids did profit educationally from busing, but on balance there were far more negatives than positives. If there was a key mistake, it was the United States Supreme Court's unwillingness to integrate all 14 of metropolitan Denver's school districts instead of just one.

Now we must put this into the past and get on with school reform.

The phoenix can rise from the ashes. In Irv Moskowitz, we have an innovative new superintendent. He is developing a plan to meet Denver's special educational needs. Yes, it will take money, but it will take community commitment, too.

September 14, 1995

Mr. President had a chat with shorty

GOOSE BUMPS.

FP—Great news, Mr. President! You're going to Denver! Good old mile-high, smile-high Denver. You'll be a mile closer to the sun. Queen City of the Plains. Imagine a great city! It's Denver. You know, I used to be mayor of Denver.

BC—Yes, I know.

FP—Let me tell you something, Mr. President, there are no more gullible people in the whole wide world than the folks in Denver. A little tax increase here, a little tax increase there, and Denver has a new convention center, a new library and a new baseball park. God love 'em, sometimes I think Denver taxpayers are generous to a fault.

BC—They'd better be generous. I'm going there to raise campaign money.

FP—No problemo. All you have to do is brag about Denver being a major league city. They love that. Butter 'em up by praising the Rockies and the Broncos. Maybe you ought to wear a Rockies cap and a Broncos jacket.

BC—You're not serious.

FP—Heh. Heh. Just kidding, boss. I was thinking, though, that when we arrive in Denver, you and I should get off Air Force One arm in arm. I'll be right there at your side when you meet the media. As a matter of fact, I could actually introduce you to the media.

BC—You're not going, little guy.

FP—Not going! Not going? I have to go. You'll need me. I'm the transportation secretary and Denver is my town. They love me in Denver. I mean, they really do love me.

BC—Not according to the latest Floyd Ciruli poll. Your negatives are right up there with such crowd pleasers as Douglas Bruce, Ross Perot and Ben Campbell.

FP—But I want to be there with you when Air Force One touches down at Denver International Airport. The first president of the United States to land at DIA. It just gives me goose bumps to think about it.

BC—We're landing at Buckley.

FB—Buckley? That's crazy. Why would you want to land at Buckley when you could fly into the world's newest, finest airport?

BC—DIA is too far out in the boondocks. It's not convenient. I'm a busy man, Shorty, too busy to spend my time gridlocked on I-70.

FP—But Mr. President, I wanted to ride with you on Peña Boulevard, which was named after me. I wanted to take you through the airport so you could see those little propellers whirling around in the train tunnels. I wanted you to walk on Italian marble and see the automated baggage system. Wait until you see the tent roof. It's supposed to look like snow-capped mountains. What a great photo opportunity! You and I and DIA.

BC—You just don't get it, do you? I would have to be out of my mind to be photographed with you at the biggest public works boondoggle in the nation's history. My God, $4 billion! Incredible. I've got that pit bull, Newt Gingrich, snapping at my heels over government waste, and DIA is a perfect example of what he is talking about.

FP—But …

BC—No buts about it. Where have you been, Federico? Don't you know bondholders have brought five lawsuits against that dumb airport of yours? I don't want to be anywhere near you when the mob arrives with the tar and feathers. They are not going to take kindly to the fool who built an airport that is less convenient and more expensive to use than the airport they had and has created the largest red-ink municipal bond debt ever.

FP—Did you say tar and feathers?

September 21, 1995

72

A chiller, a thriller, and it's here now

BLOCKBUSTER.

More spectacular than *The 10 Commandments!* More frightening than *Jaws!* More suspense than *The Bridge on the River Kwai!* More action than *Die Hard!* More thrills, more chills, more terror, more adventure than any film ever brought to the silver screen.

It's *Airport '95.*

You'll laugh, you'll cry, you'll cheer as thousands struggle through whiteout blizzards in a vain attempt to reach Denver International Airport. Only the wide screen can bring you the breathtaking panorama of a serpentine, miles-long line of automobiles at a standstill on Peña Boulevard, named after the former Denver mayor.

Few will forget Federico Peña in *A Monster Is Born,* the $5 billion production that stands as the horror film against which all others in this genre will be measured. Film historians are still in awe of that heart-stopping scene in which Peña stands before the bizarre circus tent terminal and shouts, "It's alive! It's alive!"

Several subplots are skillfully woven together in *Airport '95.* Anguished passengers are trapped in a United Express plane that takes a wrong turn and runs into a bank of unplowed snow on a taxiway. Would other planes blindly follow and crash into the ill-fated craft? Would ground crews break through to save them?

Passengers on United Airlines Flight 367 from Chicago are blissfully unaware of their harrowing escape from possible tragedy. The sharp-eyed pilot aborts his landing when he notices flashing lights on the runway where he was making his final approach. He is only 100 feet off the ground. The lights are on a Chevy Suburban driven by an airport worker who had taken a wrong turn.

It is the worst possible time for the roof of the FAA tower to start leaking. You'll cheer the guts-and-glory flight controllers when they realize their ground-control radar system is not giving them accurate positions of all planes and trucks on the DIA surface. Then the power goes off for almost two hours, forcing controllers to use a backup system "that doesn't do the whole job," as one harried official says.

Meanwhile, hundreds of small poignant dramas are playing out in the cavernous terminal building. As flights are delayed or canceled, families sip cocoa and huddle together under blankets supplied by Traveler's Assistance.

One little family from Kansas with three darling children waits eight hours for a flight to take them to Mazatlan, Mexico. Their plane is damaged when a baggage tug careens on ice and crashes into their plane.

Some passengers are luckier than others. When conditions at DIA became chaotic, more than a dozen United flights are diverted to Colorado Springs. That's the upstart little airport that proves to be an alternative to Denver passengers who want to save money while avoiding the uncertainty at DIA.

The bitter irony in *Airport '95* is the naive belief that DIA would be able to operate under the most severe winter weather conditions. In one of the most gut-wrenching scenes in *Airport '95*, one harried official tells reporters, "When snow comes down faster than you can clear it off, that's a problem."

Will there be a sequel to *Airport '95*? Hollywood insiders say there will. A producer who declined the use of his name said: "Only 5 inches of snow fell at DIA. Imagine what will happen if there is a real storm out there. We're talking blockbuster! Maybe even Julia Roberts and an Academy Award."

Airport '95 is rated R because of adult language. Don't fail to miss it.

October 26, 1995

Editor's Note: *This column pre-dated by two years the "Blizzard of '97" in which many motorists were stranded on Peña Boulevard.*

School board is due for a lesson

DIRTY WATER.

The Denver Board of Education's ultimatum that some elementary schools will be "blown up" if their test scores don't improve places an unfair burden on teachers. The strategy reminds me of an incident in World War I when French soldiers refused to attack. The high command then ordered that every 10th French soldier would be executed.

The term "blown up" is not mine. It was coined by district officials who promised some schools would have new principals and teachers as early as next fall. The new staff would be under strict orders to improve academic achievement, or else.

A number of other schools will be put on probation for a year. If there is no improvement by then, a new teaching and administrative staff would take over. No schools have been named yet, but many are in low-income areas.

Question: Does the Board of Education have any plans to replace the children's parents if test scores don't improve?

The new "blowup" strategy will be applauded by some who have the quaint notion that it will return reading, writing and arithmetic to the good old days when they were kids. If only it were that simple.

But that was then. This is now. Public education in the good old days was just that. But now, teachers are also supposed to be police officers, social workers and psychologists. Never in the history of public education has so much been expected of teachers.

The new DPS scorched-earth policy seems to embrace the mistaken belief that all children are equal when they enter the first grade and that their failure to meet standards is the fault of the teachers. By now, we should have learned that all kids are not equal at age 6. Their early childhood experiences are vastly different and the inequality can last a lifetime.

Sure, there are bad teachers and bad principals. Deal with them individually. Don't throw out the baby with the dirty bath water. DPS says that faculty and administrators in "blown-up" schools would be dispersed throughout the system. That's just great. Will they teach other teachers how to fail?

It's the family, stupid, not the teachers who are to blame. I had a friend who was an assistant principal at a middle school in Denver. When he retired, I asked him if he missed his work at school.

"Are you kidding?" he said. "I spent 95 percent of my time dealing with 5 percent of the kids. Wild horses couldn't drag me back."

If you have any doubts that the family isn't significant, take a look at the progress Asian-American kids are making in schools where test scores are below average. They find a way to excel because of their strong family support.

The failure of public education is a consequence of the failure of the American family. The family fails because of the malignant growth of the underclass in this country.

Teen pregnancies result in little kids coming into a cycle of welfare and poverty almost impossible to escape. We can't blame the teacher because unmarried kids copulate in the back seat of an old Camaro.

Sure, some of our elementary schools have problems, but blaming the faculty is simply passing the buck. What DPS should be doing is involving the teachers in the decision process, not excluding them from it.

Quote: "Don't shoot the piano player. He's doing the best he can."—Sign in a frontier saloon.

February 16, 1997

The sad, sad tale of a real swinger

FORE!

Great golfing weather! What a thrill to feel the driver in your hands, to look up the fairway and then down at the ball, to bring the club back, to hear it whistle through a perfect arc and then THWOPP! I mean really hitting that baby a ton. Sweet! You probably think I'm out there with the guys every afternoon, right?

Wrong. I do not play golf. It hurts my stomach. I discovered this years ago after deciding I was a workaholic and didn't know how to have a good time. In my typical impulsive way, I bought purple pants, clubs and spiked shoes. Then I joined a country club and signed up for golf lessons every Monday, Wednesday and Friday morning.

"You gotta picture swing, Geno, babe," the golf pro told me, "but you're not hitting the ball. Here's a bucket of of balls. Remember to keep your head down and your left arm straight. I'll see you Wednesday morning."

I'd flail away for a half an hour or so, never getting even a single ball to dribble out more than 50 feet. It was very depressing. I began to notice that on Monday, Wednesday and Friday mornings, I'd wake up with a stomachache.

I'll never forget my last lesson. I had hooked two balls into the parking lot and sliced a third into the swimming pool when a booming voice echoed down from the sky. It was a big voice, rich, commanding, mellifluous; a voice not unlike Bob Martin's.

"Geno!" it thundered. "You are not a golfer. You have a picture swing, but you can't hit the ball. Give up golf by May 15 or I am going to give you a bellyful of ulcers. Go back to work. Over and out."

"Hallelujah!" I hollered. "I am cured." Indeed I was. I quit the country club, gave my purple pants and shoes to the Goodwill and my clubs to my sons. In a final gesture of victory over pain, I threw away my pack of DiGel. The sun broke through the clouds, and in the distance there were sounds of trumpets. They were playing Aaron Copland's "Fanfare for the Common Person." "Hallelujah!" I hollered again.

Actually, I have never played a single round of golf. I just can't handle the idea of spending four hours with three jerks I don't know. It's tough enough to spend four hours with jerks I *do* know.

I have since concluded that golf is a macho thing that has a lot to do with hanging out with the guys in front of the pro shop and crunching around in the gravel wearing spiked shoes. You say things like, "Man, I hit a screamer on 18," or "I bogeyed four and five. Never up, never in," or "I got the duck hook down pat," or "I really kissed that sucker out of the sand."

Not for me. Give me four hours in the afternoon, and I'll be out at the ballpark where the sun is warm and the beer is cold. The talk will be of serious matters like batting averages, hit-and-run strategies and guarding the third-base line.

If a guy with a big voice calls, take a message. I'll get back to him.

Quote: "The only reason I every played golf in the first place was so I could afford to hunt and fish."—Sam Snead

April 23, 1987

Watch is too smart for its own good

BEEP BEEP.

The minute I saw the Casio Quartz 100M Alarm Chronograph in the L.L. Bean catalog, I knew I had to have it. It was black and had a lot of doodads. Wearing an impressive wristwatch like that would make an important statement about me. It would tell the world that I am a man who cares very much about precision.

I am a patsy for anything that comes through the mail. I have been that way since I was a 97-pound weakling and sent away to Charles Atlas for his dynamic-tension body-building program. I was fed up with having bullies kick sand in my face on the beach and run off with the pretty girls. All I have to show for it today, however, are sagging pectorals.

Even so, you can understand how impatient I was for the man in the UPS truck to deliver my new watch. I wanted to wear it so people would think I am an airplane pilot, a network TV producer, a track-and-field coach or maybe a civil engineer.

I was delighted when I opened the package. The picture of the watch in the catalog didn't do it justice. There were even more doo-dads on it than I had thought. It even had a compass. Lord knows I can certainly use that. My sense of direction leaves much to be desired. Let us leave it that I cannot find my you-know-what with both hands.

There was a brief period during the Great War that I impersonated an armored scout, a military occupational specialty in which a sense of direction is of considerable importance. I managed to bluff my way for a time by always keeping the noise ahead of me. The noise was where the Germans were. It was considered very bad form to let the noise get behind you.

One of the nice things about living in Denver is that you always know which way is west by the mountains. You take away those mountains, pal, and this old boy would have trouble getting to work. I needed the compass, and it works fine.

I couldn't figure out the other doodads, though. I tried reading the instructions in the little book that came with the watch. All I could make out was, *"Persione y sostenga 'B' en la presentacion de la hora para ajustar la hora."* What do I have here, I asked myself, a bilingual watch? I need something that tells time in English. *No hablo Español.*

Fortunately, my younger son, Jon, speaks electronics. He came over to the house and set my watch. It has a regular little-hand, big-hand dial. There is also a digital A.M., P.M. reading and a military 24-hour time. Push a button, and it tells you the day and the month. There is an alarm function and a stopwatch that computes to the tenth of a second. The fool thing even goes beep-beep every hour.

As much as I need the compass, I am thinking of going back to my old Timex. The chronograph makes too many demands on me and gives me too many choices. My life is already complicated enough without something that beeps at me night and day and answers questions I haven't asked.

Quote: "The computer is down. I hope it is something serious."
—Stanton Delaplane.

August 25, 1988

It appears age has my number

HUMILIATION.

I felt like a fool. There I was at the teller window of Commercial Federal, trying to explain to a pleasant young woman that I had forgotten my automatic teller machine number. Was it a new number? Not exactly. I got it seven years ago when ATMs came to our neighborhood. Commercial Federal was Empire Savings in those days, but when the savings and loan changed hands, depositors kept their old ATM numbers.

I realized I had forgotten the number while waiting at a drive-by ATM. It was the pressure of impatient people lined up behind me that blanked my memory. I drove away and went to a walk-up ATM, figuring that by the time I got there I would remember the number. But after three unsuccessful attempts, the ATM ate my plastic card and wouldn't give it back. I think I had some of the digits right, but they must have been in the wrong order. After I had identified myself to the teller, she wrote my number down on a slip of paper and gave it to me along with my card. I went back outside to the same ATM that took my card. I tried again with the right number, but that idiot machine kept it again.

How much humiliation does a man my age have to suffer? My head bowed in shame, I returned to the office, found the same young woman and told her what happened. She retrieved my card and explained the ATM gives you only three opportunities a day to get your number right. Then it punishes you by keeping your card.

It is common for people my age to have difficulty with numbers. Lord knows I dial my share of wrong numbers on the telephone. I make mistakes with my check balance. My problem is compounded by all the numbers I have to memorize. There is the password that gets me into my computer file here at the *Rocky Mountain News*.

We have a telephone voice-mail system that requires me to punch in my mailbox number and a second numerical password. There is a password for the database I use with my home personal computer. Add to that the password number on my home burglar alarm system. Sometimes when I come home, I blank out on the password number that disarms the burglar alarm. While the thing is relentlessly beeping at me, I have been known to punch in my ATM number or my voice-mail password, both of which the burglar alarm ignores. If I don't figure it out before the beeper stops, the cops are called.

In recent years the Social Security number is being used as a tax-payer number, an employee number, an insurance identification number and also a number to identify me from the rest of the sheep. I have had a Social Security number for more than 50 years. I even have my original card. You'd think by now I would have it memo-rized, but I can't remember the fool thing.

About the only number I am really sure of is my old Army serial number. It is burned permanently into my memory. But no one ever asks me for my serial number anymore. Who cares whatever hap-pened to old 37342310? No one, that's who.

August 3, 1989

Men's room isn't a waiting room

NATURAL CHANNEL.

Are you are offended by a discussion of the prostate gland? If so, I suggest you bail out now and turn back to Garfield. Were this column a movie, it would probably get a PG rating. That is to say it may not be for general audiences. General audiences probably wouldn't be that interested anyhow.

How can I delicately put this? Well, the prostate is a gland in males that surrounds the neck of the bladder. As men get older, the prostate enlarges, thereby restricting the flow from the bladder. This means going to the bathroom frequently. Strike frequently. Make that all the time. Incessantly.

Five or six times during the night. Back and forth all day long at work. Missing crucial scenes at the movies, excusing oneself in res-taurants, or at concerts, or at church, or anyplace.

I write from considerable experience on the subject. At work, I found myself spending more time in the men's room than in the newsroom. (That's a sort of Jesse Jackson alliteration, isn't it?) Some-times, though, I was not able to perform, left standing alone, staring at the wall, as my younger co-workers quickly arrived and departed, leaving me to imagine waterfalls, rainy days, rippling streams, foun-tains in the park, or any other liquid fantasy I could conjure up.

81

Dr. Noel Sankey, my friendly urologist/surgeon, told me to let him know when I was ready for a transurethral resection, a surgical Roto-Rooter process "through the natural channel." I won't bore you with a more detailed discussion of the process.

I had hoped to postpone the surgery until February, but as September's days "narrowed down to a precious few," as Kurt Weill's song put it, I realized I would not be able to wait. I had the surgery three weeks ago.

I only missed a few columns because I have a personal computer and modem at home, abling me to transmit my columns to the newsroom on regular telephone lines. The recuperation time following my Roto-Rooter job is three weeks to a month.

Staying home that long has not been easy for me. I don't work well at home. I need the stimulation of the newsroom. I miss my friends at the *News* and the Press Club, and all the gossip about our trade. I see new bylines in the paper I don't recognize. Some of them I can't even pronounce.

It has been nice, though, to have plenty of time to read. I have been devouring books. But even that has its limits. Yesterday, for example, I found myself zapping back and forth on cable TV between the Real Estate Channel and a public access channel on which a young woman was teaching belly dancing.

As she did, I couldn't help but remember these lyrics to an old two-beat Dixieland standard: "I wish I could shimmy like my sister, Kate. She shakes like jelly on a plate. Ever' boy in my neighborhood, now knew she could shimmy, and it's understood, that I'll never be late but will be up to date, if I can shimmy like my sister, Kate, I'm shoutin'. Shimmy like my sister, Kate, oh yeah!"

Trish did her best to brighten my day when she brought home from the supermarket a copy of *Weekly World News* with the headline, "TITANIC SURVIVOR FOUND ON ICEBERG." The subhead read, "She thinks it's April 15, 1912—and her dress is still wet!" Did we miss that story?

Sankey will tell me tomorrow when I can go back to work. I am anxious to just zip in and out of the men's room in nothing flat. That's not showing off, is it?

October 14, 1990

TNKS ILKEEP MY OLDPL8S

2MANY.

The automobile is more than a technological extension of your feet. It is also a self-propelled embodiment of your psyche. That can be the only explanation for the malignant growth of designer, vanity and other special-interest license plates. At last count, there were more than 50 Colorado license plate styles and the list keeps growing. The latest is a new design called "Colorado Denim."

It replaces our red, white and blue designer plates. Colorado Denim has numbers and letters that reflect better at night. There is the outline of a mountain range across the top, as there is on the standard green and white plates.

A new law permits all honorably discharged military veterans to display special plates even though there are already plates for Pearl Harbor survivors, disabled veterans, Purple Heart recipients, former prisoners of war and members of the Colorado National Guard.

It goes into effect Jan. 1, 1993. At this writing, there are no special plates for members of high school ROTC units, drum majorettes or aerobic exercise classes.

Nick DeBono, a Korean War veteran and commander of the Trinidad American Legion Post, waged a five-year fight to get the Colorado legislature to authorize the plates. He says 391,800 Colorado veterans are eligible to buy them at a one-time cost of $10.

I don't know what the other 391,799 veterans are going to do, but I am sticking with the old green-and-white plates, which are becoming more rare every day.

In the words of the sainted Samuel Goldwyn, "Include me out." I am not even going to get them for my 49-year-old World War II Army Jeep. I also have regular plates on my 1965 Ford truck.

The truck passes emission standards of a 1991 car. It makes you wonder what good all those expensive catalytic converters are really doing. My truck runs on any gasoline, even the cheapest. All you have to do is strain the chicken feathers out of it and start driving.

There are no data on this, but I suspect most veterans were drafted into military service. We went because we had no choice. What we did after we got there varied. Some served in mess kit maintenance battalions and others did the real fighting. Let's face it, pal, there are always a lot of free riders in the military when the shooting begins. It is very crowded in the rear echelons.

But special license plates? Come on, now. It was enough for me to get my "ruptured duck" and a GI loan on my first house. The country doesn't owe me anything for showing up in World War II. Let's get on with our lives and quit trying to bask in the fading light of old glories. We were lucky we had a country to come home to. Some of us were lucky even to come back.

There is a way guys not honorably discharged can get special recognition. They might want to go the vanity-plate route. That's the license plate where you pick out the letters on your license to say anything you want so long as it is not vulgar or obscene.

Carl Hilliard of the Associated Press thought "AWOL" might be appropriate for some old yardbird out there. Our John Sanko chipped in with the simple but eloquent "4F." It will have to be first-come, first-served for "SEKSHN8," of which there were many. I can think of one bed-wetter in our outfit who deliberately urinated his way out of the army.

Do you suppose old "Stinky" qualifies for the new plates?

July 5, 1992

Who will teach children to love?

PERVERT.

Maybe it's a generational thing, or it could be that my consciousness has not been sufficiently elevated, or perhaps I am insensitive, or just getting old, or maybe all of the above. Whatever.

Anyhow, increasingly I feel awkward in some social situations in which I encounter women I have known for a long time. It used to be that I thought nothing of putting a fatherly arm around their shoulders and giving them a kiss.

Not a big wet one on the mouth, but just a little dry, platonic peck on the cheek or forehead. The embrace was an honest expression of affection and was not motivated by a desire to cop a feel, to fondle or to jump on her bones. I certainly never did hug anyone if I detected the slightest hint of rejection.

84

I have never been a fan of Leo Buscaglia who seems to advocate nonstop hugging. Actually, I am never comfortable in churches where strangers hug each other at a certain point in the service. I don't want to hug people I don't know. I understand the symbolism, but I am uncomfortable with the practice.

Anymore, though, this old boy is just going to smile and say, "Hello." Lord knows I don't want to be dragged to the docks and accused of sexual harassment. Am I wrong that there are some people in this world who are just waiting for an excuse to make a big stink over nothing?

On the other side of that, though, I used to work with a young woman who was fond of saying around the office, "What does a girl have to do around here to be sexually harassed, anyhow?"

I have also had to revise my relationship with children. You'll never find me living in a senior citizens community where there are no children. I really love little kids. I like to be around them, to talk to them, to hold them on my lap and even give them an innocent little pat on their bottoms.

Sometimes down at King Soopers I see little boys and girls I'd like to talk to. I don't, though. I'm afraid their mothers are going to think I am a dirty old man, or a pedophile or some kind of deviate or pervert.

This is so sad. We live in a society in which our children are being taught to be afraid of almost everyone. Sure, there are horror stories of children being violated or kidnapped. Sure, there are legitimate reasons why teachers and parents drill into children not to talk to strangers, and, as it turns out, to be fearful of old people.

But children and old people really need each other. Old people have time for children. They know how to talk to them instead of talking down to them. They are able to share some of life's simple pleasures with them that young parents are often too preoccupied with themselves to understand.

It is pointless to talk about these things, I suppose. We live in a world where people are afraid of each other. We suspect the worst about folks we don't know. How sad it is for children to grow up being suspicious of those who simply want to reach out in friendship.

I have noticed that some of the the loneliest people in the world live in places where there are the most people. Watch them walk the malls in shopping centers. They want to interact with strangers but are afraid they'll be rejected.

There's not much that can be done about the human condition. We'll muddle through somehow. The children will grow up, and when they get old, will regret that they have become objects of fear and suspicion.

Too bad. Too darned bad. *February 16, 1993*

Bathroom wars between the sexes

HUNKERED DOWN.

I finally won my argument with Trish that toilet paper ought to reel off the top of the roll rather than from the bottom. It was her view that there is something insensitive, nonplused, even vulgar about having it come off the top.

But I argued that the little printed flowers on patterned toilet paper are upside down if it is reeled from under the roll. Do feminists suspect the toilet-paper industry is dominated by white males, and that's why the flowers are right-side-up when the paper comes off the top of the roll?

Obviously, all women don't buy into my belief that the over/under question is really a gender issue. The Great Northern Co. commissioned a study of 1,200 Americans to settle it once and for all. It found that 73 percent of us want our paper to come off the top of the roll.

The survey also indicated that the average American uses 90 sheets a day. That comes to 75 rolls per person a year. I'm not sure I believe that. As an old Charmin squeezer, I have noticed that there is a lot difference in the size of rolls of different brands of toilet paper. Was single or double-ply paper used?

During the Depression years, some families actually limited the number of sheets to as few as three for each application. Spinning off 10 or 12 sheets was regarded as wasteful.

The survey found that slightly more people (42 percent) tear off their toilet paper right-to-left than left-to-right (35 percent). More than half the respondents say they tear their toilet paper with just one hand.

86

Those statistics aren't valid. It depends on which side of the toilet the dispenser is mounted. Of course most people use one hand to tear the paper. The other hand is holding *The Reader's Digest* or a Victoria's Secret catalog.

Researchers studied the various ways toilet paper is applied. According to the survey, 40 percent of us are crumplers. About 30 percent are folders and about the same percentage are wrappers.

Getting back to the gender differences, I'm guessing that women use more than twice as much as men. There is the obvious reason, but women also use it as facial tissue. Both sexes use it for runny noses. Babies use tons of the stuff. Men use little bits of toilet paper to staunch the flow of blood from razor nicks.

I am not big on musical dispensers or those that emit fragrances when the roller is turned. No colored paper for me. Like Andy Rooney, I believe some things in life ought to be white and no other color. These include soap, dishes, underwear and toilet paper.

Most folks take toilet paper for granted. It's something you don't think much about until it is gone. I'm reminded of how we coped as field soldiers back in the war when no toilet paper was available. Pine boughs work, but you have to be very careful. Letters from home were often used.

This was no great sacrifice to a generation that was brought up using corncobs and the Monkey Ward catalog.

The French were less discreet and more open in these matters than we were. When we were fighting in Normandy, I can recall being involved in the solitary act of seeking blessed relief beside what I thought would be a secluded hedgerow when a group of peasants suddenly appeared from nowhere.

Solemnly, they lined up to shake hands with this embarrassed hunkered-down GI to thank him for his humble role in their liberation.

I wouldn't lie about something like that.

May 25, 1993

The truth about holiday letters

DEAREST FRIENDS:

I know it must seem impersonal to get holiday greetings in a type-written family Christmas newsletter, but it is the only way we know to bring our many friends up to date on what we have been doing this past busy, busy year. Where does the time go?

You may remember our letter last year, which took note of Fred's promotion to deputy assistant sales manager (brag, brag). And we were so proud of our perky little Missy and her straight-A grade average. We don't know where she finds time for her viola da gamba lessons. She wants to study nuclear medicine or become a Carmelite nun. Luv ya, Missy!

Our little Leonard isn't so little anymore. How that boy has grown! He lettered in four sports this year and still devotes two afternoons a week at the homeless shelter. Gosh, were we ever surprised when both Harvard and Yale offered him full scholarships.

It was a hectic year for me, too. I started baking fruit cakes for Christmas gifts in September. I know how people look forward to them. Fred says if they don't want to eat them, they can use them as door stops. (Ha! Ha!) I am still able to do my volunteer work at the animal shelter. Not bad for an old gal who still wears a size 8.

Our dog, Spunky, sends his best. (Woof! Woof!) He is such a darling and a great comfort to us when he wags his tail and looks up with those big brown eyes and smooches us with his cold nose.

But that was last year, dear friends. This year, we have decided to tell the truth for a change. Fred hasn't lifted a finger in the last eight months. He just stays home and drinks beer while he watches women's beach volleyball on ESPN. He tells everyone he is in public relations.

He was fired from his sales job for falsifying his expense account. It was something about all those $200 lunches he was supposed to be having with clients. Actually, he was having those little $200 nooners with a dishwater blonde he picked up at a doughnut shop.

Missy is pregnant. We aren't sure who the father is, but he may be a member of a rock band that blew through town last summer. I don't remember the band's name, but it had three guitars and a howitzer.

Now that she's showing, Missy has lost her job as a model at a motel in Aurora.

Leonard dropped out of school in October. He spends most of his time in the basement playing his stereo with the volume at the level of pain. The only time he leaves is to go out and get those funny-smelling cigarettes he smokes.

Me? Let's not talk about me. I have been pigging out on eclairs and cream puffs so much I can't squeeze my rear end into any of Chic's 32 jean sizes. When I worry, I eat. When I eat, I worry. So what else is new?

Our dog finally ran away. You can't blame him. Nobody ever had time to feed old Spunky. We never let him inside the house because he always relieved himself on Fred's leg.

I went out to look for him after I noticed he had broken his chain in the back yard. "Here, Spunky! Here, Spunky!" I called, but I don't think we'll ever see him again. The new restaurant down at the shopping center has a new entree on the menu—"sweet and sour cocker spaniel."

Ho! Ho!   *November 28, 1993*

It's time to stand up to NRA bullies

NEANDERTHAL.

Will the passage of the Brady Bill mean the end of the National Rifle Association, or is it the beginning of the end? Probably neither. It does send a message that members of Congress have finally been listening to the folks back home and are tired of being bullied by the NRA.

I suspect not all the gun lobby's members are in lock step with its leadership in opposing some kind of control over the sale of assault weapons. Competitive shooters and hunters are generally responsible citizens and are as anxious as the rest of us to keep people-killing weapons off the street.

You know how it is, though—you join an organization for its benefits, but you leave the policy-making to someone else. You are told over and over that any kind of gun regulation would eventually lead to confiscation of your firearms. And you also are told that Amendment 2 of the U.S. Constitution protects your right to own firearms—and it does.

The first 10 amendments to the Constitution, or the Bill of Rights, have been in force since Dec. 15, 1791. Amendment 2 was written at a time when pioneers were at risk from wild animals and other frontier dangers. It also acknowledges the service of colonial farmers who had helped win the Revolutionary War with their muskets and long rifles.

Amendment 2 is contained in a single sentence. "A well-regulated Militia, being necessary to the security of a free State, the right of the people to keep and bear Arms, shall not be infringed."

It is upon these simple words that the NRA has built its case against any kind of gun control. In their own minds, militant NRA members see themselves as a militia charged with defending us all—or, at least, themselves.

They refuse, however, to honor the qualification set down in the amendment. They ignore the words that describe the militia as "well-regulated." This self-appointed militia of wild-eyed gunslingers isn't regulated at all. Its members oppose any kind of regulation, even the Brady Bill, which requires only a five-day waiting period and a background check for prospective handgun buyers.

Will the Brady Bill solve the malignant violence in our country? "I don't think so," James Brady said, "but even the longest journey begins with a single step." Brady, who was White House press secretary, was gravely wounded in the 1981 assassination attempt on President Reagan.

Even though no "nays" were heard when the Senate passed the bill on a voice vote, Colorado's two senators, Republican Hank Brown and Democrat Ben Campbell, had opposed the Brady Bill when it was first introduced in the Senate.

Over the long haul, though, the NRA has won more than it has lost. Because of its intractable opposition to any kind of gun control, the nation is awash with people-killing weaponry.

I understand the affection some people have for their firearms. That's the way I feel about mine. I admire the craftsmanship. I enjoyed competitive shooting when I was young. I suspect that a lot of NRA members share these feelings.

It is probably too much to hope, but wouldn't it be nice if they would stand up as responsible citizens and disassociate themselves from the Neanderthal leadership of the NRA that seems to care so little for the common good?

November 30, 1993

The boom is great, unless you live here

ENDLESSLY.

Let's have a show of hands. How many think Colorado ought to have more growth? Now, how many want to see more cars on the Valley Highway? OK, raise your hand if you want to cram more kids into our overcrowded classsrooms. Next, a show of hands for those who want to breathe more carbon monoxide.

Just a couple more questions. Please raise your hand if you want more Los Angeles gangs pushing drugs in Colorado. How about more urban sprawl, higher taxes?

These questions went unanswered last week when Gov. Roy Romer and Republican candidate for for governor Bruce Benson debated growth. As *News* reporter Katie Kerwin noted in her account of the event, "Across Colorado, builders, construction workers, Realtors and bankers have celebrated growth that far outpaces the national average."

Most of us haven't joined the celebration because the quality of our lives has declined due to malignant population growth. California and Texas exiles are flooding into the state. The truth is that growth is inevitable. Growth is a lot like the national debt: There's not much we can do about it.

Former Mayor Federico Peña told us we needed a new airport to stimulate economic growth. We got the growth, but not as a result of Denver International Airport. It doesn't work and hasn't opened, and we don't know when it will.

Let's put a stop to welfare for the rich. While these guys whine endlessly about social programs for the poor, they are putting their own snouts in the public trough, too. No more tax breaks and other financial inducements to get corporations to relocate around Denver.

Republicans and Democrats have formed an unholy alliance to give away the farm. Fortunately, though, the good Lord sometimes takes pity on us, and we are spared the consequences of their foolishness.

For example, let us return to 1988. The U.S. Department of Energy announces it will build a Superconducting Super Collider and will accept bids from competing states. Boy, do Romer and his Republican pals love this deal! Colorado offers a package of highway and land incentives valued at $300 million.

But it isn't enough. Illinois ups the ante to $700 million. Texas is the winner, though, and gets the deal for $1 billion in bond money. What happens? Well, a big hole is dug in farmland 30 miles south of Dallas. The hole is still there, but Congress cancels the project and Texas is left holding the bag.

Fast forward to June 1991. Roy Romer calls a special session of the Republican-dominated legislature to help assemble a $300 million package to bribe United Airlines to build its maintenance base in Denver.

Romer and Rep. Pat Grant, R-Denver, mastermind the full-court press. United hotshots are in town, squeezing us for every possible penny and keeping us standing on tippy-toes waiting to be kissed. But we end up doing the kissing and you know where and on whom.

United tantalizes us with a new reservation center to be located at Stapleton Airport after DIA is open. But United is building its maintenance base at Indianapolis, and the reservation center is put on the back burner indefinitely.

Now, Indianapolis wishes the maintenance base had been put where the sun doesn't shine. We still have United, the 900 pound gorilla, sitting smack dab in the middle of DIA for which Roy Romer was head cheerleader.   *September 15, 1994*

Ten thumbs up for unhandymen

GROMMET.

This is All Thumbs Day. All Thumbs Day is observed on the first Tuesday in January by people who are as handy with their hands as a bear cub is with his paws.

We are the guys who were standing behind the door when manual dexterity was passed out. I grew up thinking it was a genetic problem because my father couldn't drive in a nail straight. Apparently not. My sons seem to have some aptitude with tools. I have come to depend on Jonathan to hook up my stereo and start my snow blower.

It's shameful. I grew up in the sexist times when there was men's work and women's work, and never the twain shall meet. Oh, I tried to learn how to use tools at Byers Junior High, one of the many schools I attended growing up in Denver.

There were no elective subjects then. The girls learned how to make sugar cookies and sew on buttons in home economics. The boys were required to take shop, a class that was supposed to teach us how to use a hammer without getting blood blisters on our thumbs.

My project was to build a rectangular wooden pencil box. Mine came out looking more like a Daliesque trapezoid. I got a "D" in both woodworking and metalworking. The only shop course I passed with flying colors was bricklaying.

For reasons I never understood, seventh-grade boys at Byers were required to learn how to lay brick. All these years later, I think I could still build a brick wall.

Building a brick wall is much like writing a newspaper column. You do it one brick, or one word, at a time. Maybe the schools should go back to teaching bricklaying instead of Self-Directed Learning 101.

My basement is filled with tools, particularly socket-wrench sets. I am a great admirer of the ratchet tool, although I have never actually used one.

I have 1/4-inch and 3/4-inch drills, a saber saw and a belt sander. Trish once gave me a table saw, a very serious tool I was afraid to use. My most recent acquisition was a power screwdriver.

I'm a sucker for those attache cases advertised in catalogs containing 125 different tools. I even have a collection of weird tools from Brookstone my son, Brett, has given me over the years. I don't know how to use any of them.

My problem is a childish belief that if I buy nice tools I will know how to use them to fix or make stuff. I had suffered a similar delusion that if I bought a nice camera I would be a good photographer. Didn't work.

I have always led a rich fantasy life. Sometimes on Saturday I'll slip on my Monkey Ward bib overalls and drive my old Ford pickup over to Hugh M. Woods. I'll hang around all afternoon looking at dado attachments, dowels, staple guns, drill presses, lathes and other stuff I know nothing about.

Do you watch those cable-TV woodworking programs? It has occurred to me that the guy doing the show uses $75,000 worth of power tools to make a $49 chair.

Bob Vila is my hero. He's the TV guy who restores an old chicken coop into a four-bedroom Colonial guest house with three baths, a kitchen and a wine cellar.

Ever notice that Vila never does any of the work himself? He always has an expert to demonstrate what's going on. "Bill Kenton is the carpenter on the job. Bill, show us how you are going to grommet the festarus to the kranastan."

January 3, 1995

Baseball is still our game! Give it back

SHAME.

I have taken recently to wearing an old red and blue baseball cap with the lower-case letters "db" on front. When people ask about the cap, I tell them: "It's a Denver Bears cap. If we still had the Bears, we'd still have baseball."

But of course the Bears have been consigned to the trash heap of Denver sports history. What we are left with is our $161.3 million investment in Coors Field that is really costing $215.5 million. To get where we are now, we had to kiss the rear end of every owner in the National League.

That's all history. Here we are, standing on tippy-toes, waiting for the umpire to holler "play ball" so our Fake Colorado Rockies can play an exhibition game against the Fake New York Yankees in what is probably the best ballpark in the world.

I have season tickets, but I won't be there. If you look up in the nosebleed section along the first base line and see two empty seats, they will be the Gene Amole protest against the royal shafting we are getting from the players and the owners.

They don't give a damn about us. They think baseball is their game, but they are wrong. It is our game, and they are stealing it from us.

They are thieves. It is our game because we have paid for it, and because we have strong emotional ties to it that were in place long before these pampered fat cats were even born.

The support that fans have given the Colorado Rockies is unparalleled. Are there any attendance records we haven't beaten? So what if our Rockies were a lower-division team? We threw money at them so the world would know that Denver is a major league city. Stupid.

A thousand years from now, cultural anthropologists will sift through the ashes of what we now call civilization and will conclude that the purpose of our city was blindly to support professional sports. To hell with education. To hell with the common good. To hell with public health and safety. To hell with art and music. Professional jocks were our raison d'être.

The owners are trying to break the union, and they may get the job done. They will continue to field fake major league players until the real guys start dribbling back to their teams. There will be a few marquee players first and then the lesser-known guys will be next because they need the money.

They will say to themselves that the deal we had is better than no deal at all. You have to wonder about how unified the players really are. How would they vote on any of the owners' plans that have been rejected by the union and the players representatives?

It will get ugly. There will be wounds that will never heal and friendships that will end. There will be no trust, no loyalty, no team spirit. An entire generation will pass before we can get our game back.

What a terrible shame this is. Someone once said that to understand America, one must understand baseball. The more you think about it, the more that characterization seems accurate. We live in a time when our nation seems more motivated by materialism than by the spirit of peace and freedom.

I hope I am wrong about this. I hope that I will awaken this morning to find that the players and the owners have reached an agreement and that the Fake Colorado Rockies will be replaced by the real Colorado Rockies.

For the time being, though, a pox on both their houses. They ought to be ashamed of themselves. All of them.

March 30, 1995

The hated "n" word isn't OK anymore

SELF-INFLICTED.

What is it F. Lee Bailey, Eddie Murphy, Charles Barkley, Andrew Dice Clay, rap music performers and even O.J. Simpson can say that Mark Fuhrman can't say?

The "n" word.

The "n" word is so bad that we don't use it in the newspaper anymore. About the only place you can hear it is those "def comedy jam" African-American comedy programs on cable television and on rap recordings. Some of the comedians use the "n" word almost as frequently as they use the "mf" word.

Eddie Murphy defends this kind of profane language because he says it accurately reflects African-American street talk. Richard Pryor is acknowledged by many as perhaps the most influential African-American comedian of modern times. For years, he often used the "n" word in his comedy monologues.

He doesn't anymore. A trip to Africa changed his attitude about the "n" word, and he has never used it since. Pryor not only doesn't say the word, but also says he doesn't even think it.

Some African-Americans say it is OK for them to use the word but not all right for Fuhrman and other white people to use it. There seems to be some sort of tacit agreement that self-deprecatory language or stereotypical language is acceptable within some African-American groups but not outside them.

For example, I know a lot of very funny Jewish jokes, but I can't tell them because I am not Jewish. Same thing with Italian jokes or Polish jokes. Myron Cohen, one of the funniest Jewish comics who ever lived, explained that his humor would be just as funny with an Italian accent, but he wouldn't dare tell the same jokes that way because he is not Italian.

The "n" word is perhaps the main currency of rap music. Rap is not just racist, it is sexist, too. Listen to the lyrics the rap group N.W.A. uses in "One Less Bitch:" "In reality a fool is one who believes all women are ladies; a n—a is one who believes all ladies are bitches" N.W.A., by the way, means N——z With Attitude.

As Franklin B. Krohn and Frances L. Suazo write in their article, "Contemporary Urban Music: Controversial Messages in Hip-Hop and Rap Lyrics" in the summer 1995 edition of *Etc: A review of General Semantics:* "... most white people would be surprised to find the hated word 'n——' (is) used so freely. However, words that might seem inappropriate for outsiders to use are commonly used by those within the group."

Sometimes this self-inflicted racism is communicated in code. N.W.A. had a best-selling album in 1991 called Efil4zaggin. To understand what it means, spell it backward. To add emphasis, Phoenix Suns basketball star Charles Barkley proudly proclaims, "I am a n—— of the '90s!"

Clearly, rap music, which is really rhythmic narrative, is a call for social change and an end to repression in a racist society. But some African-Americans think rap has gone too far. Writes Kevin Powell in *Vibe* magazine:

"It's made us think that being hard is the sole definition of being black in the 1990s. It's almost as if we've become the minstrels of the 1990s. White people are sitting back and saying let's watch the n—— wave guns in videos and talk, and grab their crotches and amuse us."

None of this amuses me. I am certainly not amused by Mark Fuhrman's blatant racism. Let me tell you something else: If it is wrong for him to use the "n" word, it is also wrong for all of us to use it, and that includes African-Americans.

September 17, 1995

And the winner is ... Philip Morris

BLAH.

Now that the Republicans have agreed to disagree on abortion, their national convention at San Diego can get on with the business of protecting the tobacco industry from Food and Drug Administration controls and responsibility for killing smokers.

Philip Morris is the leading underwriter of the convention and was a corporate sponsor of the Victory Train that was scheduled to arrive at San Diego Saturday. The cigarette company is also picking up the tab for a Republican beach party today.

Demonstrating that Philip Morris is an equal-opportunity influence peddler, it is also the main corporate underwriter of the Democratic National Convention later this month in Chicago through its subsidiary Kraft foods. How wholesome can you get? Aren't Democrats raising their kids on Kraft Dinners? Philip Morris also owns Post cereals and Maxwell House coffee.

According to INFACT, a national corporate watchdog organization, Philip Morris led the tobacco industry to a record $4.1 million in overall political contributions in 1995. The industry continued to lavish money on both parties this year to the tune of $1 million in the first quarter alone.

Philip Morris was the No. 1 "soft money" contributor to both parties from 1991 to 1995. Soft money can be used to promote political parties but not individual candidates.

There is increasing evidence that tobacco companies control nicotine content in cigarettes to keep smokers addicted. Public health officials want it declared a drug to be regulated by the FDA. That's why Philip Morris is sucking up to both political parties.

What do Republicans and Democrats give Philip Morris for its money? Really, now, Philip Morris isn't making these donations for good government. It isn't throwing millions around unless it gets something in return.

Let us now consider the platforms of the two parties. Actually, no one pays much attention to political platforms 10 minutes after they are approved. I have observed these deliberations up close and personal.

There is a lot of table pounding and shouting. There are hurried deliberations behind closed doors. Deals are cut, concessions are made, ruffled feelings are soothed, and the language is carefully examined, word-by-word.

Broad promises are made to protect the environment, to maintain a formidable national defense, to toughen punishment for convicted drug pushers, to take the waste out of government, to protect the income of senior citizens, to improve educational opportunity, to balance the budget, to reduce the deficit, to cut taxes for the middle class and blah, blah, blah.

Somewhere in the platform, will there be a paragraph condemning the tobacco industry for addicting kids to nicotine? Will there be a sentence or two calling for the regulation of nicotine as a controlled substance?

Don't be silly. Of course not. Somehow, tobacco regulation will be lost in the shuffle and will never see the light of day. No one will seriously propose it because everyone will know good old Philip Morris is picking up a part of the tab.

Big tobacco will continue to poison our young because it is paying off the political parties and key members of Congress it has in its pocket.

Surprise! The grumpiest old man and Slick Willy will be nominated by acclamation, and big tobacco will continue to peddle cancer.

August 11, 1996

To Broncos, fans are raring fools

SUCKERS.

Have you noticed the not-so-subtle change in the status of those who follow the Denver Broncos? We are not fans anymore. We are customers. Know-nothing boobs.

The idea is to squeeze money out of us until we are bone-dry. The Nike people have designed new uniforms so we'll have to replace our orange jerseys with blue ones. It's enough to turn Lyle Alzado over in his grave.

Let's understand one thing about our Denver Broncos: They are about money. And I suppose it will stay that way until we have the spunk to stand up and say, "No more." Without us, they are a bunch of no-neck guys with bad knees. But maybe Barnum was right and there is a sucker born every minute, and Pat Bowlen hasn't run out of suckers.

Changing traditional orange jerseys to blue is a classic example of trying to fix something that isn't broken. Good Lord, football crazies in this town loved those lurid orange jerseys. People painted their houses orange. How many women knitted their husbands gawdawful orange sweaters for Christmas?

It probably hasn't been lost on you that the "D" has disappeared from the Bronco helmet. That's the idea: Take a cheap shot at poor old Denver.

To put this as kindly as possible, is Bowlen trying to keep his options open? Is it a veiled threat that if we don't tax ourselves to build him a new luxury playground, he'll move the team to a city that will?

Maybe the Los Angeles Broncos, or the Birmingham Broncos, or the Memphis Broncos, or the Salt Lake City Broncos, or the Omaha Broncos, or the Savannah Broncos, or the Mexico City Broncos. The Aurora Broncos, maybe?

Bowlen has refused to become an American citizen. He can't even vote for the tax increase he expects us to pay to build him a new stadium. He could become an American citizen and still retain his Canadian citizenship. Why doesn't he do this? Too busy?

Does this rub you the wrong way? Are you insulted because you are being taken for granted? It's rotten that major league sports hold their fans hostage, threatening to move unless they tax themselves to support their extravagant ambitions.

There was a time when the waiting list for Broncos season tickets contained an estimated 30,000 names. Not anymore. Even though the games are technically sold out, it is still possible to get season tickets by just asking for them.

There is no question that the sports dollar is being spread dangerously thin in Denver. Avalanche games are sold out for months in advance. The Rockies continue to attract record crowds. Now that the Nuggets are putting a few victories together, their tickets are selling again.

The popularity of the Broncos faded quickly when they lost a playoff game at home to the expansion Jaguars. Just how much longer can local Broncos zealots expect 36-year-old John Elway to keep winning games in the fourth quarter?

You perhaps noticed that our raring, white bronco that rises above the Mile High Stadium scoreboard no longer appears on helmets. Instead, we have a highly stylized head of a horse with flaming mane.

If you ask me, they have put the wrong end of the horse on the helmet.   *February 9, 1997*

UPS strike touches a nerve in many of us

MYSTIFYING.

Why do most Americans, who are not union members, support the Teamsters Union in its strike against United Parcel Service? Don't they like UPS, or do they adore the Teamsters?

Actually there is little to dislike about UPS, and the Teamsters don't have what might be described as a sterling reputation in organizational and negotiating matters. It should be noted, however, that the union has come a long way since the days Jimmy Hoffa and Dave Beck were running the show for the benefit of organized crime.

One can imagine a majority of Americans backing the teachers union, or even the trash haulers, but the Teamsters? That's quite a stretch.

It is also mystifying that this support is turning up at a time when organized labor's clout has been on the decline for some years compared to the days when John L. Lewis, Philip Murray or Walter Reuther could shut down the country with a strike.

Shutting down UPS has not really inconvenienced most of us. There are alternatives like Federal Express and a beefed-up U.S. Postal Service. So what's going on here?

I'll tell you what's going on. Americans are fed up with being downsized, outsourced and phased out. They are tired of losing their "bennies" and being replaced by part-timers who do not get benefits such as health care and guaranteed pensions.

They have had enough of corporate mergers and buyouts that have left them high and dry. They are really offended when new management comes in and tells them they must reapply for the jobs they already have. They agonize that their jobs will be exported to a country with cheap labor.

They are enraged when they are pushed aside when they are 50. They are devalued when they are maneuvered into early retirement for a reduced pension even though they are still capable of doing quality work.

They are sickened by the amount of money corporate officers are paid. They don't understand why Bill Gates is the richest man in the universe. They are appalled that AT&T fired its CEO and then paid him $24 million to leave. They haven't quite gotten over that General Motors paid Ross Perot $7 million to get off its board of directors.

It's tough for them to understand why they have to take two and sometimes three part-time jobs just to make ends meet. They worry that they have no health insurance for their families. Young women white-knuckle it to work and feel guilty because they can't be full-time mothers.

They are saddened because they can't afford college tuition for their sons and daughters. They are angry because they have to take out a second mortgage on their homes to pay off their plastic debt.

They are not fools. They know that the balanced budget amendment just passed by Congress is really smoke and mirrors designed to get lawmakers re-elected, not to reduce the national debt.

While it is true that there are some companies that are good corporate citizens, there is an increasing number that are not. I think the UPS strike is just the tip of the iceberg. It has become the focal point for the anger many feel about their country and their distrust of corporate America.   *August 17, 1997*

Astaire tapped our fantasies

INNOCENCE.

As I watched the hastily prepared television specials about Fred Astaire the other night, I wondered how many other people of my generation were as saddened as I at the news of his passing. It wasn't just that America had lost its greatest dancer, it was also that some of us were losing touch with our wonderful distant memories of romantic love.

I can remember going to see the first Fred Astaire movies as Americans slowly made their way out of the Great Depression. They were delightful escape fantasies for a nation that had endured all the reality it could bear.

It wasn't until much later in life that I came to appreciate Astaire's artistry. In watching old film clips now, I am astonished at those long, uncut sequences. There were never cutaways showing just his feet, or his face. You always saw all of his body. Despite the length and complexity of those dances, Astaire and his partner, Ginger Rogers, seemed to be having the times of their lives.

When I was a kid, though, it was the romance that attracted me. I suppose I fantasized myself as dancing with Ginger. I was the one holding her close one minute, and then spinning her out to arm's length the next. It was my hand resting lightly on her trim waist and my face that was softly brushed by her blond hair.

When Astaire and Rogers danced, it was as though we were watching the ultimate romantic experience between a man and a woman. In many of those dances, she would at first resist his advances, then he would persist, and finally he would win her over. We always knew how the dance plot would be resolved, but we never tired of watching Astaire and Rogers play out their give-and-take roles.

Each time I watch those classic films now, almost-forgotten feelings come rushing back from my youth. And when they do, I count myself lucky that I was once innocent enough to believe in romantic love and in the sweet mystery of sex.

If this innocence has become passe, then it is the young who are the losers. By the time kids are 13 years old, they want to start jumping on each other's bones. The males are "hunks" and the females are "foxes" and there isn't much of a mystery about sex anymore.

I used to try to dress like Astaire, but my single-button, double-breasted suits never fit quite the way his did. When I tried to wear a tie as a belt, as Astaire did, I looked ridiculous and people laughed. I even bought a boater straw hat like his, but I never had the courage to wear it. Even worse, I never could dance a lick. Still can't.

Long ago, I resigned myself to the reality that I was not Fred Astaire and never would be. I guess I settled for the next best thing. I was able to sit back and permit him to be my personal representative with Ginger Rogers. She would never "change partners and dance with me," as the song went, but it didn't matter. Fred and Ginger were up there on the silver screen, representing all of us who still want to believe in the tender magic of romantic love.

June 25, 1987

Never let death spoil a good time

NITERY.

It is probably not accurate to report that at age 94, Temple Buell drank himself to death. Nor was his demise hastened by the baseball-bat-size cigars he chain-smoked. Certainly Buell's addiction to attractive women failed to shorten his life. It is safe to observe, however, that the venerable Denver architect did enjoy the good life. There is ample evidence to prove that.

My argument with newspaper obituaries is that they are so reverent. The only time we refer to people as Mrs., Miss or Mr. is after they are dead and no longer able to appreciate the respect we have given them. If the dearly departed were liars, cheats, drunks or scoundrels, you will rarely find this information in newspaper obituaries.

That's too bad. Some of our most colorful citizens have shuffled off their mortal coils with only a few close acquaintances knowing what improbable and sometimes outrageous characters they were. Temple Buell was such a man.

And a man he was, not the synagogue newcomers thought Temple Buell to be the first time they heard the name. No, I did not know him well. But blind luck did cast us together late one fateful night in 1954 at a restaurant then called Eddie Ott's Sherman Plaza.

Jack Mohler, then society editor for the *Rocky Mountain News*, and I had a late-night radio talk show from the corner booth of the nitery, a term we used in those days to describe such places. The program came on the air at 11 P.M. and lasted until 1 A.M. when Barney Owl's Night Owl Special came on the air.

It was an empty-headed kind of program. We interviewed celebrities, politicians and other publicity seekers. We laughed at each other's jokes and sometimes even played a phonograph record. Mohler was Denver's first male society editor and a very funny guy. The place had a reputation as a watering hole for Denver's socially elite.

One night, Mohler and I came to work and discovered that Buell, a woman who was not his wife, and a couple of other companions were in the next booth. As we went on the air, they were drinking, laughing and exchanging gossip when all of a sudden, Buell's female friend slumped over, apparently unconscious.

A physician who happened to be in the restaurant examined the woman and pronounced her dead. Her body was pulled out of the booth, placed on the floor of the adjoining aisle and covered with a tablecloth.

Mohler and I pressed on with our program, bravely trying to ignore the tragedy that had just occurred in the next booth. Buell and his friends stayed seated. As I looked up, he motioned for the young woman serving his table and ordered another round of drinks. And then another. Each time, she had to step over the body to serve the drinks. It seemed like forever, but finally 1 A.M. rolled around. Mohler and I signed off, stepped over the corpse and left.

Why am I telling this now? Well, I look at it this way—the woman is dead, Mohler is dead, Ott is dead and now Buell is dead. If I don't get the story told now, maybe something will happen and there won't be anyone left to tell it, and that would be a shame.

January 7, 1990

The airwaves lose a wonderful voice

RENAISSANCE MAN.

Is that too lavish a description of Bob Martin? After all, wasn't he just a sportscaster on the radio, a guy who described the games of the Denver Broncos for people who didn't own television sets? That's the way most people knew him, an announcer with a great voice who never let his mouth race ahead of his mind.

He was all of that, to be sure, but he was so much more. I have watched them come and go, but Bob Martin was the most gifted radio broadcaster I have ever seen, bar none. There was really nothing he couldn't do. His knowledge of classical music, drama and art was extensive. I can remember hearing him on KOA the day the great pianist Artur Rubenstein died. Bob did a short commentary that began with these words, "A great athlete died today."

He then went on to eulogize Rubenstein as an artist who had combined his incomparable musical talent with his formidable physical skills to become one of the century's foremost soloists. He talked about the strength and the stamina required to play Rachmaninoff's 3rd Piano Concerto and how this "great athlete" could do it better than anyone else.

Martin was a good communicator because he knew how to listen and how to observe. He put himself in the background and placed his subject up front. What a rare talent that is in these times of ego-centered talk-radio hosts who feed constantly on the misfortunes of others and who forget that "the play is the thing."

We worked together on the old KMYR when he and Fred Leo came to town from Illinois. Later, Bob worked for me at my station. He could broadcast with authority everything from spot news to jazz to political debate to opera, and do it flawlessly.

He came to Denver at a time when broadcasters were not considered serious journalists. We were all sitting in the back of the bus in those days. Because of Bob and a few others, broadcasters were able to gain respect as responsible members of the media. The craft of broadcasting owes a great deal to Bob for that.

What a wonderful voice he had! *Rocky Mountain News* film critic Bob Denerstein summed it up well. "I thought," he said after meeting

Martin, "If God ever speaks to me, I know his voice will sound like Bob Martin's."

He flirted with television once or twice, but stayed out. He loved radio because it involved the imagination of the listener. Bob liked his audiences and respected them. He believed radio involved people in a much more personal way than television has ever been able to do.

Even though Bob had very conservative political views, he never flaunted them or permitted them to invade his objective reporting of anything. He could laugh about them, however, particularly when Joe Finan, one of the original talk show hosts, used to chide him for carrying a picture of the late Sen. Robert Taft, R-Ohio, in his billfold.

The last time I saw Bob was when Bill Reed and I had lunch with him at the Cherokee Bar. We did a lot of laughing that day. Bill died a few months ago, and now Bob is gone. How fortunate I was to have known them both.   *February 26, 1990*

Nakkula knew the details

Gambler Harold "Murph" Cohen had been missing for three months. Underworld rumors were that the 37-year-old ex-boxer had been the "guest of honor" at a "testimonial dinner" Nov. 3, 1949, before the mob rubbed him out. Earlier that evening, he had been seen at home with his wife and Babe Didrikson Zaharias, a noted athlete.

The case slipped from the headlines as the weeks passed. And then, on Feb. 11, 1950, two boys were playing along the bank of Blue Lake, nine miles northwest of Denver. The water was clear. They thought they saw a body under about 4 feet of water near the shore. They called the Jefferson County Sheriff's Office.

Rocky Mountain News reporter Al Nakkula arrived with Sheriff Carl Enlow. Nakkula glanced at the submerged corpse and said, "That's Murph Cohen."

"How can you possibly know that?" the bewildered Enlow asked.

"Because of the polka dot tie. Murph always wore a polka dot tie," Nakkula replied. Of course he was right. The body was decomposed, but sure enough, on the tie was the monogram HMC. As Nakkula would later write in his story of the coroner's inquest, "The autopsy revealed that Cohen was alive" when he was dumped into the lake and that he "had consumed a light salad just before his death."

What a reporter Al Nakkula was. There was hardly a big story in the 1940s, 1950s and 1960s that he didn't cover. He was the lead reporter on the infamous police scandal of 1961 and '62. He worked on the case of John Gilbert Graham, the Denver man who planted a bomb on a United Airlines DC-6, killing his mother and 43 other people in 1955.

Nak had a wonderful eye for detail and an infallible memory. He knew every cop, every private detective, every bartender, every stripper, every gambler, every flack and every politician in town.

In recent years, he wasn't on the street but worked mostly around the city desk in the newsroom. He did so many little thankless jobs that no one wanted to do. His bylines were mostly on weather and holiday stories. He was also this newspaper's memory.

I was looking through our library clipping files recently and found that Nak had written almost every Colorado Day story in the last 30 years. He never complained about this drudgery. He knew what had to be done, and he did it. There was a tendency to take him for granted. But when he went on vacation, we all realized how much he really did contribute. You would hear people say, "Oh, Nak usually does that."

A few weeks ago, I brought former *News* editor Michael Balfe Howard up to the newsroom to see old friends. Nak beamed when he saw Michael who said, "Nakkula used to put out the paper when I was here."

"He still does," quickly added Rob Reuteman, the current *News* city editor.

I have no idea how many reporters, photographers and editors have passed through this old newspaper since World War II, but there is not one of them who is not saddened at the news of his death. Nak and I were pals for 45 years and often worked on the same stories.

He and I were a couple of the oldest guys in the newsroom. He used to sidle up to me every now and then and snarl out of the corner of his mouth, "Amole, don't you retire and leave me here with all these kids. I'm never going to retire. I wouldn't know how to do anything else. I'll stay here until the day I die."

He did.

April 12, 1990

Pride in country, pure and simple

BREEZY.

Fabricio ("Everybody calls me Breezy") Martinez has six daughters, seven sons and 26, "maybe 27" grandchildren. He stopped by the other day to talk about his life and to express his sadness that so many Hispanic people blame America for their problems.

It's not that he hasn't had to deal with his share of discrimination. "When I was growing up in Mead, Colorado, I would try to go to a pool hall in Longmont with my friends, but they wouldn't let me in because I am a Mexican."

Breezy prefers to be called an Hispanic, but when he speaks of his past, the word "Mexican" keeps creeping into his language. "I'm not a Mexican," he explains, "I am an American. My father was an American."

He grew up in a shack on a sugar-beet farm with his mother, father and two brothers. "We were dirt poor. My father didn't understand why I wanted to go to high school. He thought I should be a farmer like he was. But I wanted to go, and I did while I still helped him with the sugar beets."

His racial identity comes up again when he unfolds his World War II Honorable Discharge. Pointing to a little box in the upper lefthand corner, he says: "You see that? It says I am white, but now everyone calls me Hispanic. Does that make me different than white?"

Breezy served with George Company, 116th Infantry Regiment of the 29th Infantry Division. He fought in the Rhineland and Central Europe campaigns. He was awarded the Purple Heart, the combat infantry badge and the coveted Presidential Unit Citation badge.

"I got hit with shell fragments in my side and shoulder. I managed to crawl away just before a German shell hit where I was lying. My buddies thought I was either dead or missing in action. One of my brothers was also in the Army. He was wounded at almost the exact time I was. My other brother was in the Marine Corps. All of us were honored to serve America in the war," he says.

He briefly attended Colorado State University after the war. "I quit after a year. I was lonesome because there was no one like me to talk to. I lived alone in a little house."

Breezy is proud of his family. None of his sons or daughters speaks Spanish. "I told them I wanted them to talk without an accent like mine. I didn't want their accent to hurt them when they tried to get jobs. I taught them to work hard, and do the best they possibly could do with every job they did.

"One of my sons went to work for the telephone company. They offered him a big promotion just because his name was Martinez. He turned it down because he didn't feel right about it. He quit and went back to school and then went to work for the telephone company again. Now, he has the job because he deserves it and can do the work, not just because of, of, ... what you call it? Affirmative action."

Breezy is 66 and retired from his job with the U.S. Postal Service. He and his wife live near St. Anthony Hospital. They keep track of all their children and grandchildren. "I guess you could say we are integrated. The kids have married Italians, Poles, Germans, all kinds of people."

He and his wife are leaving tomorrow to visit a son in Chula Vista, Calif., who is recovering from surgery. As Breezy left, he explained his visit by saying that he wanted his story to be told "so that people out there know about people like me. None of us has ever been in any trouble. We just want to be good Americans."

February 10, 1991

Mike in the head ends ring career

MOONLIGHTING.

Did you ever happen to visit the basement locker room of Mammoth Gardens at East Colfax and Clarkson Street 45 years ago? If you did, you'll remember the smell of sweat, liniment, chlorine, old cigar smoke and the faint but unmistakable odor of urine. There were old wooden benches in front of the green metal lockers. What light there was came from bulbs shaded by metal reflectors.

That scene came into focus for me when I read Mary Chandler's Architecture column in Sunday's *Rocky Mountain News*. She reported that the Mammoth Events Center, as it is now known, is being refurbished and will be enhanced by a plaza to be built where the Clarkco Hotel once stood next door.

No one probably has kept track of Mammoth's many incarnations since it was built in 1907. The one I remember best, though, was when it was being used by wrestling promoter Tom Zaharias for his weekly matches. This was before the grunt and groan industry discovered steroids and went big time.

After the war, I was moonlighting with Tom as the announcer who introduced the wrestlers in the center of the ring. I took the job because he paid me the grand sum of $15 a night. That, added to my radio announcer salary of $35 a week, brought my income up to $50 a week. Not bad in 1946.

Tom had wrestled on the circuit along with his two brothers, Chris and George, all of whom had gristly cauliflower ears. They had all retired from the ring.

The locker room was where guys like Danny Loos, Mr. America, Bad Boy Brown, Gorgeous George and the Swedish Angel dressed for their matches and got instructions from Tom. If female wrestlers such as Mildred Burke or Juanita "Cobra Clutch" Coffman were on the bill, they had a private locker room. They dressed, buffed their nails and involved themselves in girl talk until it was time to go upstairs and tear out each other's hair.

My retirement from the ring was the result of an incident in which some of the wrestlers conspired to teach one of the guys on tour a lesson. He was tough and mean and refused to follow the script. He tried to really injure his opponents, particularly Bad Boy Brown who was a bleeder. Bad Boy would bleed profusely from even the slightest injury.

A match was set up between the tough guy and the Swedish Angel. It was payback time, and the Angel came out of his corner like a raging bull. The match was supposed to go three falls, but it lasted only seconds. The Angel really put a hurt on him, grabbing his arm and twisting it so hard that his shoulder was dislocated.

We got him downstairs and stretched him out on a bench. Bad Boy sat on his chest while Mr. America and I pulled and jerked his arm back into place. He bellowed at the top of his lungs.

The guy was out of action for several weeks while his shoulder healed. The night he returned to action, he climbed through the ropes and came to the center of the ring. Recognition flashed in his eyes. He grabbed the microphone from me and ripped it from the cord suspending it from the ceiling.

Then he slammed it to the side of my head, sending me to the canvas like a sack of wheat. Tom climbed through the ropes and dragged me out of the ring and carried me down to the locker room where I regained consciousness.

For a time I'd occasionally see him on the street. We didn't speak.

August 27, 1991

Reliving the days in an old hotel

WE LAUGHED.

Max Hummel is being remembered for his Cherry Creek delicatessen and his successful catering business, but my memories of him go back a lot farther. Max was 92 when he died last Friday.

What an imposing figure he was in 1939 when he was the maitre d' of the Pioneer Room at the old Cosmopolitan Hotel at 18th and Broadway. I can see him now, standing ramrod-straight at the door of the dining room.

There wasn't a hair on his head. He wore steel-rimmed glasses and was immaculately dressed in a perfect-fitting dinner jacket and starched formal shirt. His bearing was that of a Prussian general, even though he served only as a German army cook in World War I.

Max was in command of the Pioneer Room, though. Every busboy and every waiter knew it. He was their captain, and they were his soldiers. He demanded perfection from them and he got it. He taught them how to be attentive to diners without being intrusive. They learned something else from Max, too. They learned pride. Pride in service and workmanship was not so uncommon then as it is now.

I was still in high school when I went to the work at the Cosmo as a lobby porter at $2.34 a day. It was the lowest rung on the hotel hierarchy. There was no one below me. My job was to empty ashtrays, sweep away litter and dig the spit and cigar butts out of the sand urns in front of the elevators.

Ultimately, I advanced to service elevator operator, lobby elevator operator, bellboy and then captain of my shift. We worked one day from 6 A.M. to noon, and back at 6 P.M. to midnight. The next day it was just noon until 6 P.M. When a new shift came on the floor, we all wore clean white gloves and marched in formation to our posts. It was sort of like the changing of the guard at Buckingham Palace.

The hotel chef was Henri Pettijean, who operated the kitchen with the same iron hand that Max exercised in the dining room. On slow days, the bellboys would try to figure ways of getting inside the kitchen's walk-in refrigerator. Once the door was closed, we would scarf down as many French pastries as we could.

Henri knew we were doing it but could never catch us. Sometimes hotel guests would have us refrigerate corsages until the next day. This was a perfect excuse for raiding the refrigerator. When one of us would walk in the kitchen carrying a corsage, Henri would drop everything and follow us into the refrigerator. Then he would glower at us as we put the corsage on the shelf right next to the chocolate eclairs, parfaits and petits fours.

What a great time that was! I learned more about life, death and love in that hotel than I ever did in school. I also learned guile, hustle, con and other survival skills that have served me so well in later life.

Back in the 1930s, there was a movie called *Grand Hotel* making the rounds. It was about the many little dramas being played out among hotel guests. I always thought a more interesting script could have been written about the people who work in hotels.

The old Cosmo was dynamited into history on May 20, 1984. I saw Max quite often in the years since we worked together. We loved retelling stories of what went on behind the lobby, in the kitchen, behind the bar and in other parts of the hotel the guests never saw. We laughed at the way we were then, and what we had become since.

I'll miss you, Max.   *March 26, 1992*

He drifted into Telluride and struck a lode of love

HONKYTONK.

This is a love story. It is also a story about salvation, family, art, treasure and luck. But more than anything else, this is a story about love.

Love was about as far from Jim Shane's mind as it could be when he blew into Telluride more than 100 years ago. Like so many others who found their way to this bawdy little mining outpost, Shane was thinking about money. "Gold fever," they called it in those days.

They came from all over the world. The "Rooshins" and the Finns were there. There were a few Chinese and some Italians. Big mines, like the Smuggler and the Tomboy, would come later. But in the 1880s, the prospectors were shoveling and picking along every creek and hillside in San Miguel County.

Folks didn't know much about Shane except that he had never done much hard work. They could tell that by his hands. There were no callouses, just the sensitive hands of an artist, which was his real vocation. That's why he could never get a grubstake, or financing, for his prospecting ambitions.

Before my Uncle Frank Wilson died 20 years ago, he tape-recorded an oral history of Telluride that included Jim Shane's story. He was a great storyteller. Frank owned the Busy Corner Pharmacy, Telluride's only drugstore for almost 50 years.

"Shane finally drifted down into the honkytonk section of town and met a girl by the name of Audrey," Frank said. "I don't know what her last name was, but she was a whore at the best parlor house in town, the red brick two-story house on Pacific Avenue."

Their relationship was a commercial one at first. She suggested they become partners and go into the mining business and finance it by selling a life-size nude portrait of her that he would paint.

"What he got for the painting, I don't know," Frank continued. "But he sold it to a local bar and got himself a sack of beans and bacon and went out on Deep Creek, about 8 miles west of town, and staked a claim. He brought back ore samples that were very rich."

Their relationship deepened into love. Because Shane knew nothing about mining, they decided to sell the claim to an eastern mining company. "Jim built her a nice brick bungalow directly across the street from the old gymnasium. He made an honest woman out of her, and they were married. They lived in Telluride the rest of their lives."

Audrey's portrait turned up over the years in about every saloon in Telluride: the National, the Diamond, the Roma, the Beer Garden and eventually in a private gambling club on the second floor of Frank's drugstore. When the Colorado attorney general cracked down on private gambling, the club was abandoned, along with Audrey's portrait.

Enter my cousin, Robert Wilson, and his wife, Mary. They cleaned up the painting with soap and water (mischievous kids had drawn a mustache on Audrey). She was then displayed in the drugstore over the player piano. After Frank sold the store, the painting was hung on the second floor of the New Sheridan Hotel.

There were several hotel management changes, and the portrait took a beating over the next 20 years. Someone jabbed a ski pole into it. Unruly teen-agers from a church group got out of control one night and ripped the painting from the wall and used it to barricade one of the rooms.

Audrey was battered and vandalized. Robert was about ready to give up and junk the painting. His daughter, Kim Sheek of Mancos, would have none of that. The painting was sent to the Rocky Mountain Conservation Center in Denver to be restored. The center is a self-supporting, nonprofit department of the University of Denver that offers a full range of art conservation services.

Rocky Mountain News photographer Frank Murray and I met Kim and her sister, Kristen, at the center to see the portrait for the first time since its restoration. We were all startled at the color, the detail, the size of Shane's work. Even though the painting was an idealized portrait of a whore, we were seeing her through Shane's eyes. She was no longer a woman of the streets but someone to love and to cherish.

There are no Wilsons left in Telluride anymore. Uncle Frank and Aunt Gladys are dead. One daughter, Betty Jo, lives in Detroit. The other, Billee Mae, lives in Oceanside, Calif. Robert and Mary live in Montrose. Their daughter, Karen, lives in Cortez. Kristen lives in Longmont and Kim in Mancos, where Audrey will be taken.

"I couldn't stand to lose Audrey," Kim told me. "She has become a part of our tradition. It's worth all the time and trouble to get her back again." Because Kim teaches art in a Cortez high school, it is proper that she be granted permanent custody of Audrey.

There are not many of the old people left in Telluride. With all of its skiing and festivals, it certainly isn't the way I remember it as a boy. The drugstore burned down two years ago.

I suppose that if Audrey was still on display there, most folks wouldn't know or care who she was or why the portrait was painted. They would just think she was a nobody. But she's not. She has become a member of our family.

July 26, 1992

Denver shines in Akers' eyes

TRUST.

After watching Carl Akers for the first time, a friend visiting from the East asked why he was Denver's No. 1 television personality. "He is us," I answered without hesitation. That was it. When Denver watched Carl on TV, it was like looking in a mirror.

I have lost track of how many pompadoured, powdered and pampered TV newsmen have come and gone in this town during the past 40 years, but none ever achieved Carl's popularity. Long after he had retired from Channel 9, opinion surveys continued to show him as Denver's favorite newscaster.

If he were to walk into any Denver television station today and get a job, it would be sweeping out the place. The image-conscious, focus group-oriented, ratings-worshiping, consultant-dominated broadcast executives would not give him a second look as an anchorman.

With his craggy face and the wisp of hair carefully combed across his bald dome, Carl came across like your favorite uncle. He had great eye contact with the camera, and when you looked into those eyes you saw trust. When Carl gave you the news, you knew he was telling you the truth.

We have been friends for all of those 40 years. There was a time when I almost became Carl Akers. Channel 7—then KLZ-TV—had just gone on the air in 1953. I had moved over from Channel 9 to Channel 7 and was anchoring the weekend news. Carl was anchoring the Monday through Friday 10 P.M. news.

Carl refused to wear a tie, believing that the tie had nothing to do with the news. He didn't want anything cosmetic about his presentation. Hugh Terry, Channel 7's general manager, took him off the air, replacing him with a guy who turned out to be a drunk.

In what must have been sheer desperation, news director Sheldon Peterson offered me the job. Unknown to Channel 7, I was secretly involved in applying to the Federal Communications Commission for a license to operate a Denver radio station. I confessed this to Peterson and told him I couldn't accept.

I fully expected to be fired because Channel 7 had its own radio station and I would be a competitor. But Terry kept me on in an act of generosity I shall never forget. He said I would need the money. He was

116

sure right about that. I advised him to sweet-talk Carl into wearing a tie and get him back on the air, which he did, and the rest is history.

My favorite Carl Akers story involved a dinner party Jack Carver and his wife were giving for Akers, Warren Chandler and me and our wives. We met first at Carver's house in Lakewood. After a few drinks, the plan was to split up in two cars and drive to the Black Forest Inn in Black Hawk.

Akers and Mary Lou rode in my car with Trish and me. As I headed for the Sixth Avenue Freeway, Carl, who prided himself on his knowledge of Colorado backcountry, said, "No. Don't get on the freeway. I know a shortcut that will get us to Black Hawk before Carver." After directing us up Arvada side streets and down Golden back alleys for what seemed like forever, Carl finally said. "Hell, I don't know where we are. We're lost." We finally got to Black Hawk 45 minutes late.

Even though he was well-paid, Carl never had a shot at the big money television news personalities get today. I'll tell you one thing, though, as a friend and fellow news slave, this old guy is worth his weight in gold. Glad you are feeling better, Carl.

And that's 30. *August 4, 1992*

Behind zebra suit, a fine, decent man

BLEEPING.

Being a professional football referee is like being a member of an order of cloistered nuns. You can associate only with other officials. When you travel, you are given a list of hotels, restaurants and nightclubs that you are not permitted to enter. You are forbidden to have friendships with coaches or players who might be in games you work.

It has been that way for Pat Haggerty for 28 years, and now it's over. He is retiring after becoming one of the best-known and most-respected referees in pro football history.

He is also Bear Valley's neighborhood celebrity. Pat's family and mine have been next-door neighbors for all of those 28 years. We have watched our kids grow up and move away. We shovel each other's sidewalks and cut each other's lawns when the other guy is out of town. We are good friends, the best of friends.

And so Trish and I will be there June 19 at the Stapleton Airport Red Lion Inn when Pat's pals from all over the nation get together to honor him, not for just being an outstanding referee, but also for being a fine, decent human being. It's the sort of thing most folks don't think about when they watch the guys in zebra shirts throw yellow flags.

Those split-second decisions are second-guessed by sportscasters and fans who have the luxury of slow-motion, freeze-frame and re-verse-angle video replays on which to base their wisdom. It's different on the field where the violence is in real time and where the position of the official is everything.

Pat was so good at what he did that he was chosen to referee three Super Bowls. It might have been four had he not been disqualified in 1978 when the Broncos went to their first Super Bowl. Officials can't live in cities where either team plays its home games. He was selected to officiate at playoff games 26 out of the 28 years he was in the league.

He could write a book, but probably won't. In it would be that inci-dent when Chicago Bears coach George Halas ran out on the field and picked up Pat's yellow penalty flag and wouldn't give it back. "I go to church with you on Sunday morning," Halas roared. "I get down on my knees and pray with you on Sunday morning. And what do you do to me Sunday afternoon? You throw a (bleeping) flag at me!"

Or there was that time when a horde of tacklers finally pulled down the elusive Walter Payton, Chicago's dazzling running back. When he didn't get up, Pat ran to him and said, "What's the matter, Walter, are you hurt? Can't you get up?"

"I can't," Payton replied.

Pat looked down and saw that Payton's tacklers had ripped off his pants, displaying his almost-everything. It took a convoy of Chicago Bears players surrounding the embarrassed Payton to get him off Sol-dier Field and into the locker room for new pants.

And then there was that game in St. Louis between the Cardinals and the Saints. I was on a TV crew filming the game. Pat was wired with a cordless remote microphone. He was crouched in the back-field, behind St. Louis quarterback Jim Hart, when a myopic New Or-leans linebacker blitzed into the backfield, taking out Pat instead of Hart.

118

There were a few seconds of awful silence, and then I heard Pat's voice. He was gasping for air as he said, "Somebody get that s.o.b.'s number!"

I don't know if there are any tickets left, but you can call 'Bama Glass, another Denver Zebra, to find out. His number is 420-6037.

June 1, 1993

Recalling Coit, attitude and all

GONZO.

Everyone has to be somewhere. My somewhere is the newsroom. If I hadn't been here 10 years ago this month, I would never have known John Coit when he logged on as a columnist for the *Rocky Mountain News.*

None of us knew what to expect. We should have known he wouldn't fit the mold because he showed up for his job interview wearing a three-piece suit, sneakers and a red baseball cap. John came to the *Rocky* from a Norfolk, Va., newspaper.

Ralph Looney, our editor then, had been judging a national writing contest when he spotted Coit's work, mostly long magazine pieces. He had never written a column, but Looney thought he could, and John was hired.

"Writing a column," Ellen Goodman once observed, "is the world's hardest work that doesn't involve heavy lifting." John faced even a tougher challenge. Denver didn't know him and he didn't know Denver.

But he hit the ground running and had an immediate impact on *News* readers, finding universal themes that somehow touched us all. He didn't just write about bikers, veterans, hobos, skid row derelicts, the homeless, the rich and the poor, he lived their stories, too.

He got snockered in Aspen with Lily Tomlin, rode a boxcar with Ted Conover, went biking on a Harley hog with Vinny "The Blade" Terenova, spent the day with Gov. Richard Lamm, "shot the breeze" with Henry Kissinger and quit smoking for the 15th time.

That just scratches the surface. John was his name, but diversity was his game. Was it ever! We never knew which John Coit would show up until he walked through the door. He might be wearing the uniform of an infantry captain, or a pin-stripe suit, or an earring, or a motorcycle jacket, or camouflage fatigues.

It is my theory that there was more than one John Coit. It wasn't a case of multiple personalities. He was multiple people. One day he was an old man. The next, a little boy. John's loyalties were with the chronic underdog. His work was explosive, unpredictable.

The column became his psychiatrist. He told it the most private things about his abusive father, his marriages, his children, everything. Readers loved it, and him.

The happiest and most important day of his life was New Year's Eve 1985, when he married Susan O'Malley in the lobby of the *Rocky Mountain News*. The wedding was televised. The KIMN chicken was there. A motorcycle gang showed up as did an assortment of reporters, editors, veterans and the just plain curious. Susan, a saleswoman in the *News* advertising department, was beautiful in white.

Just 11 days later, she would wear red at his funeral in Holy Ghost Church. He died at 38 of what appeared to be too much living in too short a time. A Samoan chief in native dress placed a floral lei on his coffin. "Amazing Grace" played on a bagpipe echoed through the sanctuary. Glen Close Jr., a Vietnam veteran, read a poem that ended with: "What's mine is yours. Because—hey, bro—I've been there, too."

His death shocked young reporters because it was an in-their-face reminder of their own mortality. In my column the next day, I would write, "He was outrageous, kind, funny, maudlin, moving, righteous, jaded, innocent, clever, clumsy, honest, self-indulgent, egotistical, modest, gonzo, excessive and often hung over. He was whatever his column said he was on that particular day. But more than anything else, John Coit was a talented writer."   *July 20, 1993*

St. Dominic's merits recognition

THE SIDE DOOR.

There were old north Denver ghosts haunting me last week while I sat alone at the back of St. Dominic's Church. I was there for the funeral Mass of Minnie Mattedi, a dear friend and neighbor who lived in the same block as our old home on West 23rd Avenue. She and her husband, Joe, were so good to my mother all those years after my

120

father died. When Mom was dying, Minnie was there at the hospital to pray for her. And so I wanted to be near her family to demonstrate my love and respect.

Just driving down West 29th Avenue from Sheridan, I got choked up thinking of what it was like growing up in that old neighborhood. I thought of Glen Deaner, Ed Mangei, Sam Hartzell, Karl Boldt, Betty Brauer, Joe Paulson, Paul Epstein, the Haggertys, Jimmy Battaglino, Dick Whitlow, Chink Alterman, Dick Binder, Ralph Paul, Jack Angell, Billy Reed, Gloria Stewart, the Cito brothers, Ernie Capillupo and so many others.

Old St. Dominic's has been a rock for parish faithful in that neighborhood for generations. There is no fancy statuary, no stained-glass windows depicting the life of Christ, no oil paintings. The floor is one of those imitation vinyl mosaics you get at Color Tile. And yet for me, a non-Catholic outsider, there was a strong spiritual presence there, a sense of community.

By contrast, the Cathedral of the Immaculate Conception seems sterile, even with its stunning windows, brilliant white marble sculpture and magnificent stations of the cross. Workers are putting on the final touches so it will be ready for Pope John Paul II when he visits Denver for World Youth Day.

But somehow I can't get old St. Dominic's out of my mind. I want something special for its hard-working priest, its nuns in polyester slacks and its parishioners like Minnie and Joe who have loyally served their church so many years.

World Youth Day will be a series of well-organized photo opportunities showing the pope kissing the ground, praying as he holds his sterling-silver crucifix, saying Mass for thousands, surrounded by an ethnic mix of fresh-faced kids, greeting dignitaries, conferring with President Clinton. You know the drill.

But one night, wouldn't it be wonderful if he would put away his white cassock and dress like an ordinary priest. Then, without fanfare, slip away to St. Dominic's in an old Chevy. No cameras. No microphones. No press.

He could go in the side door, taking a wide berth around that big white dog that barks a lot in the back of the church. Then he would surprise the daylights out of the parish priest and join him in saying Mass for the few faithful, mostly old people, who would be there.

121

The pope is being presented to us as some kind of visiting king. He has been preceded by a display of the wealth of Vatican art. All of this says the church is more about royalty than it is about meeting the spiritual needs of ordinary folks. We should remember that Jesus wore a crown of thorns, not jewels.

Of course the pope won't go to St. Dominic's. Vatican officials have a thousand reasons why he can't. There won't be any surprises. But wouldn't it be wonderful if there were? I am sure it must be difficult for him to break out of the security of his isolation.

Being an outsider, I don't believe in his infallibility but I do hope that beneath all of his elegant trappings of power and prestige, there is still a simple parish priest who hasn't forgotten why he took his vows. I would want this kindly man not to just put on a performance for the cameras but rather to take a private moment to be the shepherd of a small flock. *July 25, 1993*

Let the sun shine for Ed Bowman

DIRTY MINDS.

Weatherman Bowman has Lou Gehrig's disease.

I don't know how to say it any other way. I wish there were a kinder, more gentle way of reporting that one of this town's most beloved citizens has been stricken with one of the cruelest ailments there is.

Amyotrophic lateral sclerosis, or ALS, is all of that. It is, as my friend Cecil Neth once wrote, "an inexorably terminal neurological disorder." There is no cure. ALS withers away the skeletal muscles. Eventually, the victim becomes totally paralyzed, unable to speak, breathe or swallow.

Most everyone knows ALS as the disease that claimed the life of New York Yankees first baseman Lou Gehrig. After he became afflicted with it, Cecil began to refer to it as "Cecil Neth's disease." Now it has become "Ed Bowman's disease," too.

In the more than 50 years I kicked around in the broadcast game, I met a lot of interesting characters, but Ed Bowman was unique. He was not the first television weather reporter in town, but he is the one most people remember best from TV's formative years.

At one time or another, Eddy worked on Channels 4, 2 and 7. He also did weather reports on his network of small AM radio stations, mostly in eastern Colorado, Nebraska and western Kansas. If you ever saw or heard him, you'll never forget Weatherman Bowman.

He didn't have Doppler radar, satellite TV, mountain cams, or other electronic gizmos that are stock and trade of TV weather reporters today. Eddy really knew weather, but he also relied on woolly bear caterpillars and other natural indicators.

He figured precipitation probability by computing the number of cows in a field lying down to those standing up. When we worked together, he tracked my arthritis to predict storms. Eddy never claimed to be a fancy meteorologist. He was, dammit, a weatherman.

Folks loved the weather maps he drew on the air. I never knew how he could be saying one thing to the camera while simultaneously writing something completely different on the map. His "trough aloft" maps became collector's items. He had a great cult following.

Psychiatrists had a field day interpreting them as though they were Rorschach splotches. They saw his troughs as phallic symbols and his puffy clouds as pneumatic women's breasts. Eddy dismissed all of this by saying, "I can't help it if those guys have dirty minds."

He was as much a character off the air as he was on the air. A veteran flyer from World War II, he flew an old open-cockpit Ryan plane with his pixie face out in the slipstream. He owned a motorcycle with a side car. He sometimes wore riding boots and breeches. He was Waldo Pepper and Smiling Jack all rolled into one.

Stubborn as a mule, though. When General Electric fired him after his years of loyal service at KOA, he refused to have even a GE toaster in his house. When we worked together on TV, there was a GE electric water cooler in the office. Eddy wouldn't drink from it.

I suspect there are a lot of people who love Weatherman Bowman as I do and might want to let him know how much they care. His son, John, tells me he enjoys cards and letters. His address is 2481 S. Ivanhoe Place, Denver 80222. During my recent illness, many people wrote to me. Those cards and letters meant a great deal to me, and I still have them.

Could Weatherman Bowman accurately predict the weather? You bet he could.

January 16, 1994

Yelland's on a par with nobody else

LITTLE SQUIRT.

About golf, I know zilch. About Starr Yelland, I know plenty. That's why I wanted to be on hand this week at Green Gables Country Club when he was inducted into the Colorado Golf Hall of Fame.

Despite failing health, old Starr charmed the daylights out of the audience. At the end of his anecdote-filled acceptance remarks, he cried. So did I.

Starr's devoted wife, Patricia, was there. So was his daughter, Leslie, and his sister, Patty, who lights up any room just by walking in the door. A lot of his old pals from Channel 7 had a great time telling and retelling old radio and TV war stories about Starr and how he used to raise hell because he didn't have enough time on his sportscasts for golf scores.

As I was soaking up all of this, my mind kept drifting back to our salad days when he was an announcer at KOA on California Street and I was the night man across the alley on Stout Street at KMYR. After work, we'd hoist a few at Mozart's.

Remember all these old radio guys: Gil Verba, Ivan Schooley, Bob Young, Bill Balance, Clarence Moore, Ed Brady, Milt Shrednik, Tor Torland, Evadna Hammersly, Cecil Seavey, Happy Jack Turner, Ed Bowman, Bob Palmer, Chuck Collins and Shorty, Sue and Sally?

Most folks think of Starr only as a TV guy, but he was wonderful on the radio. He was Denver's first telephone show host on KLZ. What he did, though, didn't resemble in any way the adversarial babble that passes for talk radio these days.

Instead of taking calls from listeners on his "Party Line" program, Starr did the calling. I was fascinated one night when he called W.C. Handy in Memphis. It was the old man's 90th birthday. Starr talked him into digging out his old cornet and playing his composition, "St. Louis Blues," over the telephone. Wow! You don't hear radio like that anymore.

Starr has a basement full of richly deserved awards and trophies, but there has been pain along the way, too. He was devastated in 1968 when his 17-year-old son died from injuries incurred two years earlier in a roller coaster accident. Somehow, Starr managed to go on TV every night with never a hint of the anguish he was suffering.

The death hit me pretty hard, too. I knew the boy when he was in diapers. When Bill Reed and I were broadcasting DU hockey games, Starr would bring the little squirt up to the press box and plop him on my lap while we were on the air. The kid would giggle and whoop it up when the Zamboni resurfaced the ice between periods.

Starr survived serious coronary problems. His wife, Helen, called me after his heart attack. I rushed over to St. Joe's and saw him in the critical care unit. He looked awful. I thought he was going to die, but he snapped back after bypass surgery and was on the air again in record time.

When Starr called me to tell me Helen had died, I wondered just how much can this guy take. He's a fighter, though, and is still fighting. It should be noted here that there have been three wonderful women on his side: Leslie, Helen and Patricia.

He's been a wonderful pal all these years. He and Helen were at my wedding 29 years ago at Point Loma in San Diego. Last year when I was in the intensive-care unit at Porter Hospital, I was dimly aware of Starr crashing through the door to tell me he was on my side.

Hey, Starr, it's great you are in the Colorado Golf Hall of Fame, but I want you to know that you are in the Amole Hall of Fame, too.

June 16, 1994

Bob McPhee struck by his convictions

CONTEMPTIBLE.

Was Robert McPhee the Last Angry Man? I don't know, but he will do until someone angrier comes along. His son, Mike, stopped by last week to tell me his father had died.

I wasn't surprised. Dusty Saunders and I had seen Bob crossing Tremont Place just a few weeks ago. I thought he looked terribly drawn and tired. He had told me in 1992 that he had prostate cancer.

As old guys will do, we compared infirmities and concluded that life doesn't get any easier. The next day he dropped off a copy of a letter he had written to James Joy, the executive director of the American Civil Liberties Union in Colorado. In it, he made the case that suicide should be a civil right that can be exercised "without undue trauma."

125

He added, "The public has been almost hopelessly brainwashed by centuries of religious dogma that preaches the disallowed redemption of one who commits suicide.

"Thus millions are left with no lifestyle and forced to needless suffering while waiting for the inevitable. Thus are health-care costs recklessly expended with unlimited and expensive—but perfectly legitimate—treatments, which only briefly postpone mortality."

While Bob often described himself as "a contender for world-class champion agnostic," he was better known as an intractable opponent of mindless development and downtown's foremost windmill tilter. He was a gadfly and an iconoclast. His fiery commentaries were frequently printed in the *Rocky Mountain News* and *The Denver Post*.

In a letter he wrote to former Gov. Richard Lamm, he began, "I have in mind your contemptible cowardice." Of former Mayor Federico Peña, he wrote, "The developers own (him). What really hurts is when somebody from an ethnic minority gets in there and is absolutely putty in these guys' hands."

In a *News* interview, Bob said, "The Democrats don't want to get out and lead. They want to get on TV with 30-second slogans." Of Republicans, he said, "Most of them are simply stupid, insensitive, mean-spirited people who are just after the buck."

My relationship with Bob got off to a rocky start. He submitted a commentary piece to Vincent Carroll, editor of the *News*' editorial page. It was a merciless attack against me. For 750 words he raged against me because I had sold my interest in a radio station and put the money in the bank.

Vince came to me and said, "My God, we can't print this. It's too vicious. What did you do to upset McPhee?" I told him I didn't know but I suspected he was pigeonholing me with the developers because I had made a few bucks.

Actually, I thought he was right about most things, including suicide. We finally got better acquainted and enjoyed an easy, friendly relationship. We read the same authors, particularly E.L. Doctorow. I agreed with him that downtown needed more residents.

Bob lived out his last years in his downtown apartment. To some, he seemed reclusive, but he really wasn't. His companion was an ancient computer into which he poured his thoughts, ideas, criticisms and his heart. I'd often see him on the 16th Street Mall, soaking up the atmosphere of his beloved downtown.

At the end, Bob remained true to his convictions. He died where and when he wished, and by his own hand. I'll miss him. Because he was a world-class champion agnostic, I have no idea where his soul resides, but I hope he is resting in peace and without pain.

January 14, 1996

The tears we shed, we shed for Greg

SLACK.

The chair on the other side of my desk is empty. I can just barely see it through the flowers people have been bringing all morning. It will take me awhile to get used to the fact that Greg Lopez won't be sitting there anymore.

Reporters have been stopping by to tell me that his death "just isn't fair." It certainly isn't. Sitting here, trying to figure out what to write about him, I keep wondering why the good often die so young.

Greg was good, all right. In searching my memory, I couldn't come up with a single instance in which he said anything unkind or insensitive about anyone. He was eternally in love with people.

But you know that from his stories. He was a wonderful listener. He loved the language of ordinary folks and incorporated it so skillfully in his columns you could actually "hear" their voices. He was a master of his craft.

When their daughter was stillborn in September 1994, Greg and his wife, Kathleen, were overwhelmed by grief. Friends and relatives came by to comfort them.

"Almost all of them said there was nothing they could say," Greg wrote. "Some had gone on to say there must be a reason these things happen. You can choose to believe that or not, but you can't choose when you will believe it and when you won't."

Not long ago I brought a picture to work of my infant grandson, Jacob. Greg looked at it and smiled. I told him that he and Kathleen ought to try again to have a baby, that there is nothing in life so gratifying as being a parent. He said, "Oh, yes, we will."

What a wonderful father Greg would have been. His death is a tragedy not only for us who knew and loved him but for all the lives he would have touched in the promising future that was stolen from him.

People often ask why I don't retire. I tell them it is because of writers like Greg that I still want to work. No, it doesn't make me any younger to come into the newsroom everyday to work with young people, but it does rejuvenate my spirit.

I learned a great deal from Greg. I thought of him not only as a friend but also as a teacher. His writing was uncluttered and to the point. He wrote to express, rather than to impress. This is a skill many writers never master.

It was good we sat together in the newsroom. Mine is an opinion column. His was about what other people feel and think. We thought our work complemented each other. There is a bitter irony in Greg's death. Last September 3, the headline on Greg's column was, "NOBODY CUTS ANYBODY ANY SLACK ON THE ROAD." He re-created an experience he had while driving on Interstate 25. He was listening to a baseball game between the Colorado Rockies and the Pittsburgh Pirates.

Always a careful driver himself, Greg watched what other drivers were doing on the crowded freeway. "A man with a red car with a green fender clapped his hands, took a drink from a bottle of Budweiser and kept swallowing until it was finished. A man in a BMW slapped the steering wheel … "

It was someone in a BMW who forced Greg's truck off I-25 Sunday night, killing him instantly. No one cut Greg, or his family, or his friends who loved him, any slack.

In our journalism world, there is an unfortunate perception that we neither bleed nor cry. We do. Greg was very special to us, and we shall always miss him.   *March 19, 1996*

Mayor loved city down in his bones

SLOGGERS.

We met in Maureen and Bob Stapp's home 40 years ago. It was a party for some of Bob's newspaper and political pals. I knew about Bill

128

McNichols, of course, He was chief of staff for his brother, Steve, when he was governor.

We small-talked our way into a corner and compared notes about where we were during World War II. He served in the Fourth Armored Division and I was in the Sixth. Both divisions were in Gen. George Patton's Third Army, and so we had plenty to talk about.

Bill was a replacement during the Battle of the Bulge. At 33, he was older than his battalion commander, too old to fight as a dogface. But, there were heavy casualties, and the Army replaced them with anyone who could walk and carry an M-1.

We talked, laughed and then we wept. OK, so we were having a few. That night, as we left, he put his hand on my shoulder and said, "Good night, old slogger," and I said, "Good night, old slogger." That's the way it was between us from then on.

After his death at 87, Mayor Bill is being remembered for his brick-and-mortar accomplishments like the 16th Street Mall, the Denver Art Museum, the Denver Center for the Performing Arts and new city parks. The city is not the same without him. He had Denver in his bones. How he loved this city!

The old slogger and I didn't agree on everything, though. We parted company on the proposed Winter Olympics of 1976. He really wanted those games here. I raged against them on television commentary. Voters rejected the Olympics in 1972 by a ratio of three to two. It was a bitter defeat for him.

I raised hell when he took $750,000 of federal revenue share money to put new lights on Mile High Stadium so Howard Cosell would do *Monday Night Football* from Denver. I opposed a $25 million bond issue for east stands at Mile High. The 10 percent seat tax to finance it was supposed to be temporary, but we still have it even though the bonds were paid off years ago. There is nothing so permanent as a temporary tax.

Still, we never let our disagreements affect our friendship. Every time we'd meet, a big grin would split his face and he would say, "Hello, old slogger." Even during periods when he and the media were barely speaking, his door was open to me. I would always get wonderful quotes from him, like, "The county commissioners are out there poisoning the wells." He thought he had a deal with them to support a Boundary Commission proposal instead of the Poundstone

Amendment which froze Denver's boundaries and its tax base. He believed he was betrayed by them. Both amendments passed. "It wasn't enough to hang me, they had to shoot me, too," he said.

Twice he submitted plans for a metropolitan services authority but was turned down by suburban voters. They feared any kind of metropolitan government would lead to desegregation of their schools. The white flight to the suburbs was draining the city of its middle-class families.

Then we were hit by the energy bust. McNichols remained in command. It was his steady hand on the tiller that guided us through. He never considered running for higher office. To Bill, there was no higher office than Denver mayor.

Goodbye, old slogger.   *June 17, 1997*

Gun-totin' governor shot down scandals

SNAKE PIT.

You can imagine how I felt one night sitting alone at the Denver Press Club bar when this big cowboy came busting through the front door and was heading straight for me.

All of a sudden he slapped leather and pulled two .45-caliber Colt Peacemaker revolvers. Pointing them directly at me, he snarled, "Amole, you gave Palmer Burch seven more minutes on your television program than you gave me."

Burch was Colorado state treasurer and the Republican candidate for governor, and, of course, the big gunslinger was Colorado Gov. Stephen L.R. McNichols who had just returned from the annual *Denver Post* train to Cheyenne Frontier Days. It befitted his celebrity status when newspaper headline writers always referred to him as "Steve."

He didn't shoot me that night, but he did defeat Burch in the November general election. After serving six years, Steve was finally defeated by John Love in 1962.

It was said then, as it has been many times since, that Steve was the best governor this state ever had. I believe that, even though most governors in my lifetime have been effective, decent, well-intentioned men.

It was pleasant the other day to sit down with Steve and Sam Lusky to shoot the breeze about nothing and everything. In the process, I learned for the first time how he wound up in charge of the investigation into Denver's notorious 1962 police scandal.

There had never been anything quite like it anywhere. Fifty of "Denver's finest" were convicted of grand theft and sent to prison. The "burglars in blue," as they were called, were masterminded by the Adams County sheriff, himself a former FBI agent.

Steve recalled that Palmer Hoyt, editor and publisher of *The Denver Post*, and Jack Foster, editor of the *Rocky Mountain News*, had called to arrange a secret meeting with him. "I couldn't imagine why these two mortal enemies of each other would want to meet with me together."

What they wanted was to inform him that reporters for both newspapers had turned up massive evidence of a breakdown of law and order in the Denver Police Department. And they wanted Steve to order a state investigation. "Hell, I couldn't do that," Steve said. "Denver is a home-rule city. For me to do that, I would have to have a request from the city."

The next day he got it in a letter from Manager of Safety John Schooley. Mayor Richard Batterton had previously described the scandal as a "few rotten apples in the barrel." Following a final report of the state investigation, Steve lined up the crooked cops and personally relieved them of their badges and guns.

But that was only one incident during his six years as governor. If he is remembered for nothing else, it will be for the "giant step forward" in the way Colorado met its mental health responsibilities. The Colorado State Hospital at Pueblo was truly a snake pit until Steve initiated in 1959 a massive effort to change its policy from custodial care to one of treatment and rehabilitation.

He invited me to Pueblo the day the doors were unlocked. I saw men and women leave hospital wards where they had been confined for 20 years without so much as stepping out the door. Unforgettable.

Again, Steve, thanks for everything.

September 14, 1997

I'll take dumplin's with a side of brie

HOME COOKIN'.

I hope I'm not getting the reputation of being the resident OF (old fogey) at the *Rocky Mountain News.* What the heck, I like brie cheese, Tina Turner, Saab automobiles, chicken fajitas, Wynton Marsalis and little kids named Tyler, don't I? But I draw the line when it comes to squeezing lime juice into my beer, or gagging down a couple of other trendy culinary distortions that are showing up on restaurant menus.

Trish and I stopped by Bennigan's the other evening for a quick dinner in the non-smoking section. The minute I saw the "warm salads" selection in the new menu, something inside me snapped.

"Lawsy me," I said to her in my stage whisper, "Don't that beat all? That's real home cookin', hain't it? Reminds me of when I was jest a little bit of a bucko, playin' out in the cold and snow in my grandmaw's back yard."

"Keep your voice down. People are staring at us," Trish said without moving her lips.

"Us kids were rollin' around in the snow, makin' a snowperson, throwin' snowballs at one another, and jest plain havin' fun. Then that wonderful old lady would come to the back door and holler, 'You kids come on in out of the cold, now. It's time for supper and your old grandmaw has some real rib-stickin' fixins settin' right on the table.'"

"You mean? You mean?"

"'Yes,' Grandmaw would say, 'You come on inside and wash your hands 'cause we're havin' warm salad.'"

To me, a warm salad sounds as though it is something Phyllis Diller might whip up for Fang.

Have you been to those rooty-toot restaurants that feature nouvelle cuisine? Nouvelle cuisine, by the way, is a method of food preparation in which the French have reinvented the cucumber, and the green beans and broccoli are undercooked, and the whole shot costs you "Twenty-three Dollars."

Anyhow, a waiter who identifies himself as Stanley minces over to your table and says, "Hi. Let me tell you about our special. Chef Bruno has prepared a simply delightful chilled raspberry soup for today. We all think it is absolutely scrumptious!"

Chilled soup made of raspberries? Scrumptious? Come *on* now. Soup ought to be made out of beans, onions and smoked ham hocks. Or maybe tomatoes, celery, carrots, peas, potatoes, barley and big chunks of beef shank. And it should be so scalding hot you have to blow it before you can eat it.

While we are on the subject, we should get together and file a class-action suit against anyone who makes a cold pasta salad. To me, there is nothing so unappetizing as a cold, wet noodle, unless of course, it is cold, leftover pizza for breakfast.

All food should come in traditional shape and form. I can remember trying to explain to Lloyd Knight, my old radio sidekick, about how to determine the circumference of a circle. "You just use the mathematical formula of pi r square," I said to him.

"Pie are NOT square," Lloyd replied indignantly. "Pie are round. Cake are sometimes square, but pie are always round."

July 2, 1987

Memories spring from seltzer gift

EGG CREAM.

I had seen seltzer bottles in the movies long before I ever used one. There was always a seltzer bottle and a decanter of Scotch whisky on the table in English drawing-room comedies. Somewhere in every Marx Brothers film was a sketch involving a seltzer bottle, usually squirted by Groucho smack dab down the decolletage of a busty old dowager.

And so when I started working as a bellboy at the old Cosmopolitan Hotel back in the 1930s, I knew how to squirt someone with a seltzer bottle. We'd find them partially filled in the halls with the dirty room-service dishes in the mornings. The bellboys would run up and down the halls, spraying each other in seltzer bottle duels.

My next contact with seltzer bottles came in 1951 when I was staying at the old Tokyo Correspondents Club at No. 1 Shimbum Alley during the Korean War. It was a sort of home away from home for reporters from around the world who were supposed to be covering the Korean War. We'd spend a couple of weeks at the front and then straggle back to Tokyo for weekend R&R.

The Russian Embassy was just a few steps away. We amused ourselves by squirting the guards and the NKVD (now KGB) agents with seltzer bottles. We never squirted the correspondent from *Tass*, the Russian news agency, because he was supposed to be a noncombatant. Actually, no one believed he was a newsman because he knew very little about journalism. He knew a great deal about drinking, however, and used to hang out at the Correspondents Club bar where vodka was cheap.

All these seltzer bottle memories flooded back when a box was delivered to my desk the other day containing two Sparkletts Seltzer bottles, a new syphon seltzer product in a plastic container with a reusable plastic "spritzer" on top. It looks quite a bit like the seltzer bottle we knew in the olden days.

European Jewish immigrants introduced seltzer to this country around the turn of the century. The price for a tall glass of unflavored seltzer was 2 cents, prompting publisher and humorist Harry Golden to name his best-selling book of anecdotes about New York's Lower East Side, *For 2 Cents Plain*.

For a penny more, a person could buy an egg cream. The recipe for an egg cream is to combine 1 ounce of Fox's Ubet chocolate syrup, 1½ ounces of whole milk and seltzer in a 12-ounce glass. Add a scoop of vanilla ice cream and you have an ice cream soda. There was no egg in an egg cream.

The old glass seltzer bottles all but disappeared during World War II because most of them were manufactured in Czechoslovakia. According to the poop sheet sent to me with the Sparkletts bottles, only a few mom-and-pop companies still bottle and deliver seltzer in old recycled seltzer bottles.

Sparkling water has become very trendy. I am told that there is even a bar in Beverly Hills that serves nothing but an array of the various brands of bottled water.

Quote: "Water? Why did you bring me water? I said I was thirsty, not dirty."—Lloyd Knight.

May 23, 1989

Wars and diets exact their price

TRADE-OFF.

The Idea Fairy was sitting on an old brick, next to the telephone on my desk, when I walked into the newsroom.

FAIRY—Did someone throw this at you?

ME—No. Bob Denerstein brought it to me from Telluride. The brick is from my Uncle Frank's old drugstore that burned down just before the Telluride Film Festival. Bob said he was lucky to get it because the town was cleaning up after the fire as fast as possible to get it ready for the film festival.

FAIRY—You were very fond of your uncle, weren't you?

ME—Yes. What a storyteller! He was a captain in the 89th Infantry Division during World War I. He once told me he led his company into battle astride a big, black horse. The fighting raged all night. It was so bad that when the sun came up the next morning, the horse had turned to white.

FAIRY—Incredible!

ME—One of these days I am going to write a long article about him and his recollections of Telluride history.

FAIRY—You ought to do something like that to get your mind off the airport, the baseball stadium and the automobile race. You're getting awfully crotchety. Maybe it's your diet.

ME—My diet?

FAIRY—According to a story in *The New York Times*, people who lower their cholesterol sometimes become more aggressive.

ME—You mean, chicken, fish and Egg Beaters are making me crotchety?

FAIRY—Scientists have found that people who lower their cholesterol, in some groups, have more accidents, suicides and homicides.

136

Apparently, reducing cholesterol doesn't reduce their mortality rate. They don't live any longer, they just die from different causes.

ME—Are you saying that I am less likely to to die of heart disease, but more likely to take the big sleep in an automobile accident?

FAIRY—That is oversimplification, but you get the idea. Come to think of it, I liked you better when you drank martinis and pigged out on pot roast, corned beef and cabbage, and steak smothered with pork chops.

ME—Do you suppose these fancy scientists of yours have it all backwards? Maybe dieters are aggressive, mean, cantankerous, stubborn, ill-tempered, curmudgeonly, sarcastic and cynical simply because they are tired of eating chicken and fish. I have had it with chicken teriyaki, chicken Hawaiian, chicken Marsala, chicken picatta and chicken mozzarella. I am also tired of eating fish that looks like something that washed up on the beach at Sloans Lake.

FAIRY—Be grateful for what you have. At least you are not eating combat rations in Saudi Arabia. What do you think will happen over there? Will we go to war?

ME—A lot of people are talking it up. I guess we don't know what the bottom line is yet.

FAIRY—Bottom line?

ME—There is a trade-off. How many barrels of Valvoline do we get for every American boy who is killed? American parents and wives want to know. The Defense Department will have to send out telegrams saying, "There is good news and there is bad news. The bad news is your son was killed in action. The good news is we liberated an oil field for the Japanese and the Germans."

FAIRY—Boy, you are cynical, aren't you? By the way, what did you have for lunch today?"

ME—Chicken delight.   *September 13, 1990*

Chocoholic admits dark addiction

DOG DROOL.

Somewhere in James Hilton's *Lost Horizon*, a philosophy is expressed of moderation in all things, even in moderation. I try to be that way about chocolate. You know, a Hershey's Kiss here, a Mr. Goodbar there, and on special occasions, a cream-filled Godiva truffle.

On Valentine's Day, Trish gives me a heart-shaped box of See's assorted chocolates. We always get a 3-pound box of See's for Christmas. I scarf an occasional dollop of Haagen-Dazs dark chocolate ice cream. Mostly, though, I'm pretty much under control.

OK, so I have a little problem, but I'm working on it. For a long time, I was in denial. But I couldn't keep covering it up like the ugly little secret it is. There were times I would lurch through the front door as late as 8 o'clock at night, just reeking of Tootsie Rolls and Jell-O chocolate pudding.

My problem was going on an occasional chocolate binge. I'd start with Duncan Hines chocolate brownies. Then I would down a parfait or two. Next I would hit a few Milky Way fungoes and then segue into hot fudge sundaes, finally passing out on chocolate-covered chocolate doughnuts or devil's-food cake.

It got so that chocolate was dominating my life. I put it before my home and family. I'd wake up in the night and secretly devour a couple of Klondike chocolate ice cream bars. I even got to hanging out with the Baskin-Robbins crowd. I knew I was sick when I started to stash M&Ms in the bathroom.

But I'm recovering. Or at least I was until the new Dove bars came along. Have you tasted the Dove bars yet? First it was just the bars. Now they have come out with those seductive Dove Miniatures in either dark or milk chocolate.

Don't just bite into it and gobble! What you do is put one of those little squares on your tongue and hold it there until it dissolves. It isn't just the flavor, it's also the silkiness, the aftertaste. How quickly they melt away. It isn't possible to eat just one.

I knew I would have to come up with a strategy to keep myself from becoming hopelessly addicted. I was just starting John Grisham's new novel, *The Client*, when I decided to ration myself to just one Dove Miniature per chapter.

What I failed to compute was my dog, Oreo, who is as loopy over chocolate as I am. You'd have to expect that, I suppose, from a dog who is named after a chocolate cookie.

I would quietly try to remove the foil wrapper from a Miniature as I was reading. But it didn't matter where in the house Oreo was, or how quiet I was, she'd come roaring up the stairs and right up to the side of the bed and blow her hot dog breath on me and dribble dog drool on my hand. She'd fix me with those big brown sparkling eyes and I would have to pop the Miniature in her mouth.

How can she hear that? Or is it the chocolate aroma? She wakes up out of a sound sleep, or scratches at the door if she's outside. Maybe it is some kind of primordial instinct. Whatever. I have to share. I've tried to palm off Girl Scout Samoa cookies instead, but Oreo knows the difference.

Well, anyhow, Oreo and I were up half the night and I'm almost through with Grisham's book. It was partly because the book is very good and partly because I couldn't stop eating the Dove Miniatures.

Quote: "When someone new comes to Denver and asks me about my favorite bar in town, I always tell him, 'It's Hershey with almonds.'"—Mark Wolf.

March 18, 1993

Life with just tofu is not worth living

MARTOONIES.

Trish keeps asking me if I feel better. Better than what? She means better than how I felt before we began counting grams of fat. Actually, I don't feel any better—maybe even a little worse.

But look at her. The pounds are melting away and her clothes don't fit anymore. Her eyes sparkle and she has pep in her step. She looks great. But here I am, just as pot-bellied as before. I have not lost an ounce.

It doesn't make sense. We are regulars at Healthy Habits. We are devoted to low sodium, no cholesterol, no MSG foods. I eat so many salads my friends call me "Old Lettuce Breath."

She and I eat the same food for breakfast and dinner. I can't figure it out. Do you suppose it could be the ham hocks, beans and cornpone I eat at the Press Club for lunch? It brings to mind that old Moldavian proverb I just made up: "Man cannot live by tofu alone."

Maybe it's a decade thing and has something to do with the '90s. The last of the great decades was the 1940s. It's been downhill since. The '50s were boring. Things went to hell in the '60s. The '70s people were self-absorbed. The '80s generation was devoted to greed. And now we have the '90s and a generation of puritans willing to starve themselves to death so they can live a few days longer.

Do you suppose they are preoccupied with their mortality and want to live forever? I have tried to explain to them that death isn't so bad. It means no more arthritis, and everyone gets to ride in a Cadillac.

But they don't buy it. They insist on punishing themselves by squeezing into spandex pants and wearing little ladybug helmets to go out and find a hill to climb on their mountain bikes.

In the olden days, regulars at the Press Club bellied up to the bar for boilermakers. Now, they sit there and suck up iced tea and Diet Cokes and try to remember when they had their last real belt.

Trish is fond of reminding me that the reason I have so many aches and pains now is because I didn't take care of myself when I was young. She's right, of course, but I do have those wonderful memories. When the shadows get long for the '90s crowd, what sort of sterile retrospection will occupy their idle hours?

There is something to be said for the old adage that it is better to have loved and lost than not to have loved at all. This is the theme of *The Bridges of Madison County*, a best-selling 171-page novel written in just 14 days by Robert James Waller.

It's about a *National Geographic* photographer and a married farm wife who have a four-day affair that sustains them for the rest of their lives. The book was a quick read, but I thought it was hokey, overwrought.

I kept wondering why the woman's husband didn't notice that funny little smile on her face when he and the kids came back from the state fair. "Anything happen while we were gone, honey?"

"No. Not much," she answers. "Just the same old, same old." Didn't he wonder where all the brandy went?

To each his own. Thank God I have the '40s to remember. There we were, sitting flank-to-flank at the old Shaner's bar on 17th Street. We were sipping Timmy's five-to-one Beefeaters martoonies and digging Johnny Smith playing "Moonlight in Vermont." Calories? Carbohydrates? Triglycerides?

You must be kidding. *July 15, 1993*

Ketchup menace: The plot thickens

MANLINESS.

I call it The Great Ketchup Conspiracy. It must be a conspiracy, because there is no other explanation. It doesn't matter where I go to eat, I always have to break in a new bottle of ketchup.

I hate that. It's bad enough to break in a new bottle of ketchup at home, but to be served one at a restaurant is asking too much. It happens to me all the time. That's why I think it's a conspiracy.

In every restaurant there is a lookout who observes me getting out of my car. The word is then whispered to the kitchen: "Amole's coming in. Quick, get out a new bottle of ketchup so we can watch the old boy make a fool of himself."

It starts innocently enough. As soon as I am settled at my table, a smiling young woman approaches and says, "Hi! My name is Vicki. I'll be your server."

"Hi!" I respond. "My name is Gene. I'll be your customer."

"Let me tell you about our 'catch of the day' seafood special," she beams.

"Not necessary," I tell her. "Just bring me a medium-rare cut of prime rib and ketchup."

"You're not going to put ketchup on our prime rib," she frowns disapprovingly.

"Yes, I am!" I say, mimicking the little guy in the Bud Light TV commercials.

Then comes the inevitable new bottle of Heinz ketchup. I know it's new because I have to twist hard to get the lid off. Then the struggle begins. First, I try holding the bottle with my right hand and delicately tapping its neck with my left forefinger. Nothing.

Next, I invert the bottle and shake it. Still nothing. My face reddens as I shift the bottle to my left hand and begin slapping its base vigorously with the palm of my right hand.

Thwop! Thwop! Thwop! It is quiet now, and I can feel eyes on me from everyone in the restaurant. Somewhere behind me, I know that Vicki and the other servers are whispering and giggling at my plight.

Thwop! Thwop! Thwop! Then all of a sudden, SPLAT! At least a third of the bottle gushes onto my plate and into my lap. You know the drill.

Some years ago in this space, I cheered the development of the plastic squeeze ketchup bottle. Mal Deans, a former managing editor for the extinct *Philadelphia Bulletin*, was writing a novel and working here part time as our readers' representative columnist. He took me to task for what he described as my "sissy attitude" about ketchup bottles.

"You're not a man if you can't handle an ordinary ketchup bottle," he snarled. "The country's going soft if we have to resort to squeeze ketchup bottles."

A fine one he was to talk about manliness. At the time, his wife was managing editor of Boulder's *Daily Camera* newspaper. When she went to out-of-town conventions and meetings of managing editors, Mal would go with her.

I asked him what he did while his wife was busy with convention activities. "Oh, there's always plenty of things planned for the spouses," he said, "like teas, fashion shows, luncheons and card parties."

Actually, Mal was a decent sort about most everything except food. Being from Philadelphia, he was a great booster of scrapple as the breakfast of champions. He got me to try it once, but I regretted it almost immediately, especially after I read the label and discovered what it is made of. It tasted gawdawful ... even when covered with ketchup.

July 3, 1994

A taste of death? Pass the burritos

LEGACY.

Dr. Jack Kevorkian, the Michigan pathologist known as "Dr. Death," told reporters Wednesday he had assisted in the failed suicide attempt of Gene Amole, a Denver newspaper columnist. Amole, 71, a writer for the *Rocky Mountain News*, told Kevorkian he was "up to here with phone calls, threatening letters and too many assistant managing editors" and wanted to "end it all." He also said he was sure he would "never live long enough to see Denver International Airport open anyhow."

Spurning a lethal injection or a sniff of carbon monoxide gas Kevorkian used to help 20 others die, Amole said he wanted to overdose on chile rellenos and burritos smothered with green chili. He said he got the idea after Michael Jacobson, who heads the Center for Science in the Public Interest, alleged that some Mexican food is loaded with fat.

Jacobson has made similar charges about Chinese and Italian food, school lunches and motion picture theater popcorn. Amole said he never considered committing suicide by eating school lunches. "I refused to eat watery macaroni and cheese and brown betty when I was a kid, and I'm not going to do it now."

Kevorkian emerged shaken from the rusty old Volkswagen bus where the assisted suicide was to take place. "The old man is like a Timex watch," the retired Michigan physician said. "He just keeps on ticking. His lungs don't work. He has just one eye and only a one-fourth of a stomach, but he continues to pig out on refried beans and chimichangas."

A *Hard Copy* television reporter interrupted Kevorkian to ask if Amole has said anything. "Not much," Kevorkian answered. "He did complain that Michigan bartenders don't know how to make a decent margarita, but other than that, he just nibbles on tortilla chips and salsa while he waits for another order of tostadas."

Heredity may be keeping Amole alive. His great-grandfather died at 91 despite a lifetime of eating chicken and dumplings every Sunday and pork ribs and kraut the rest of the week. He had his own teeth when he died.

In one of his columns Amole wrote: "The afternoon after his funeral, friends and relatives gathered in the parlor. I was just a little boy at the time, but I can remember hearing everyone talking about how Grandpa had his own teeth. I do not take this legacy lightly. I floss and use the toothpick after every meal."

Kevorkian said he would no longer practice euthanasia by enchilada. "It takes too long," he said. "I don't have time to sit around waiting for a cholesterol buildup in the arteries, or the triglycerides to shut down the coronary-artery system. Besides, it's boring in there, watching him shake on the Tabasco sauce and slurp up the guacamole.

"I figured death wasn't imminent when the old guy started playing mariachi and ranchera tape recordings on his boom box and doing the pasodoble around his sombrero. I asked him if he had any last words and he said, 'Dos mas tequillas solo, por favor.' Earlier he had told me that if the Mexican food doesn't kill him, he wanted me to order some Italian food.

"I can't understand why he is still alive. We gave him bags of theater popcorn laced with animal fat and palm oil, and all he did was complain that there wasn't enough butter on it. And then, if you can believe this, he wanted more salt. I thought that if all those grams of fat don't kill him, the salt certainly will.

"I really don't know what to say about this. Amole has set back the assisted suicide movement many years."

July 21, 1994

Here's my beef about fast food

GLOP.

I am thinking of filing a class action suit against McDonald's because the Big Mac I order isn't like the one Michael Jordan eats on TV. Larry Bird and Charles Barkley also get better looking Big Macs than I do.

Understand, I'm not being shorted on ingredients. I get the "two all-beef patties, special sauce, lettuce, cheese, pickles, onions on a sesame seed bun," but they are all squished together so you can't tell whether it's a hamburger or a small animal you ran over on the highway.

Same thing with the Quarter Pounder with Cheese. I got one the other day, and the top half had skidded off the bottom half. I couldn't get it back together because the melted cheese was so sticky.

Actually, my last Big Mac attack was years ago. I learned to hate them when I was working in radio and moonlighting here at the *News*. I'd finish with my morning radio program and then grab a Big Mac to eat while driving downtown to write my column.

Ever eat a Big Mac while driving? Then you know how the special sauce dribbles on your shirt and on the crotch of your pants. French-fry grease makes your steering wheel slippery. You lurch into the office reeking of junk food.

It's not just McDonald's that's guilty of false advertising. Burger King's Whoppers bear little resemblance to the advertising pictures.

144

Wendy's Dave Thomas may fix his chicken sandwiches the way he likes them but try to get old Dave to fix you one like his.

My most recent fast-food adventure was last week. Trish, who's counting fat grams, saw the Taco Bell commercial on TV where Robert Stack is sitting in the back seat of a car and a big bruiser is driving in front. Stack in his best Eliot Ness voice tells about a new Taco Bell burrito that is low in fat.

"Let's give it a shot," Trish said. So we went to the Taco Bell near Southwest Plaza. I knew it was a mistake when we walked in the door. Tables were dirty. There was confusion in the kitchen and a guy in back hollered to the cashier, "Don't sell anything with lettuce in it!"

We each ordered the low-fat Burrito Supreme and Diet Pepsis. The drink machine was out of Diet Pepsi. When I took the wrapper off my Burrito Supreme it sure didn't look like the one Robert Stack's driver was eating.

Actually, mine didn't look like a burrito at all. I'd rather not discuss with you what it looked like. Got a problem with that?

Do you like lasagna? So do I, but it is Trish's lasagna I like, not what they served me recently at the Olive Garden. The picture of Olive Garden lasagna looks great so I ordered it.

What I got was a shapeless glop in the middle of my plate. The pasta was not *al dente*, not even close. The pasta was almost invisible because the lasagna was overcooked.

Oh yes, I ordered a glass of Merlot, which I thought would be nice with lasagna. The waiter brought me some kind of sissy blush wine, white Z, I suspect. I said to the waiter—a big lug—"This is not Merlot."

He glared at me and said. "That's Merlot. That's what Merlot looks like." And then he turned on his heel to go out to the kitchen to get my glop. The salad was nice, though.

Something else: I don't care how Donald Trump eats his pizza.

Quote: "Do you know on this one block you can buy croissants in five different places? There's one store called Bonjour Croissant. It makes me want to go to Paris and open a store called Hello Toast."
—Fran Lebowitz.   *May 18, 1995*

RADIO AND TV DAYS

Time to unleash the radio animal

ART DECO.

It must have been about 4 A.M. I couldn't understand a word he was saying, but Adolf Hitler was in our old Delco console radio in the living room. The hypnotic quality of his voice drew me closer to the speaker. His speech was punctuated with cheers and shouts of *"Sieg Heil! Sieg Heil!"*

The next day in the lunch room at North High School, Ralph Paul told me he had awakened in the middle of the night and had heard the same short-wave broadcast. It was September 1939, and we had been listening to the beginning of World War II.

I thought of all this a couple of weeks ago while rummaging through the basement of our old house on the north side. The ancient Delco had been disassembled, and its parts were scattered around the storeroom. There were so many memories associated with the radio that I decided to see if I could get it fixed.

My pals at Reichert TV Service put the radio back together, replaced a part or two and turned it on. By gosh, darned if it didn't warm up and sound as good as ever. There isn't any FM, of course, but the short- and medium-wave bands worked as well as the regular AM broadcast band. Hitler was gone, however.

When I got it home, I went over the walnut veneer cabinet with lemon oil, and the old Delco looked as good as it did more than 50 years ago when Pop brought it home. I guess you could say it is an art deco style, with one of those slanted "No-Stoop, No-Squat, No-Squint" dials, on top of which is a green tuning eye.

In some primitive religions, objects, as well as living things, are said to have souls. If that is true, my old Delco has a soul. When I think of all the history that has come out of its speaker over the years and all the programs that made us laugh and cry, I have no choice but to believe it is true.

When I was gone during the war's darkest days, my parents found strength each night when Mutual Broadcasting Co. commentator Gabriel Heatter began his newscast with "There's good news tonight!" They listened to Ed Murrow broadcasting from a London rooftop during the Battle of Britain.

Before I went away, how I loved hearing *Vic and Sade, Club Matinee, Col. Stoopnagle and Budd, Walter Winchell, The Lux Radio Theater, The Joe Penner Show,* Fred Allen's *Town Hall Tonight, Inner Sanctum, One Man's Family, The Mercury Theater on the Air,* Glenn Miller and a whole bunch more.

I have kicked around over the years in TV, newspapers, magazines and radio, but I am really a radio animal. I got that way the first time I heard a human voice over Grandpa's crystal set. It was a miracle to me that I could hear a voice from someone so far away. I still think it is a miracle; all those voices, all that music, all those sounds swirling around me all the time.

I wonder what happens to old radio signals. Do they die, or are they still out there in another dimension waiting to be heard again? I don't know, but if they do return from the twilight zone, I will know where to go to hear them.   *May 12, 1988*

When television used to be fun

UTILITARIAN.

There was a time when television wasn't the deadly serious business it is today. In its early years, it was adventurous, irreverent and sometimes wacky. It was particularly so at Channel 2, Denver's first TV station.

The building on Lincoln Street was never meant for television. It was a small warehouse with an office up front. The main studio was on the east side of the building with a door leading to the alley. There was another door in the corner of the studio that opened onto a tiny janitor's closet where there was a toilet and a wash basin. It was the kind of strictly utilitarian john one would expect to find in a warehouse.

Its proximity to the studio was the basis for one of the most elaborate practical jokes I have ever witnessed. It involved three good friends of mine—Bill Reed, Tim O'Connor and Andy Cohen. Reed was the radio play-by-play announcer for the Denver Bears Western League baseball team. Cohen was the field manager for the Bears, and O'Connor was a cameraman and floor director for Channel 2.

During baseball season, Cohen and Reed had a 15-minute interview show that went on the air at about 6:30 P.M. Cohen was a born entertainer. Reed was a perfect straight man, guiding him into hilarious anecdotes of his playing days in the major leagues.

One night, the engineers rigged the studio monitor Reed and Cohen used on a separate circuit that would be seen only in the studio. It didn't go on the air. Just as the show began, Cohen and Reed looked at the monitor in shock and disbelief. What they saw was not themselves, but O'Connor sitting on the toilet, reading a newspaper.

There was a look of astonishment on Reed's face. Cohen bit off the end of his cigar. Both tried unsuccessfully to recover and to speak. They looked at each other, but their eyes were drawn back to the monitor screen showing O'Connor, with a bored expression on his face, casually turning pages in the newspaper. In the background was the muffled laughter of the studio crew.

I have laughed to myself over that story three times in recent months. The first time was last November when we carried a story that Cohen had died in El Paso, Texas. Last week, I thought of it again when O'Connor's sister called to tell me Tim had died up in the Pacific Northwest. And I thought of it again yesterday when Charles Reed called to tell me his father, Bill Reed, had just died after suffering a heart attack.

Bill and I had been close for many years. We went to North High together, were bellhops at the Cosmopolitan Hotel, and we worked in radio and TV together. I broke in Bill on his first radio job. In recent years, we'd have lunch every couple of weeks over at the Cherokee Bar and laugh at the things we did and didn't do, and at the way we were. And we were able to laugh at what has happened to us, too.

As my world gets smaller, I become more grateful for guys like Bill, Tim and Andy. What a rich experience it was to have known them and to have shared in their fun.

You're right, pal, they don't make guys like those anymore.

July 6, 1989

Country-western suits a cow town

GOOD-TIME BUDDIES.

In case it escaped your notice, Denver's favorite radio station plays country and western music. In the spring Arbitron audience ratings just released, KYGO-FM registered an 11.3, the highest audience rating of any local station for nearly 13 years. Not only that, but KYGO has been first in four of the last five Arbitron surveys.

This is good news for those of us who contend Denver is an overgrown cow town and ought to be proud of it. But you know how it is, some folks keep trying to put the silk pants on us and make us into something we are not. There is nothing wrong with being an overgrown cow town. After all, this is the West.

There is a lot of crossover from pop music to country and western, which has changed considerably over the years. At the dawning of my radio career, I did a show called *Rhythm Rodeo*. It was a breeze as long as I remembered to play "Old Shep" at least once a day.

We played mostly cowboy music, favoring the Sons of the Pioneers, Rex Allen, Bob Wills and his Texas Playboys and a smattering of Ernest Tubb, Merle Travis and his Coon Hunters, Tex Ritter and Waylon Jennings.

I also announced transcribed syndicated radio shows with Shorty, Sue and Sally, and Dusty, Pammy and Sue. And also with good old Cap'n Ozie Waters, the Colorado ranger, who opened every show with, "You get a line and I'll get a pole, and we'll go down to the crawdad hole, honey, baby mine."

The importance of country music never sunk in until I went into the Army down in the Mojave Desert. The first Saturday night I was there, everybody gathered around a radio to hear The *Grand Old Opry*. Roy Acuff and his Smoky Mountain Boys were performing "I Heard the Crash on the Highway, But I Never Heard Nobody Pray." Most of our outfit was made up of good old boys from rural Missouri, the Ozarks, Tennessee and Georgia.

"Is that bleep-kicking music the only thing you can get on that radio?" I hollered. "How about some Benny Goodman?"

Poor timing. Acuff had just started singing, "What a beautiful thought I am thinking, concerning the great speckled bird." It was as though I had interrupted the Lord's Prayer or the national anthem. I was stuck with every bleep detail for weeks.

Since then, I have cultivated a taste for country music. That may seem strange coming from a former owner of a classical music radio station and a lifelong devotee of almost any kind of jazz. Aretha Franklin can sing almost anything, and I'll love it. I can even tolerate some rock music. A group I liked a few years ago was the Who. Some of their stuff could have been written by Bela Bartok. Pink Floyd was sort of interesting. Cajun music is irresistible. I'm a big fan of Queen Ida and Doug Kershaw.

But when I am herding my old '65 Ford pickup around town, I usually punch up KYGO-FM. Pickups and country music go together. I also have a tape of K.T. Oslin I play. She is my current favorite country singer. There are generous doses of reality in her songs. In one of them, she laments, "I'm tired of your good-time buddies spillin' beer all over my clothes." She crosses over into the pop field, too. I notice that MTV uses some of her videos.

By the way, did you hear what happens when you play a country and western record backwards?

The guy gets his girl back, his job back and his truck back.

July 23, 1991

Replaying Denver's golden age of TV

DOUG'S LIP.

Television Channels 2 and 9 are celebrating their 40th anniversaries. Since I was present at the birth of both, I thought it appropriate to try to remember bits and pieces of what it was like in 1952 as Denver entered the television age.

Channel 2 was on the air first. Its call letters then were KFEL-TV. It was owned by Gene O'Fallon, a portly, white-haired little guy who also owned KFEL, an AM radio station.

I had a late-night movie program on Channel 2 the first week it was on the air. None of us knew diddly about television, so we just made it up as we went along. I came on after Jack Fitzpatrick's 10 P.M. news.

Channel 2 tried to preserve the illusion that Jack had memorized the news and was speaking extemporaneously.

His copy had been typed on clear plastic sheets that were projected on the wall behind the cameras. Old Jack was doing his best to try to read the copy without moving his head back and forth as he finished each line. The reproduction was blurred, and Jack was squinting at it through his bifocals.

So many great memories. Husband and wife Doug and Willie Taylor had an afternoon cooking show. Doug was merciless in his criticism of Willie's cooking. Something always seemed to burn. One day, Willie had enough of Doug's lip and hurled an egg at him on the air.

And then there was Les Barry's kids show sponsored by Carlson-Frink Dairy. Les got the surprise of his life on one program when he was giving a small radio to a little boy as a contest prize. The kid was so nervous that he vomited all over Les and the radio.

There was no videotape in those days. Everything was live, and a lot of unintentional funny stuff happened all the time on *Snicker Flickers, Fred 'n Fae,* the *Murphy-Mahoney Amateur Hour, Bill Reed Sports* and *Mass for Shut-ins.*

Now that Channel 9 is hyping its fancy new studios at 300 Logan St., my mind goes back to its first studio at Speer Boulevard and California Street. It was literally a storefront with low ceiling, board floors and no ventilation. I was on Channel 9 the first week it went on the air, too. I also was in that studio the last night before it moved to West 11th Avenue and Bannock Street.

It was blazing hot under those old scoop lights. Only the talent (me) was wearing anything but shorts. I was dressed in coat, shirt and tie. The temperature under those lights must have been over 110 degrees. Between commercials, I'd run across the street and drink a glass of beer at the Cherry Creek Tavern. The beer never made it to my bladder. I would sweat it out immediately.

On my last commercial about safe-deposit boxes for Central Bank, I was supposed to ignite an insurance policy to illustrate what might happen to valuable documents in case of fire. The fool thing flared on me, and I had to drop it before it burned my hand. It fell from the ashtray and onto the floor. I had to finish the commercial while smoke and flames were billowing up in my face as the floor crew was scrambling to put out the fire.

The next night, we were in the comparative luxury of the old United Motors Service building. When Channel 7 opened, Jim Lannon, Jim Edson and I left Channel 9, taking our limited expertise to the city's newest TV station, which was located in an old Packard agency building on Speer Boulevard.

Those were great times. People would watch anything, even a test pattern. The fun went out of television when the networks optioned prime time and videotape replaced live TV.

May 5, 1992

Tarzan: the good, the bad, the sequel

JUST FRIENDS.

You will be pleased to learn that a sequel will be filmed later this year to 1984's *Greystoke: The Legend of Tarzan*, probably the best of all Tarzan movies. I hope the producers have the good sense to sign Christopher Lambert to reprise his role as the Jungle Lord in *Greystoke II*, or whatever it is called.

Greystoke was the most realistic of all the Tarzan movies, if a story about a guy who is brought up by apes can be said to be realistic. In it, you'll recall, Tarzan sampled civilized life in England and found it so uncivilized that he went back to the jungle to hang out again with the apes.

The other fairly recent Tarzan movie was directed by John Derek and starred his wife, Bo Derek, as Jane. It was terrible. It may be the worst movie ever made, even more awful than *Ishtar* with Warren Beatty and Dustin Hoffman. I will never understand how a guy can direct a movie that shows his naked wife romping in slow motion with an orangutan.

The first screen Tarzan was Elmo Lincoln in 1921. His Jane was Louise Lorraine. Herman Brix played Tarzan in 1935, swinging through the trees in a Guatemalan jungle. Larry "Buster" Crabbe played Tarzan but is best remembered as a bleached-blond Flash Gordon in the Saturday afternoon movie serials.

The Tarzan with whom my generation identifies was Olympic swimmer Johnny Weissmuller, who starred in 12 ape-man movies. I was just a kid when the first one came out. Every little boy in town was running up and down the alley, pounding his chest and trying to imitate the Tarzan yodel.

Skeeter Bribach and I saw the movie at the old Alameda Theater on Pearl Street. We giggled at the scene where Jane, played by Maureen O'Sullivan, jumped in the river. As she did, a tree branch caught her dress, ripping it off. There were underwater scenes showing her swimming with absolutely nothing on.

Skeeter and I didn't know it then, but we were watching one of the few prints of that film containing the nude scenes. They were cut out of almost all of the prints. In all the years later, I wondered if I had actually seen O'Sullivan in the buff or whether I just imagined it.

There was a documentary on cable television recently about the old MGM studios. The controversial underwater scenes were shown again and I was reassured that at least a part of my memory remains intact.

I am happy to report that Edgar Rice Burroughs' Tarzan books are now in the Denver Public Library. They weren't for years because a minor official had decided that Tarzan's relationship with Jane was not platonic.

Burroughs wrote *The Tale of Tarzan of the Apes* in 1912, *The Return of Tarzan* in 1915, *The Beasts of Tarzan* in 1916, *The Son of Tarzan* in 1917, *Tarzan and the City of Opar* in 1918, *The Jungle Tales of Tarzan* in 1919 and *Tarzan and the Untamed* in 1920.

Burroughs died at Tarzana, Calif., in 1950, but the Burroughs family corporation has been cranking out Tarzan movies, books, television shows, and comic strips anyhow. The name "Tarzan" has been registered as a trademark and any use of it for commercial purposes will get you sued by ERB Inc., a corporation Burroughs formed in 1923.

Why are we so fascinated with Tarzan? Are we trying to get in touch with our primordial instincts? I used to work at a television station with a female chimpanzee named Buttons. We were just friends, though. The relationship never went any further than that.

June 30, 1992

154

A click will cure your TV headache

INTERACTIVE.

I'm not ready for *Police Academy XIV*, or *Emmanuelle Goes to Porky's*, or *I Was A Teen-age American Ninja for the FBI*. Are you also up to here with *I Love Lucy* reruns, Australian football and Pete Rose selling his autograph on *Home Shopping Club?* We're in for more of the same.

This raises the question of why technology always develops faster than our ability to utilize it. An example was the announcement last week that application of the new compressed digital television technology will supply us with 500 cable TV channels instead of the 61 we now have.

We have scraped the bottom of the barrel for program material on cable channels now in use. The availability of even more threatens us with a redundancy overload.

There have been nights at my house when the pickings have been so slim that I have found myself watching *The Full-Figure Workout* or reruns of Denver City Council meetings. That's sick, pal, really sick.

Most men I know routinely use the remote tuner to watch several basketball games at the same time. This annoys their wives who view the zapper as just another way men exercise power over women.

Because Denver has become the cable TV capital of the universe, we will be among the first to have the new technology. John Malone, president of Tele-Communications Inc., said, "Television will never be the same. Programmers are already approaching us with ideas that would have been entirely unrealistic a few years ago. For starters, imagine choosing from more than 20 college football games in a single afternoon." Imagine also choosing a new wife.

That must have been the thinking when NBC offered its triplecast of Olympic coverage and lost more than $100 million. It is so easy to sit around the office and hypothesize what you think the great unwashed want.

If there is one thing I learned in the 50-something years I spent in the media wars, it was never confuse public taste with mine. Convincing yourself is easy. Proselytizing the masses is another matter.

We have a football glut on TV already. My pulse no longer races when I hear Chris Berman holler, "HE ... MAY ... GO ... ALL ... THE ... WAY!" I don't know how ABC did with its pay-TV coverage of college football games, but I suspect not well.

It is my guess that the cable-TV people, who are essentially distributors, not programmers, are looking at the new technology as a way to expand home marketing services that interactively separate us from our money.

There simply is no venture capital to develop sufficient entertainment programming to utilize hundreds of cable channels. Production costs are high, and with advertising revenue spread even thinner, it isn't likely that program material can be developed that will pay for itself.

The trick is not just putting on a television program, it is producing one that people will watch. It's like the tree falling in the forest and making no sound because there is no one there to hear it.

TV audiences are becoming so diluted because of cable and VCRs that the networks' power to command a mass audience is diminishing. Increasing the number of cable channels will accelerate the process.

I have become very interactive with my television set. When I can't find anything I like, I turn off the fool thing and go to bed.

December 8, 1992

Clean-air myth goes up in smoke

CHEAPSKATES.

Note to newcomers: If an old fuddy-duddy with dog breath tells you he can remember when Denver's air was crisp and clean and free of pollution before the flatlanders came to town, tell him he is full of baloney.

Henry W. Toll Jr., who is both a physician and an attorney, popped a little pamphlet in the mail the other day proving my contention that polluted air is not a new problem. I recently wrote a column in which I claimed that the city has had a brown cloud from its very beginning in 1859.

We live in a temperature inversion-prone area. Long before we were here, layers of warm air were trapping pollutants in the colder surface air during winter months. We are stuck with these atmospheric conditions and nothing is going to change that.

The pamphlet was published by the City Club of Denver on July 24, 1924, and was titled, *Smoke Abatement in Denver.* Toll's father was president of the club at the time. "The curtain of smoke which frequently blots out the scenery surrounding the city, and which, in certain sections, obscures the city itself, obviously impairs Denver's development as a tourist city," the pamphlet said.

Sound familiar? So will this: "Your committee finds that physicians are united in declaring that smoke is extremely detrimental to the health of the community. That the smoke and its attendant nuisance impairs comfort goes without saying."

Denver's first attempt to control air pollution began in 1917 when the City Council passed an ordinance creating a Smoke Commission.

A smoke inspector, who was paid $1,200 a year, passed out citations to those accused of contributing to illegal smoke density. Fines of $10 to $100 were provided but seldom levied. The smoke inspector judged the gravity of the offense by gauging the shade of gray of the smoke.

Some of the worst offenders included: Brown Palace Hotel, Albany Hotel, Daniels and Fisher, Beatrice Dairy, Public Service Co. and "almost every large apartment in Denver."

Since coal was used for most industrial and residential heating, people were urged to use cleaner-burning anthracite, rather than the softer bituminous coal. As I recall, anthracite was $5 a ton and bituminous was about $3.50.

Fuel companies delivered coal by dumping it in your front yard or back alley. Then you used a wheelbarrow to carry it to a window where there was a chute to the basement coal bin. You could tell the neighborhood cheapskates by looking at the color of smoke coming out of their chimneys.

Natural gas has since replaced coal as our primary method of heating. Public Service Co. of Colorado still uses coal in its steam generation plants to produce most of our electric power. Up until the mid-1970s, it used natural gas, but switched to coal because of the energy shortage. Now, it's being urged to return to gas to help clean up the air.

I guess everything that goes around, comes around, including temperature inversions and all the gook trapped in them.

January 12, 1988

Cooks had rivalry greater than Gart

POIGNANT.

Sometimes it seems as if Denver is a big Monopoly game with corporations and holding companies merging, buying out each other or simply going out of business. Often lost is the human side of these stories. Last year, the May Co. closed The Denver stores, and Neusteters went out of business. This year, Gart Bros. Sporting Goods and Dave Cook Sporting Goods are merging, ending years of rivalry.

But if we are talking real rivalry in the sporting goods game, we need to go back a few years when the intense competition in this town was between Max Cook and his younger brother, Dave. Their alienation split one of Denver's oldest Jewish families right down the middle.

In 1890, their father, Harry Cook, came to the United States from Commona, Poland. The family name was "Barg" then, but as was so often the case, immigration officers didn't understand Polish and wrote down the name "Crook" instead.

Harry lived under the old West Colfax viaduct, as did so many other Eastern European Jewish immigrants. Jews from Germany and other Western European nations settled on the more prestigious east side. Jews from Poland and Russia tended to be traditional or conservative in their beliefs. Those from Germany were more liberal.

Crook, as Harry was then known, collected and sold rags and bottles. Later, he opened Crook's Russian Baths at West Colfax Avenue and Clay Street. When no customers came, a friend explained to him that the word *crook* meant *criminal*. That's when the "r" was dropped from the name.

Harry's son, Max, worked for and later bought Solomon Jewelry Co. He purchased some surplus cash registers and World War I German Luger pistols and then bought out Tritcher's Hardware, which had a large fishing equipment stock. The sporting goods business began to evolve. His younger brother, Dave, went to work in the store, but after a family dispute in 1924, they separated.

Dave opened a store on Larimer Street, and Max moved uptown, locating his store on Glenarm Place between 16th and 17th streets. Through the years, Max absorbed many smaller sporting goods firms, as did Dave. Max liquidated his business in 1961 when his store was demolished to make way for the 30-story Security Life Building.

The sibling competition was bitter. Max and Dave hardly nodded to each other if they accidentally found themselves in the same group. The brothers refused to advertise in the same newspapers or buy advertising on the same radio stations.

The alienation lasted for 27 years, ending in 1951 when Dave was near death in Rose Memorial Hospital. Max went to see him. In what must have been a poignant moment, they embraced and decided to forgive each other for their long-standing differences. When Max died in 1970, some of Dave's sons were among the pallbearers. The rivalry finally ended, and the two sides of the family were able to come together again.

Old wounds are slow to heal, however, and some painful memories still remain.

March 17, 1988

For Bonfils, time mocks immortality

RASCALITY.

The 56th anniversary of Frederick G. Bonfils' death slipped by Feb. 2 without any public notice, all of which contributes to mounting evidence that immortality is pretty hard to come by. You wouldn't have thought so at the time had you looked at the front page of *The Denver Post*.

Every story was edged in black. The banner headline read, "FREDERICK G. BONFILS, EDITOR AND PUBLISHER OF *POST*, DEAD." Another headline blared, "COLORADO HAS LOST ITS GREATEST CITIZEN," and another, "PRESIDENT HOOVER DEEPLY GRIEVED BY F. G. BONFILS DEATH."

If Bonfils' demise did nothing else, it caused a temporary truce in one of the many newspaper wars between the *Post* and the *Rocky Mountain News*. Only three months earlier, Bonfils had sued the *News* for libel. The *News* had printed a speech by Democratic state chairman Walter Walker, calling Bonfils a "vulture," "public enemy," "slimy serpent" and "a contemptible dog."

"The day will come," Walker said, "when some persecuted man will treat that rattlesnake as a rattlesnake should be treated and there will be general rejoicing."

After the suit was filed, the *News* asked that Bonfils be found in contempt of court for refusing to answer its questions during a pretrial deposition hearing. In its report of the suit, *Time* magazine reported that the *News* published "with impunity" some of these allegations:

"That he operated a crooked lottery in Kansas City under different aliases."

"That he conducts a theater which offers lewd dances, smutty jokes."

"That when asleep he requires a constant companion to waken him lest, talking in a nightmare, he reveal some of his shady transactions of the past."

160

"That he hi-jacked and blackmailed Henry Sinclair and his associates of $250,000 in 1924 on a threat that he would expose their Teapot Dome activities."

But when Bonfils died, his libel action and the *News'* countersuit were dropped. There was no question that many of Bonfils' land deals were crooked and that the big winners in his lottery schemes were his pals. He did blackmail Denver merchants into buying coal from a company owned by the *Post*.

And how did the *News* report Bonfils death? With restraint. It paid tribute to his "challenging virility." The thrust of the story seemed to acknowledge that his energy outweighed his rascality and his beneficence somehow atoned for his arrogance.

Bonfils ceased being a scoundrel at the last possible minute. Just as he was about to die, he was baptized a Roman Catholic by the Rev. Hugh L. McMenamin, who said at his funeral three days later: "And I shall always remember with untold satisfaction that his oft-expressed desire to die within the fold of the Catholic church, a desire that he expressed only a few hours before his passing, and was not denied him."

Quote: "I have spent a lot of time searching through the Bible for loopholes."—W. C. Fields.   *February 14, 1989*

Middle East crisis could be good thing

EASY STREET.

Readers of this column don't need to be told what an incurable optimist I am. With me, the glass is never half-empty, it is always half-full. Don't tell me about dark clouds. I am strictly a silver-lining kind of guy. That's why I have been trying to focus on the bright side of the crisis in the Middle East.

Bright side? You betcha. We have only to return to the late 1970s and the early 1980s to recall Denver's oil boom glory days. Remember the downtown skyline? It looked like a roost for giant iron cranes. Skyscrapers were going up so fast we couldn't keep track of them.

Canadians dumped hundreds of millions of petrodollars into Denver because they were afraid the industry would be nationalized at home. We began to think of ourselves not as the Queen City of the Plains, but as the ENERGY CAPITAL OF THE WORLD! Wow!

The construction industry was in tall cotton. Sprawling condominium subdivisions were being thrown up purely on speculation. People were astonished to find their modest little homes had quadrupled in value.

The town was filled with fast-lane petroleum guys in silk suits. They were big spenders and big tippers. Everywhere you looked, it was money, money, money and more money.

Remember the wildcatters? The town was crawling with them. Marvin Davis was the king of the wildcatters. He was so rich he seduced people like Henry Kissinger and Gerald Ford to attend his lavish charity Carousel Ball.

Davis had a Rolls-Royce hood put on his golf cart. His Cherry Hills Village home was protected by a private police department. The corner booth at the Palace Arms restaurant in the Brown Palace Hotel was reserved each day at noon for him. His desk in the Metro Bank office was almost as large as a tennis court.

And then there were the landmen who fanned out across the West, hustling farmers for mineral rights to land that was mortgaged to the hilt. They were followed by the smoothies who were pasting together limited partnerships so investors could pour their life savings into dry holes. "You can write off your losses," they hissed in confidential tones. The oil shale boom? I have forgotten whether Rifle was to be a city of 100,000 or 300,000. There were environmental concerns over what to do with huge amounts of spent shale after the oil was extracted.

Surely you remember a Colorado governor who was piloting his private airplane over a section of the Western Slope where the shale was to be mined. His wife was seated next to him and said after looking out of the window: "I can't understand what the big deal is. This is nothing but Godforsaken land, anyhow."

A reporter in the plane's rear seat preserved her views for posterity by putting them in the newspaper. I have purposely avoided identifying the governor because I am fond of him and wish to spare him further embarrassment.

And so you see, there is no such thing as bad news. It is all a matter of perspective. I know you will come around to my way of thinking on this. A little petroleum shortage is really a good thing.

In the meantime, let me tell you about this little limited partnership I am putting together. I know a guy who has a lease on a piece of land in the Julesburg basin that can put us all on Easy Street ...

Bumper sticker: "Lord, please let me have another oil boom, and I promise not to blow it this time."   *August 12, 1990*

Let's try to muffle the coming boom

DISAPPOINTED.

How much is enough? Strike that. How much is too much? That's better. We ought to be asking ourselves this question now because the Front Range is about to have another population explosion.

The signs are everywhere. We have survived the great oil crisis and are putting the latest recession behind us. Instead of businesses moving from Colorado, they are moving in. We are better off now than many East and West Coast cities.

The popular explanation for the turnaround is to credit the new airport, convention center, baseball team and other so-called economic generators. And of course the usual booster organizations are stepping forward to bow and smile and claim credit.

The real reason for the recovery is our abundance of office space and the availability of affordable housing. If I had a business located in California and had to pay outrageous rental for office space and pay my employees enough to afford $250,000 houses, I would be looking around for a better deal to lower my overhead. Colorado has a better deal.

The consequence of overbuilding offices and homes here during the early 1980s is helping us now to attract businesses from both coasts. Our climate and excellent recreational facilities are significant, too.

Is there a flip side to this? Yes. Families moving here will bring environmental pollution with them. There will be more traffic on our overburdened streets and highways. We'll have to build schools and infrastructure to accommodate them.

The problem is that we don't have a clue as to how much growth our economy and environment can sustain. There ought to be a way to determine this, and I believe there is. We have produced technology that is endangering our environment. Why can't we use technology to save it?

Can we develop a computer model of the Front Range that would tell us how many more people our temperature-inversion-prone environment can support? How much water will they need? How many cars will they drive? How much money will be necessary for capital improvements? There are probably existing databases from which the model could draw.

We need to be selective. What kind of industry should we attract and what kind do we reject? There are a lot of studies that address some of these questions, but I suspect there is hidden bias in most them. What we always do is reach a conclusion we want, and then we create a study that supports it, i.e., the new airport.

We know how to export Colorado's agriculture and minerals. Now we need to learn how to export our brain power in the computer age.

I was disappointed to read the other day that former Gov. Richard Lamm is on the board of the American Water Development Inc., which wants to drain 200,000 acre-feet of water annually from an aquifer in the San Luis Valley to support population growth in Denver's suburbs. How does Lamm know how much growth metro Denver can support?

He doesn't, and neither does anyone else. That is why I suggest we try to find out. Have other cities established computer models that have helped them plan for expansion? If so, let's find out how they did it.

Why should we be so hungry for growth that we Californicate our town until it becomes another Los Angeles? This time around, let's diversify our economy so that our next boom won't become a bust.

August 29, 1991

That blue light first flashed here

BALLOONS.

When it comes to ethnocentrism (characterized by or based on the attitude that one's own group is superior—Webster), we take a back seat to no other city. After all, it was right here in Denver, on Curtis Street, that O.P. Baur invented the chocolate ice cream soda. A chef at the old Manhattan restaurant on Larimer Street deep-fried the first onion rings.

164

The cheeseburger was born in Denver, as was the Anholt safety ashtray. Jack Kerouac, Neal Cassady and Allen Ginsberg became the world's first beatniks in Mile High Denver. Buffalo Bill got drunk regularly at Denver's oldest restaurant, the Buckhorn Exchange, West 10th Avenue and Osage Street. The Community Chest, now United Way, was founded in Denver.

World War II hero Audie Murphy used to hang out at the Senate Lounge in the Argonaut Hotel on East Colfax Avenue while his quarter horses raced at Centennial Turf Club. Jack Benny's announcer, Don Wilson, went to North High, and Douglas Fairbanks Sr. went to East.

Here's one you probably didn't know:

The first Kmart "Blue Light Special" was flashed in Lakewood!

Eat your heart out, Tom Noel.

I have this on no less of an authority than Bob Anderson, one of the Kmart workers who conceived the blue-light idea. It took place 30 years ago at the first Kmart store in the Denver area, No. 4101 at 7325 W. Colfax Ave.

"Self-help department stores were a new idea," Anderson writes. "We had a whole new merchandising system. I was managing menswear. We had to have a fast turnover for it to work.

"When we had slow-moving items, we had to move them out. We announced '15-minute specials' (on the store's public-address system), but customers couldn't find where they were. We tried helium balloons, beach balls suspended in the air over vacuum cleaners, but customers still couldn't find us.

"We rigged up a cart used to carry shirts and other items to the counters where they were to be displayed. There was a tub on top and a shelf at the bottom. We put a car battery on the shelf, a chrome tube through the middle of the cart with a blinking red light at the top.

"We would move it from department to department, and on Saturdays and Sundays, we kept it going all day long. It was an instant success. The Fire Department made us change the light from red to blue because the color red had the exclusive function of marking exits.

"The district manager saw it and put the system in all his stores. Within six months, flashing blue lights were in every Kmart store in the nation. I'll bet that even the Kmart historians don't know how it got started, but I do—and now you do, too.

"The story might bore the hell out of people, but it is an event in the history of merchandising and perhaps the closest thing I have to achieve celebrity status."

Not only that, but the "Attention, Kmart shoppers" announcements over the stores' PA systems are still the stock and trade of comedians who stand in front of brick walls on cable TV and think they are making people laugh by using the MF words.

We are indebted to celebrity Bob Anderson for the information. Now, if we can just find out how "red-tag sales" started. My earliest recollection of them was 40 years ago at Nessie Nides' appliance store on East Colfax during one of her frequent "sell-a-brations."

October 8, 1992

Bad taste once was temporary

SMART ALECKS.

I hope I don't live long enough to see Civic Center screwed up any more than it already is. It has really taken a beating over the years from automobile races, overpriced food fairs that give you the trots, and dippy architecture. Why don't we just leave it alone and let it sit there looking nice the way Mayor Speer intended.

But no. Some lame brain has commissioned a bunch of flatland architects to come up with a master plan for what we are now calling the Civic Center Cultural Complex. Venturi, Scott, Brown and Associates of Philadelphia want us to erect 20 110-foot stainless steel towers along 13th Avenue, west of Broadway.

It's not clear what these towers are supposed to be or do. Are they windmills, oil derricks or phallic symbols? Whatever they are, I don't like them. I also don't like it that we let Eastern smart alecks call the shots on our Civic Center. Would they let us send our guys back there to paint Constitution Hall pink and solder up the crack on the Liberty Bell?

On the other hand, we are capable of wretched excess on our own. We peaked out in that category 35 years ago when Denver was about to celebrate its centennial. The town went crazy. Men let their beards grow. Joe Alpert's did a land office business selling cowboy boots and big hats. Radio stations played hootenanny music.

166

For symbolic overload you couldn't beat Civic Center. First, the usual City Hall Christmas decorations went up. At the same time, Pioneer Village was built across Bannock Street from City Hall. It was supposed to look like the Denver of a century earlier. There were false-front saloons, a stable, a bank and a general store.

But that was the Denver of yesteryear. What about the future? Well, sir, we thought our bright destiny would firmly be linked to nuclear holocaust.

We were proud of the new Martin plant just south of town and prevailed upon its management to erect a Titan intercontinental ballistic missile smack dab in the middle of Civic Center. All 90 feet of that big sucker were spotlighted at night from thrusters to warhead.

Wait, there was more. The Statehouse wanted to get in on the act. A ramshackle log cabin suddenly appeared on the Capitol lawn across Broadway. It was claimed to be the meeting place of the first territorial legislature. Actually, it was an old Chinese hand laundry trucked up from Colorado Springs.

The setting looked incomplete to members of the Cactus Club, an eating and drinking society. Its spiritual leader, poet Thomas Hornsby Ferril, bought an old privy for $45 and placed it behind the log cabin.

Do you get the picture? There was Rudolph and the other reindeer, assorted cherubs and angels, the baby Jesus with Mary and Joseph, the three wise men, Pioneer Village, gunslingers and dance-hall girls, the Titan ICBM, the Chinese laundry and the privy. It was a cultural amalgam unrivaled for bad taste.

During the noon hour each day, "Away in the Manger" and other Christmas carols were piped over the public address system and were punctuated by the sounds of gunfire from mock shootouts in front of Pioneer Village.

At least, we took it all down when the madness ended—something we wouldn't be able to do with those fool towers the smart alecks want to put up.

November 16, 1993

Matchless visit with Baby Doe

REUNITED.

The old woman was dressed in rags. A floppy hat was pulled down almost over her eyes. She was sitting in a chair tilted back against the side of a weather-beaten shack on Fryer Hill. Cradled in her arms was a rifle. She told us not to come any closer. We didn't.

Grandpa wanted to see Baby Doe Tabor again, and so my father drove us to Leadville in his 1927 Dodge. As we lurched along Tenmile Creek Road, Grandpa talked about how he had taken flowers to her many years ago. "She liked snowball flowers the best," he said.

You can imagine how surprised I was when we finally got there and Grandpa said the raggedy old lady was Baby Doe. I couldn't understand why a woman who looked like that would be called Baby.

But then I was just a kid of 8 or 9 and didn't know the story of how wealthy Horace Tabor had divorced his straight-laced wife, Augusta, to marry Elizabeth McCourt. She was a comely young woman from Central City, someone he would always call Baby Doe.

Everyone called Tabor "Haw" because his initials were H.A.W. He had struck it rich mining silver in Leadville. Tabor became a U.S. senator. He went broke in 1896 when the bottom fell out of the silver market. As he died, his last words to her were, "Hold onto the Matchless," his mine that he believed contained a mother lode of silver.

We must have spent an hour with Baby Doe. Grandpa did all the talking. She smiled and said she remembered him when he was a kid and brought her flowers. They talked about the old days before the turn of the century when Denver was still a roughneck frontier town.

Then we left. All the way back home, Grandpa didn't say much. He looked out the car window and seemed lost in his thoughts.

That day surfaced from my memory when I read Marc Shulgold's story in *Weekend Spotlight* about the return to the Central City Opera House of Douglas Moore's opera, *The Ballad of Baby Doe*. I had seen the opera a couple of times. There's some lovely music in it, particularly the aria, "Willow Song." Beverly "Bubbles" Sills sang the role of Baby Doe in the New York premier of the opera.

A few years after our visit to Leadville, Baby Doe was found dead in her little shack. The newspapers headlined her death with Page-1 stories, recounting her riches-to-rags romance with Horace Tabor.

Photographs showed her, not as the wizened bag lady I remembered, but as the pretty young woman who stole Tabor's heart and stood by him until he died.

Her body was discovered by two neighbors, Tom French and Sue Bonney. She was lying on the floor, frozen to death. It was bitter cold that March. Coroner James Corbett said she probably had been dead for two or three weeks. Baby Doe and Tabor were finally reunited alongside each other at Mount Olivet cemetery.

They had a daughter they named Silver Dollar. A film about the Tabor family was made after Baby Doe died. It starred Edward G. Robinson as Tabor.

Baby Doe's vigil went unrewarded. There was no silver in the Matchless. When she finally died alone, the love story ended. The spirit of the early West died with her. She never gave up, though. She was proud, refusing all offers of help.

It was left to *News* columnist Lee Casey to write the epitaph I shall always remember, "Baby Doe remained constant. It was the world outside that had changed."

July 2, 1996

This dog really put her foot in it

CHUCKLED.

The checkout lady at Walgreens looked at me kind of funny. One of her eyebrows even arched. I guess she probably doesn't see many 65-year-old guys buying the economy pack of three dozen Trojan condoms. For the briefest of moments, I reveled in what she might be thinking.

But, let's go back to the beginning of the story. It was last weekend that my dog, Oreo, and I were walking in the park. It is a daily ritual we both enjoy. Somewhere, she stepped in broken glass and cut her right rear foot. Oreo didn't seem to notice, but she was bleeding profusely, leaving bloody paw prints along the walkway.

When we got home, I tried to stop the bleeding but couldn't. The wound was too deep. The only thing to do was take her to Anderson's Animal Hospital, which has cared for our dogs, cats, parakeets, gerbils and other Amole wildlife over the past 23 years.

As gentle and as nice as they are at Anderson's, Oreo flat out doesn't like the place. She started to whimper the minute we pulled into the driveway. I finally dragged her out of the car and up on the porch. Oreo stood up on her hind legs and put her front paws on my shoulders. Yes, she is that large. Then she grabbed my arm with both paws and tried to pull me back to the car, licking my face.

Once inside, Oreo cried pathetically. As they dragged her away, quivering and panting, the look on her face was one of having been betrayed. I felt worse than awful.

The vet said Oreo would be given an anesthetic and stitched up. I could pick her up that night. Anderson's is open 24 hours a day.

She was pretty groggy when I returned a few hours later. The doctor said, "Whatever you do, don't let the bandage get wet. We don't want to get her paw infected."

You know what happened Tuesday. Snow and more snow. Well, sir, just how can you keep a big dog in the house without letting her out in the back yard regularly to you-know-what? You can't. You put a sandwich bag on her paw, secured by a rubber band, that's what you do. The fool thing kept falling off, though.

That was when the condom idea hit me. Why not simply roll on a condom over her bandage? It just might work, I thought to myself, recalling the many uses we found for condoms during World War II. We used them to keep the dust out of our machine gun barrels, as balloons for little French kids, to cover leftover cans of C-rations, etc. Why not a dog's paw?

Too thin. The condom broke almost immediately. My wife, who declined the use of her name for this column, said, "Maybe we should try Trojan-Enz Lubricated, Trojan rib textured, Trojan Naturalube or Naturalamb."

Getting back to the lady at Walgreens, I thought I handled the purchase very adroitly. "Heh, Heh," I chuckled. "These aren't for me. They are for my dog." *November 20, 1988*

Gene, Gene, the dancing machine

DIPPING.

The television said yesterday morning that the mambo is coming back. The mambo is a dance that was popular 30 or so years ago. I couldn't do it then and am not about to try it now. When the orchestra plays anything faster than a waltz, I head for the sidelines.

As I remember the mambo, it was a Cuban dance that evolved from the rumba, which I couldn't do either. The cha-cha came along in the 1950s. My problem with it was that I either had one cha too many or too few. Having the right number of chas was very important to the success of the dance.

I come from a long line of poor dancers. My father—a tall, skinny man—looked like a drunken stork on the dance floor. I asked him once why he didn't dance very well. "Because," he replied, "my mother made me wear long underwear."

"What's that got to do with it?"

172

"Everything," he explained. "When I danced, the long underwear made me sweat. When I sweat, I stinked. And when I stinked, the girls didn't want to dance with me."

My mother wanted me to acquire the social graces my father lacked, so she enrolled me and my pal, Skeeter Bribach, in a summer dance class taught in a lady's basement rumpus room near Wash Park. We went just once but never came back. We'd dress up like we were going every Saturday morning, but would fish for crawdads instead in the Wash Park lily pond.

I have had cause since to regret playing hooky from dance class. High school proms and tea dances were very painful for me. I never mastered the East High Hop, a dance popular in all Denver high schools.

East got the credit for it because East was very snooty and a trendsetter in those days. East was where Carl Stern and "Flying" Fritz Fairchild played football. Anything East did, North, West, South and Manual had to do.

It's difficult to explain the East High Hop. The boy faced one way and the girl sort of arranged herself on his left hip at a right angle. There was also some dipping done by experienced practitioners. No one would go to the prom with me because I couldn't dip.

In the Army, I went to the Hollywood Canteen one night to dance with Betty Grable or Lana Turner. The only movie star I saw, though, was Zasu Pitts and she was passing out punch and cookies.

Overseas in England before the invasion, our battalion played host to a British WAAF outfit, the female version of the RAF. I made a stab that night at learning the Lambeth walk with a lance corporal named Maggie. It was a dance, I was told, that "any idiot" could do. I couldn't. My version looked like "Wrinkle Belly" McCleary doing the side-straddle hop, a calisthenic exercise now called the jumping jack.

Maggie kept trying to Lambeth walk me out of the Quonset hut behind the motor pool. She was whispering, "You will take me to America, won't you?" I have lost track of all the dances "everyone" was doing that I couldn't do. There was the shag, the Lindy hop, the Suzy-Q, the conga, the monkey, the twist, tango, the Charleston, truckin', disco, carioca, polka, schottische, two-step and I don't know how many others.

One of my dance partners confessed to me that my dancing was bad enough, but what bothered her the most was that I was counting in her ear all the time.

Quote: "Dancing is wonderful training for girls, it's the first way you learn to guess what a man is going to do before he does it." — Christopher Morley. *July 16, 1991*

Oxygen-dependent and proud of it!

TANGLED.

It's about the hose in my nose. The rhyme is something like, "When Rose blows her nose on her clothes, her hose shows."

Was it Gertrude Stein who said, "A hose is a hose is a hose"? And when Juliet looked down from her balcony at Romeo, did she whisper: "What's in a name? That which we call a hose by any other name … "?

Actually, the technical name for the hose in my nose is a nasal cannula. You've seen them on people. It's a clear plastic tube looped around the ears and under the nose with two little nozzles that fit in the nostrils. The loop is joined to a tube under the chin and attached to an oxygen tank.

I have been wearing one for a couple of months. The pulmonary fibrosis for which I'm being treated has made me oxygen-dependent, and so I'm hooked up to an oxygen tank 24 hours a day.

Understand, I'm not complaining. It certainly beats the alternative, which is not being able to breathe. Sure, it's a nuisance. The long hose attached to the large oxygen tank I have at home gets twisted and coils around my leg like a predator python. Our dog, Oreo, gets her legs tangled in it sometimes, and people step on it, but I'm learning to accommodate myself to the inconvenience.

I was surprised at the number of oxygen-dependent people who have written to me. Sadly, some confessed they are too embarrassed to go out in public. When I looked at myself in the mirror the first time, I was reminded of something my mother told me when I was in the first grade.

I had been slow in school. I couldn't cut out a paper gingerbread boy like the other kids or follow the teacher's visual instructions. She suggested that my eyesight should be checked. Sure enough, that was the problem, and so I was fitted with glasses that made me look like a frog peering through a thick cake of ice.

But I didn't want to be the only kid at Alameda School with glasses. "Look," Mom said, "if you have something like that, you can't do anything about. Don't hide it; feature it." That's what I did. It wasn't long before other kids were asking their parents why they couldn't have glasses, too.

Years ago, when I drove Corvettes, it was cool to wave at other Corvette drivers. Maybe that's what we cannula wearers ought to do. You know, just a little wink or salute to tell the other person you understand. Maybe even polite high-fives.

One of the letters came from Shelley Rhym, a jazz drummer and friend of many years. I used to dig Shelley at his bottle club down in the Points. His paradiddles, ratamaques and Rhym-shots were impeccable. He's hooked up to oxygen now because he had to breathe so much secondhand cigarette smoke in nightclubs. Shelley said I can stop by his place any time for an oxygen refill from his tank.

I guess the point of all of this is that oxygen-dependent people shouldn't stay at home and worry about how they look. Hey, if you can't see well, you wear glasses. Folks who have hearing problems wear hearing aids. Same thing with oxygen. It's OK to wear a cannula. It's not the end of the world to be oxygen-dependent.

At the Red Lobster the other night I saw a pretty young woman wearing one like mine. I thought she looked great. Pretty hair. Nice eyes. Lovely skin. I rejoiced that she was out with her family, having a good time.

Honk if you need O.   *November 14, 1993*

News media part of D.C. arrogance

INCESTUOUS.

There were nothing but crumbs left from the Nixon story when I came to work yesterday. Over the weekend, hotshot television pundits had spaded up almost every known aspect of the former president's life.

They played back Watergate, protests of the Vietnam War, his "enemies list," Nixon's relentless pursuit of Alger Hiss, his campaign

175

against Helen Gahagan Douglas, the "kitchen debate" with Nikita Khrushchev, his foreign policy successes, the "Checkers" speech, the debate with John Kennedy, his appointment of Gerald Ford as vice president. Did I miss anything?

Poor old Henry Kissinger probably hasn't had a wink of sleep since Nixon died. They had the poor old guy on every TV network. He was evaluating the late president's stewardship of American foreign policy. Surprise! Kissinger characterized him as a genius.

It was impossible to watch all of the retrospectives. But in none of those I saw was an interview with Spiro Agnew, Nixon's choice as his vice president. Strange. He was forced to resign after pleading no contest to tax evasion charges. He blamed "nattering nabobs of negativism" for Republican problems.

It wasn't long before television coverage became redundant. The same things were being said over and over by different people. We are left with two Richard Nixons, the bad guy and the good guy. Take your choice.

One analysis broke the monotony of the Nixon coverage for me. Cokie Roberts, who works for ABC and National Public Radio, was doing a stand-up thumb-sucker when she said that the problem with Nixon was that when he was in Washington, he didn't "fit in."

All those years as a congressman, senator, vice president and president, Nixon somehow just didn't "fit in." That was his problem, Roberts said. To myself, I said, "My God, it's our fault. We elected a president who didn't fit in. We should have known better. The Washington establishment does not take kindly to folks who don't fit in."

Roberts knows about fitting in. She has lived in Washington almost all of her life. Her father, Hale Boggs, was House majority leader until he died in a 1972 plane crash.

Her mother, Lindy Boggs, also served in the House of Representatives. Her brother, Thomas Hale Boggs, is an influential lobbyist in Washington, and her husband is a former Washington correspondent for *The New York Times*. That's really fitting in.

Anyone who watches *Washington Week in Review, The McLaughlin Group, The Capitol Gang, This Week With David Brinkley, The Today Show, Evans and Novak* and any of their clones knows that celebrity journalists make a living by interviewing each other.

They sometimes safari a few miles beyond the Beltway but try to get home before dark. The name of their game is Inside. The more inside they are, the more power and influence they have.

This is true for Washington politicians and journalists. They feed off each other. One cannot exist without the other, and at cocktail time, the relationship becomes incestuous.

They are the oligarchy that really runs things in this country. Those of us who live outside their Beltway, do not participate, nor are we counseled. We are only spectators to their private little games. Like Richard Nixon, we don't fit in.

If Roberts is right, next time we elect a president, we should clear the candidates with her to see if they fit in.

April 26, 1994

We miss you, Jakeob, Alie, Mayra and ...

DEAR JAKEOB,

I thought I'd take a few minutes to drop you a line and bring you up to speed on the investigation of your murder. It seems like yesterday your body was found beside an old cottonwood stump in Jefferson County. Actually, it was July 22, 1991. You had been stabbed 24 times.

There's never a day I don't think of you, Jakeob McKnight. I drive by where you were murdered on my way to work and coming home. I know that place well. It's just a little west of South Wadsworth, and south of West Yale Avenue. Trish and I have ridden and walked that bike path all the way up to Kipling many times.

I wish you could see that open space now. We've had a lot of rain this spring and everything is so green and beautiful. Old Bear Creek is running bank-full since the sun has started to melt the snowpack in the hills.

When it gets a little warmer, your pals will be splashing again in that pool under the willows near Estes Street. I'll bet you did that when you were alive. Was there a rope that swung out over the creek? Maybe I saw you there. I was the old guy on the red bike. Of course I didn't know anything about you until you were murdered.

Remember the wooded area just west of the open space? I surprised a couple of deer there one summer morning. Blue herons nest in some of those trees, and in the evening you can hear beavers splashing in the creek. What a great place for kids to play and grow up.

I wish I could report some progress in the investigation, but I can't. John "Felix" Chinn and Tom Judge are still suspects, but police have no evidence linking either of them to your murder. Both admit talking to you that day but deny knowing who killed you. You know, of course, but you can't tell us.

Each time I pass that place, I shudder when I think about how you died. To be stabbed over and over again must be a terrible thing to endure. Those of us who care about you hope death came swiftly and with as little pain and suffering as possible.

The old cottonwood tree where you were found has been burned. Burning it helped your friends and family cope with your death. By the way, a little bench with your name on it has been dedicated to your memory. You will never be forgotten, Jakeob.

I can't explain why there is so much killing going on around here. When I started in this business, a murder was front-page news. Now, there are so many to report they don't rate much space in the newspaper anymore. The other day, we had three in just one story.

Some folks complain there is too much crime news in the paper. I guess they figure if they don't know about crime, somehow it will go away. You and I know better, don't we, Jakeob?

Other children murdered in recent years include Heather Church, Alie Berrelez and Mayra Lopez. Little Christopher Abeyta and Anthony Moya were stolen from their homes.

And who can forget little Mikey Manning, the Boulder toddler who was murdered in 1982 because he wet his pants? His mother reported him missing but broke down 10 months later and took police to where his body had been thrown away in a plastic trash bag.

The police are still working on your case. I am so sorry we let you down by not making society safe for you and other kids. That's it for this time. We miss you, Jakeob, and love you very much.

Sincerely,
Geno.

May 24, 1994

Psychobabble can't excuse pushy parents

WAR AND LOVE.

We are not supposed to grieve over the death of little Jessica Dubroff in an airplane crash because she was doing what she wanted to do. At least that's what her mother, Lisa Hathaway, tells us.

That's disgusting. How any mother could so easily rationalize the senseless death of a daughter is beyond me. There is no way that her death was justified by what was a cheap publicity stunt.

It wasn't just a little girl who was killed. It was all she would ever be, all she would ever do, all she would ever dream, all she would ever love, all she would ever learn, all the children she would ever bear. All of that died with her when that plane crashed in a storm at Cheyenne last week.

The evidence suggests Jessica was being used by her parents to milk the event for all the publicity they could get. They were even trying to dicker with *National Geographic* to do a spread about their plan to have Jessica set a cross-country flying record.

Come on, now, was this really Jessica's idea? I don't believe it. The family even had T-shirts and baseball caps made that said, "From sea to shining sea—April 1996." They had set up a post office box for financial contributions.

Hathaway said children should make their own choices. In a masterpiece of new age babble, she told the *San Francisco Examiner*: "People tend to be very parental with children. ... (Their) natural state is a state of non-fear. There's no fear. Fear is not a reality to them. That's taught. Emotion is what they're taught, and thinking is taught, and neither of those is a natural state."

This tragic story reminded me of a book I had read in 1982, *The Disappearance of Childhood*, by Neil Postman. Somehow I lost the book. I called the Tattered Cover and was delighted when they told me a new edition was published by Vintage Books last year.

Postman believes the whole idea of childhood as a special class of people is really less than 400 years old. In America, the precise marking of a child's age is "a relatively recent cultural habit, no more than 200 years old."

For all they knew about civilization, the ancient Greeks had no moral or legal restraints on infanticide. Aristotle did suggest, however, that there ought to be some limits established for the killing of children.

I find it interesting that Jessica was 7 when she died. In the Middle Ages, the age of 7 was when children became adults. It was a non-literate world, and by 7, children had developed sufficient language skills to be considered adults.

J.H. Plumb writes, "There was no separate world of childhood. The 7-year-old male was a man in every respect except for his ability to make war and love."

When we observe the disappearance of childhood today, it seems as though we are journeying "back to the future," or back to the Middle Ages. Aren't we forcing on our children, as Jessica's parents did, adulthood before they are physically and emotionally prepared for it?

We have taken play from little boys and substituted organized athletic leagues with uniforms and equipment "just like the pros." And as Postman writes, "Twelve and 13-year-old girls are among the highest-paid models in America. In advertisements in all the visual media, they are presented to the public, in the guise of knowing and sexually enticing adults, entirely comfortable in the milieu of eroticism."

How sad for them and for all of us.

April 18, 1996

Monkeys can get quickly to business

BLUENOSE.

Have you been following the story about the baby spider monkey at the zoo? The little guy was rejected by his mother, and so folks who work there are taking care of him. They feed him with a bottle and take him home at night.

They are very good about these situations. Remember Klondike and Snow?

Those little polar bear cubs became nationally famous as the zoo keepers nurtured them until they were able to fend for themselves.

And then there was the baby kangaroo. The poor little bloke was also rejected by his mom. The zoo folks did their best to keep him alive, but it was all for naught. He died.

The baby monkey seems to be getting along fine. Adult spider monkeys can be quite a handful, all of which reminds me of a spider monkey story to end all spider monkey stories.

It took place some years ago at Pasadena, Calif., where my second cousin, Edna, lived with her husband, Warren. I don't know how Pasadena is now, but then it easily qualified as a contender for the bluenose capital of the world.

Did it ever! Pasadena was solidly Republican. Not many children playing in the street. The residential areas were immaculate. The lawns, trees and shrubbery were carefully manicured. Everything had to be just so.

Anyhow, Warren came home from work one day with a spider monkey named Jasper. Since he was a boy, Warren always wanted a pet monkey. It was probably a foregone conclusion that when he met a sailor in a Los Angeles bar with a monkey perched on his shoulder, he would try to buy it. The sailor had probably sneaked Jasper into this country on the sly, and he sold it to Warren for $25.

Warren kept the little primate in the garage until he had a large cage built in the back yard. Jasper loved it. He had his own baby blanket, and Edna would fix him a big fruit salad every day. Warren would have to tuck him in at night so he would go to sleep.

Occasionally, though, Warren would let Jasper out to frisk around in the yard with a long chain attached to his collar. It was on such a day that the lady next door stopped by for a glass of lemonade.

She was a largish woman and very proper. She, Edna and Warren were sitting on lawn chairs and making polite conversation. Jasper was dragging his blanket around the yard, ignoring the three of them. He thought it was great fun to put the birds in the tree to flight.

Suddenly, with no warning at all, Jasper dropped his blanket and made a beeline for the neighbor lady. He was so quick, that Jasper. The three of them seemed frozen in their lawn chairs as Jasper put both of his little hands under the lady's skirt.

Of course she screamed. Jasper grabbed her ... well, he grabbed her underpants and began to pull. Then Edna started screaming, too, only at Warren. "War-ren, War-ren, do something!"

Poor Warren had no choice but to reach under the woman's skirt and try to pry Jasper's fingers away from her underpants. "Let go, you rotten little b——d, let go, I say!" he shouted.

Finally, Jasper took a final tug and then went back to frightening the birds. The woman gamely tried to regain her composure. She stalked out of the back yard and went home.

Early the next morning, workmen arrived to build a 15-foot-high stone wall with barbed wire on top to separate the back yards.

July 27, 1997

THE WAR THAT NEVER ENDS

The zigzagging condom debate

OVERWHELMING.

It is with more than passing interest that I have been watching the great condom debate. At its center is the question of whether condoms should be hawked on radio and television. The issue was raised after it was determined that condoms offer protection against spread of the killer AIDS virus.

Manufacturers put on their sincere faces and asked broadcasters to permit the advertising of condoms because of their prophylactic qualities. "We are not interested in promoting them for contraceptive use," they said. "We want our people to use them to protect our nation's health."

Sales of condoms are sharply higher, causing the manufacturers to fight each other for market share. Since the guy at the drugstore doesn't ask his customers if the condoms are to be used to prevent disease or to prevent babies, no one really has accurate information on why they are used.

My mind flashed back 43 years to a time when I was required to have 60 condoms in my possession. That's 60. Six-oh. There was no opportunity then for philosophical discussion of birth control, disease prevention or the morality of pre- or extramarital sexual experiences. The government ordered me to have 60 condoms, and 60 I had.

America was at war and was about to send her fighting men to assault *festung Europa,* the evil domain of Adolf Hitler and his Nazi thugs. In short, we were gonna cross the English channel to try to kill them before they killed us.

There was a combat supply for everything we carried: ammunition, first-aid packs, C-rations, boots, socks, underwear, canteens, blankets, shelter halves, gas masks and, yes, even condoms. The number 60 was never explained. I wondered on whose experience it had been projected. Did this mean we were in for a long war, or a short one? Did we come here to make love or to make war? Sixty was difficult for us to put into any kind of perspective. Personally, I found the number overwhelming.

The Army was convinced that ooh-lah-lah diseases were epidemic in Europe. Supreme Headquarters wanted us properly equipped with GI condoms if we ever felt tempted to whisper, *"Voulez vous zigzig avec moi?"* Incidentally, we thought the term *zigzig* was French. The French believed it to be American. Whatever its origin, everyone seemed to know what *zigzig* meant.

I remember thinking how sad it was that some young soldiers would lose their lives before they had the opportunity to lose their virginity. Why is it we send our innocents to die for their country instead of the old geezers who have been in some big towns and have heard them some sweet talk?

As it turned out, very few condoms were ever used for their intended purpose. They wound up keeping dust out of barrels of Browning .50-caliber machine guns. How do you like that for phallic symbolism? They also kept cigarettes dry and served as a temporary cover for half-eaten cans of meat and beans.

My favorite alternative use was blowing them up as balloons for little French kids who were celebrating their liberation.

February 10, 1987

To forgive and forget just isn't possible

DESENSITIZED.

Holocaust Awareness Week ends today. As it passes, I wonder how much longer people will remember, or even care, about the systematic slaughter of 6 million Jews by the Nazis during World War II. When the last survivors of the concentration camps die, our only direct link to this monstrous event will be gone, too.

None too soon for some, I suspect. No, not the crazies who claim the Holocaust was a hoax, nor the thugs who vandalized Denver synagogues and Jewish community centers last week, but the millions of everyday people who would just as soon forget the whole thing. "Enough, already," they quietly say to themselves.

No one in his right mind would openly object to Holocaust remembrance, but I suspect there are many who have become desensitized to it over the years and have come to think of it as an aberration, or something that happened to another people, at another time and in another place. Ancient history.

Perhaps it is my age, but I find it sad when major historical events slip from the collective public memory to disappear into books, or are filed away with the lights and shadows of grainy old motion picture film. In my lifetime, I was profoundly affected by the Great Depression and World War II. But after my generation is gone, who will remain to testify about the hunger, the pain, the despair and the fear?

When I talk to young Jewish people about the Holocaust, I see in their eyes that they really don't comprehend it despite the best efforts of their parents to sustain the memory. I don't know, but I suspect some of these young people even have to cope with the guilt of not feeling so strongly about genocide as do their fathers and mothers.

As historians try to put the Holocaust into an emotionless, academic perspective, they trace its roots to the Versailles Treaty that ended World War I. Anti-Semitism slowly developed over the years, they say, as the masses of Germans accepted its consequences, one little injustice at a time.

For me, it was the worst kind of nightmare suddenly come true. I had general knowledge that Jewish people were poorly treated in Germany before World War II, not unlike, I believed, the discrimination against blacks in America. I was not prepared for the enormity of the horror, however, until the Army division with which I served stumbled upon the Buchenwald death camp near Weimar.

Even though we had come through hell, as Gen. George Patton would later write of his Third Army, none of us was prepared to confront the ghastly crimes our German enemies had committed against their fellow human beings. All these years later, I cannot think of it rationally. I have tried, but I cannot rid myself of the hatred I still feel.

Could it happen again? Given mankind's predilection for repeating its own atrocities, I suppose so. That's why it hurts so much when I hear people who seem anxious to forgive and to forget. I am not able to do either.

May 3, 1987

One soldier's war:
Gene Amole remembers World War II

The adjutant came into the headquarters tent at Camp Lucky Strike in France and put a bottle of Johnny Walker Red Label on the makeshift desk in front of me. He didn't say anything. He just put down the bottle and walked out. I never saw him again. I was acting sergeant major of a battalion being sent home to be demobilized. It was our last day in Europe, and the guys were sitting around in front of their pyramidal tents chanting "We wanna go home! We wanna go home!"

I showed the bottle to the headquarters company first sergeant and told him we'd get together after chow that night and drink it. As I remember the incident, some local Calvados also was involved. My memory is vague about other details of that night, but I do recall that he and I shot out the tops of some of the tents with a Thompson submachine gun. At the time, it seemed like the right thing to do.

The next morning I stood bleary-eyed at the bottom of the gangplank and checked off the names of the men as they boarded the troop ship for home. I'd holler their last names and they would respond with their first names and middle initials. No one mentioned the Tommy gun incident. We were going home after the Normandy, northern France, Ardennes, Rhineland and central Europe campaigns in the European Theater of Operations. It had been almost two years, and home was all we could think about.

Three weeks later I was back in Denver. Mom, Pop and Grandpa were waiting for me at the top of the passenger ramp at Denver Union Station. I tried to hug them all at the same time and still keep my duffle bag on my shoulder. My mother was crying as she counted the battle stars on my ETO ribbon. I was alive and home. The war was over and I wanted nothing more than to put it behind me forever.

It wasn't long, though, before I began to realize that it would never be over for me. Eight of us went to war from the little north-side neighborhood where my family had lived since the turn of the century. Only three of us came home. Facing the mothers of the boys who were killed was tough. They smiled and hugged me and told me how glad they were to see me, but in their eyes I could see they were wondering "Why?" Why couldn't their sons have come home instead

186

of me? I didn't know why then, and I don't know why now. I actually felt guilty that I survived.

At first I didn't realize what a bundle of nerves I had become. A sudden clap of thunder or an automobile backfire would humble me to my knees. I was embarrassed one Saturday at a University of Colorado football game in Boulder. A weekend warrior flying a Navy fighter plane suddenly buzzed Folsom Field during the game. Instinctively, I fell on my belly and rolled under the seat. My girlfriend didn't know what to do. People all around our seats were looking at me when I finally came out and sat down again. I tried to laugh it off as I brushed away pieces of popcorn, peanut shells and candy wrappers clinging to my coat. But I couldn't. It was difficult to sleep. I would awaken suddenly and my heart would pound. I would shout in my sleep and my legs would twitch. I still have sleeping problems. World War II is slipping from public memory, though. When my old division association monthly newsletter arrives in the mail, I note with sadness that the "Taps" column gets longer, and the number of active members gets proportionately shorter. Cancer, coronary disease, diabetes, emphysema and an array of other ailments are accomplishing what German guns were unable to do all those years ago.

When I read their names, I don't see pictures in my mind of the old men we have become. There is no greater bonding of men than exists between those who have gone to war together. The fading snapshots in my memory are of the boys we used to be. Real wars are not fought by men as they are usually portrayed in motion pictures. There were no make-believe soldiers like John Wayne or Ronald Reagan. Most of the real soldiers were just civilian draftees. Kids. It was a war of our kids fighting their kids.

How quickly 50 years have passed since I was a 16-year-old sophomore at North High School when the war began. The day after German troops moved into the Polish corridor to capture Danzig, I stayed up all night to listen on short-wave radio to Adolf Hitler's speech to the German people. I couldn't understand anything he said but was fascinated by the magnetic, almost seductive quality of his voice. I don't know how I knew it, but I was convinced that I would be there when the time came to fight Germany. It was my destiny and I always knew it. I was drafted into the Army when I was 18.

All these years later, I am still unable to resolve my feelings about the war. I suspect I am not alone. Of course we had to put an end to the Hitler madness. If war can ever be justified, it certainly was then. It was the peak event in my life. It left an indelible mark on me. I don't know how it is with others who fought in distant battlefields, but even as some of my memories fade, there is a sort of anxiety deep inside of me that won't go away.

What is so disturbing is that I can't explain what the war was like, or exactly how I feel. During the war, I occasionally had an opportunity to see newspaper clippings by correspondents who reported on some of the battles in which our division was involved. There was little resemblance in what they wrote and what I saw. Somehow, the real fighting in the war was a terrible secret shared only by the few who actually were there. The media sanitized the war for the folks back home.

In published accounts of our battles, I saw nothing about the medic in our battalion who used wire cutters to cut the fingers from dead German soldiers to steal their rings. By the end of the war, he had several hundred. There were no accounts of how unarmed German prisoners were sometimes gunned down for no reason at all. German atrocities were publicized. Ours were not. There were war criminals on both sides. I didn't read anything about the women and children we sometimes accidentally killed. No one wrote a story about a half-track driver in our outfit who blamed God for letting the war happen and smashed every crucifix he could find. It was never made a part of any record that one of our battle-weary soldiers got up in the night just two weeks before the end of the war and killed four members of his crew as they slept. They were listed as "killed in action." No one wanted to explain to their next of kin that they had been murdered by one of our own.

What astonishes me now is how accepting we became of these horrors. We had become desensitized to the agony around us. I have to confess, though, that there were times when our armored division was on the move, and the ground shuddered under our tanks, and the blue flame splatted from their fishtail exhausts in the pre-dawn gloom, that I was exhilarated by all the power surging around us.

Five years after the war, I returned alone to Utah Beach in Normandy where we had landed. I walked along the sand and tried to remember the day the big LCTs came ashore and we rolled out on the beach. I poked around in some of the old gun emplacements. There were still some scuttled ships offshore. Then I went over to the nearby American Military Cemetery. I was overwhelmed with grief when I saw the 10,000 grave markers of American servicemen killed in Normandy.

In the Korean War, I was a civilian correspondent, determined to write convincingly about what it was like to be a combat soldier. But even with my background as a GI, I was no better at reporting the Korean "police action" than correspondents had been in World War II. In his *Red Badge of Courage,* Stephen Crane did better than all of us when he described the madness as "the red animal—war, the blood-swollen god."

But of course it wasn't like that all the time. War can be boring, so boring I have seen dog soldiers hunkered down, reading the labels of C-ration cans as though they were pages in a book.

There was also plenty of humiliation to go around, like an incident on our first night in beleaguered Bastogne during the Battle of the Bulge. We were all nervous. The word was out that the enemy had infiltrated our position dressed as American soldiers. We all had memorized our passwords and countersigns. I was assigned as a guard to maintain contact with a parachute regiment a couple of hundred yards on our right flank. Three rifle rounds fired in quick succession was a signal for help. It was bitter cold and the snow squeaked under my boots as I walked. I had made one trip to where the paratroopers were and was on my way back when I heard a noise in a barn.

"Come out with your hands up or I shoot," I hollered.

More noise, but no one came out.

"Kommen Sie hier, schnell!" I ordered.

Nothing.

Forgetting the signal, I fired.

Bam! Bam! Bam!

A half dozen of our guys immediately converged around me. We kicked in the door, and there stood a horse, trying to stomp away the cold in the barn. Fortunately, none of my shots hit the poor old nag. For days, no one would let me forget how I had bravely captured a Belgian horse.

No civilians were left in Bastogne. Just a few animals. There was a small shell-shocked brown puppy that adopted me. I called her Lulu. Her favorite food was C-ration meat-and-vegetable hash. Our guys loved her. I have often thought that they felt "safe" in making her an object of affection. They could say things to her that they couldn't say to people around them. There was nothing else to love in our lives. When we finally moved on to the East and the Siegfried Line, Lulu came along on our Jeep. She stayed with us for about a week. I gave her to a captain from another outfit moving back toward Bastogne.

I remember little things like that so vividly. There is so much I have either forgotten, or have forced out of my memory. About 10 years ago, my battalion commander and his wife came through town. He called me up and we agreed to meet for dinner with our wives. We were talking about old times when suddenly, he turned to my wife and said, "Trish, I almost got your husband killed." He proceeded to describe a skirmish I had completely forgotten, but remembered when he started to talk about it. I have often wondered how many other incidents I have hidden away in the darker recesses of my memory.

We all learned to live with death. It was omnipresent. We looked, but we did not see. In the beginning it wasn't that way. Some tried to deny it, like a young soldier I knew who wouldn't abandon his dead buddy. We had been shelled from our position, but the soldier refused to leave. A medic and I took an ambulance out to bring them in. There he was, with the remains of his friend cradled in his arms.

"He's going to be all right. I know he will," the soldier sobbed.

There was a three-inch hole in the right temple of the dead soldier. You could see the brains, and yet his friend could not confront that reality. These little vignettes were played out against a setting too large for the human imagination. The war in Europe was on a scale not known either before or since the conflict. It was a spectacle that always seemed to extend from horizon-to-horizon, from earth-to-sky. The destruction of some towns and cities was so great that an undamaged building was a rarity. Nowadays, one can look into the sky and see one, two, or maybe three airplanes. In the war, there were hundreds of them, in wave after wave. It wasn't crowded at the front, though. There were amazingly few people doing the actual fighting.

Me? I was just there. I used to think to myself that they didn't really need me. My participation, I reasoned, wouldn't change the outcome one way or the other. But of course everyone else was thinking the same thing. There wasn't a time that I couldn't look around and see someone who had it worse than I did. Even though in some cases the Germans had better equipment, we outnumbered them and we had tremendous air support. When it was finally over, the soldiers in my division were proud of what we had done.

We resented that the burden of the fighting was being borne by so few. We sometimes were able to identify ourselves with the enemy rather than with those back home, or even troops in the rear echelons. When we took prisoners, I would look into their faces and see my own. They were as frightened as I was. They were sleeping in the same mud and snow as we were. They didn't want to be there any more than we did. The brass were calling the shots. We were just doing what we were told. "Just following orders" was the universal excuse for everything.

From the distance of a half-century, World War II has become the "good war." It was a time when the diverse peoples of our nation were drawn together by a single purpose. Gen. Dwight D. Eisenhower described it as a "crusade." The nation was mobilized. Nothing less than victory was acceptable.

I think of it that way, too. Every now and then I'll hear an old recording of Helen Forest singing with Harry James' band, "Kiss me once, kiss me twice, and kiss me once again. It's been a long, long time." And then my mind conjures up the longing to go home; the instant joy of V-mail at the front; USO shows; crazy weekends on pass in L.A.; the flowers pretty French girls gave us in Brittany after the St. Lo breakthrough; watching Joe Louis box at Camp Cooke, Calif.; listening to President Roosevelt's "fireside chats"; seeing "Kilroy or Clem was here" signs everywhere; hearing Roy Acuff on the barracks radio singing "The Great Speckled Bird"; getting snapshots in the mail of the "victory garden" back home; Betty Grable pinups; A, B and C gasoline ration automobile stickers; trying to sleep in the baggage rack of a Greyhound Bus; scrap metal drives; War Bonds; and gold stars hanging in living-room windows.

I guess your perspective of the war depends on who you are and where you were. To professional warriors, it was a deadly, high-stakes game. To the people at home, it was a noble cause. But it was pure hell to the poor bastards with fouled pants, lying face-down in a slit trench while a barrage of 88s was slamming in.

I have come to the conclusion that all wars are the same to combat soldiers. You can be killed as dead in a just war as you can in an unjust one. The official end of World War II in Europe was May 8, 1945. But to those who actually fought in it, on both sides, it will not end until the last of us finally find our peace in death.

September 10, 1989

No matter what it's written on, notes to GIs are pieces of home

THE GIFT.

We were standing in a circle looking at the package. The guys were all hunched up because of the bitter cold. The Germans had captured some of the supply trucks carrying our holiday letters and packages from home, and so mail deliveries were sporadic during the Battle of the Bulge 46 years ago. Even so, one package from my girlfriend managed to get through. The other GIs didn't get anything, not even a single Christmas card.

It was natural, then, that they would want to be a part of the package-opening ceremony. And of course there was the delicious speculation of what the package might contain. The heft of it suggested canned delicacies of some kind. One guy thought there might be fruitcake inside. Another envisioned a tin of carefully wrapped chocolate brownies.

"There's no way they could get a pastrami sandwich and a bottle of Bud in there, could they?" one guy asked. "I heard about a dog soldier over at the 44th Infantry whose folks actually sent him canned fried chicken," someone else chimed in. "Go on, Slim, open it," urged the kid next to me.

And so I did. Carefully, I slid the blade of my pocket knife under the Scotch tape stuck to the brown wrapping paper. There was a box inside wrapped with Christmas paper imprinted with holly wreaths. "Quit screwing around and open the damned package!" the kid demanded.

I ripped off the rest of the paper and opened the box. Silence. The soldiers stared down at what was inside. A great sorrow descended over us. I could feel tears of disappointment about to well up in my eyes. "Geez," the kid hollered, "It's a (bleeping) book!"

Indeed it was. A big, green, hardback book. It was *The Music Lover's Encyclopedia* by Deems Taylor. I opened the cover and written on the fly leaf were these words: "Thinking of you at Christmastime. Fondly, Beverly."

Fondly? What kind of fondly is that? There I was, somewhere in Belgium, up to my butt in snow, filthy dirty, stinking like a dog, frost-bitten feet, hungry, battle rattled, scared out of my wits and wondering what in the name of God Beverly thought I was doing out there.

The bright side, of course, was that if someone happened to ask me what a portunal-flaut was, the information was right at my fingertips. We found a practical use for the book, though. Shall we say it met a domestic need we all had—one page at a time.

Beverly was gone when I finally got home. I never saw her again. She'd married a draft dodger and was living somewhere in California. It was just as well. Somehow I always knew there was no future in our relationship.

The only thing I kept from the book was the page on which Beverly was thinking of me fondly. I would get it out every now and then and look at it and try to remember how it was between us.

That's the way it is when you are a GI far away in a Godforsaken land. Every letter is like a little piece of home you can carry with you wherever you go and whatever you do. You can get it out and read it over and over again.

Soldiers like to get newspaper clippings, snapshots, anything about home. Going home becomes a major preoccupation. The next best thing are letters from home. A little hint of Chantilly on the paper is nice, too.

Keep writing, as often as you can.

December 16, 1990

Scenes of war give way to snapshots

BAD DREAM.

Most of the war experts I have encountered have one thing in common: They have never fought in one. But this doesn't prevent them from laying out grand strategies that envision a quick victory by the

United Nations over Iraq. The United Nations, by the way, is a euphemism for American GIs.

I have disqualified myself as an armchair strategist because I have never been able to see the big picture. The reason I can't see the big picture is because I have been to war—two of them. To me, war has always been a lot of little pictures of people killing each other and defenseless civilians.

The grand strategies for a quick and almost bloodless victory over Saddam Hussein involve massive air strikes. Have we forgotten that those nightly 1,000-plane raids over England by the German Luftwaffe in World War II failed to bring the British to their knees? The raids only deepened their resolve.

In the Korean War, there was hardly a building left standing in North Korea, and yet the best we could do was fight the North Koreans and the Chinese to a draw. In Vietnam, we bombed, strafed and napalmed anything that moved. We hammered them night and day from the air. We lost.

There was one good thing about losing. We didn't have to keep an army of occupation there for 40 years. What happens if we defeat Iraq? Will it mean another American army of occupation? Has anyone considered that we simply can't afford to "win" another war?

I keep thinking that this whole thing is a bad dream from which we shall all awaken. Maybe there is a way out. Maybe Saddam Hussein will chicken out. Maybe at the last minute, President Bush will find that his conscience won't let him push the button. Maybe all those prayers for peace will work. Maybe, maybe, maybe.

But the machinery that is pushing us into war seems to be out of control, or on "automatic pilot," as one of our writers puts it. It has taken on a life of its own and is answerable to no one. It gains momentum every day. We are told that action after today's deadline is likely to be sooner, rather than later, even though we have been told that our military forces won't be ready until next month. It's frightening.

If it does happen, we must unite behind our servicemen and women whose lives are on the line. We can't abandon them the way we did our troops who served in Vietnam. They are our family. We owe them our loyalty.

Sure, I hope that "surgical air strikes" can end the war quickly and that there will be few casualties. If not, then my thoughts will be with the poor bastards with the M-16s who are going to have to walk in there and kill the enemy face to face. I'll be thinking of the tank crews in their "iron coffins" that are stalled because intake air filters are jammed with sand.

My spirit will be with the advance guard of an armored combat team in a terrain where every sand dune looks like every other sand dune, and where every Arab looks like every other Arab. I'll be thinking about the poor devil whose machine gun bolt jams because of sand.

And when "incoming" artillery and mortar fire starts hammering at our positions, I will know the nameless fear that will grip each soldier. Sadly, I also will know the sorrow that each death will bring. I will know the horror of seeing the young disfigured and maimed in the prime of their lives. And for what? Those are the little pictures I'll see.

January 15, 1991

Farewell, again, little pigtails

WILDFLOWERS.

I was rummaging through the desk at home the other day in search of a missing W-2 income tax form when I saw Erica Wagner. There she was, looking up at me from the bottom of a drawer, a 7-year-old German girl with blond pigtails and a skinned knee.

Her photograph was with some other old pictures, a pocket New Testament and a photocopy of my Army discharge. Funny I should accidentally find her photograph. Just a few weeks ago I was talking to Steve Caulk about her and how we met shortly after World War II.

It was the summer of 1945 and my unit was stationed at Neu Isenburg, a small town near Offenbach, south of Frankfurt am Main. Frankfurt was in ruins, but little Neu Isenburg had escaped war damage. We were billeted in houses near the center of town. Our field kitchen had been set up and we were still chowing outside with our mess kits.

I spotted Erica the first day. She and some other children had gathered to watch us eat and then would scurry over to the garbage can to salvage what they could after we were gone. I was never able to get used to seeing that.

One day I motioned for Erica and her little brother, Wilfried, to follow me where no one would see us. I gave them some of my food. From then on, I got extra large helpings and shared with Erica and Wilfried. They got my PX candy rations, too. I was able to bum some C-rations for Erica to take home.

As we gradually returned to garrison duty, I was the sergeant in command of the color guard that raised and lowered the American flag in front of headquarters. Erica was there every morning and every night. When the flag came down in the evening and I dismissed the color guard, Erica would run over to be with me.

She, Wilfried and I would take long walks. Sometimes we would just sit on the steps in front of where I was staying. I would try to teach her to speak English and she would sing little songs to me in German. Wilfried, a wistful little guy, would just sit and listen.

Late one night, I was awakened by the guard. It was about midnight. He said there was a woman outside and she wanted to talk to me. In those days, it was against Army regulations to fraternize with Germans. But I pulled on my pants and slipped out the front door.

She was a small woman, standing in the shadows. Through an interpreter, another woman, she tearfully asked me if I would take Erica and Wilfried back to the United States with me. She said she was alone, out of work and didn't know how she could possibly raise her children in the aftermath of the war. Erica and Wilfried loved me, she said as her voice trailed off into tears.

I tried to explain that it would be against regulations to take her children. "God," I said to her, "I'm not even supposed to be talking to you." She left. I couldn't go back to sleep.

A few days later I was transferred to another division. We were to leave early in the morning. Somehow, Erica found out. Just as I was throwing my duffle bag up into the back of the truck, I saw her. Her face was scrubbed clean and her pigtails were pulled tight. She ran over to me and jumped up into my arms.

She was crying and trying to tell me something in German. And then she handed me a little bouquet of wildflowers she had picked. I put her down as she was rubbing the tears out of her eyes. "Auf Wiedersehen," I said. Erica turned and ran away. I never saw her after that.

March 21, 1991

Soldiering isn't for everyone

HONOR.

The controversy over whether American women should be sent into combat reminds me of a political convention I was covering years ago that was debating whether the voting age should be lowered from 21 to 18. A hot-eyed lobbyist in his teens approached Gene Cervi and me, shouting, "If I'm old enough to fight for my country, I ought to be old enough to vote."

Cervi, a scrappy old political journalist, roared back at him: "You're not old enough to do either one."

As I understand the feminist view, women in the military services aren't being considered for top command roles because they lack combat experience. If the playing field for promotion is to be level, women should be permitted to fight alongside men.

A good combat record helps career soldiers get promoted. That's why there are so many decorations passed around after the shooting stops. I once saw a bird colonel get a Purple Heart for spraining his ankle. Look at the fruit salad on Norman Schwarzkopf's chest. He didn't get to be a four-star general by serving in the Quartermaster Corps.

Women who want to serve in combat are really saying they are willing to kill to get ahead. Killing is the business of soldiers. They have to be able to look the enemy right in the eye and kill him. Put out his lights. Waste him.

Are career goals that important to the women who yearn to serve in combat? When soldiers think about combat, they worry about getting killed or wounded. They pray for the courage to face those possibilities. That's not the point, said Gen. George Patton. "The idea," he told World War II GIs, "is not to die for your country but to make the other s.o.b. die for his."

Virtually anyone can be trained to be a killer. It's a matter of conditioning. You do it without thinking, and after it's done, you try not to ever think about it again, except there is no way you can really forget it. You are a killer. You may be able to keep other people from knowing your dark secret, but you know it.

Some people carry this knowledge through life better than others. By rationalizing, you can tell yourself that the killing was justified. The other guy meant to kill you. You were just following orders. It was your duty. You did it for God and country. But down deep inside you know that another human's life ended because of you. You did it. You killed.

It's easier if you are up in the air and dropping bombs or launching missiles. This is killing in the abstract. Down on the ground it's different. You get to see the consequences of your action up close and personal.

Because the government censored media coverage of the Persian Gulf War, the public was never permitted to see the ugly side of it. War was sanitized and presented to us as a great patriotic adventure. It is a different matter for those who do the killing.

In this context, bucking for promotion seems almost ludicrous. What is career advancement when measured against this kind of horror? Is making captain or major really worth it if you have to kill to be promoted?

I don't think anyone should have to kill. But if it must be done, let the men do it. Soldiering is an honorable profession, but it isn't for everyone. Women are uniquely enabled to give birth and to nurture life. In my book, there is more honor in that than there is in taking it away.

June 23, 1991

Poor chaps itched to fight, but ...

EXPLODING.

A cardinal rule for telling a believable war story is to give it credibility. "I was only two steps behind the chaplain when we hit the beach," illustrates the point. By involving the chaplain in his story, the old soldier can fabricate almost anything and some people will actually believe it happened.

Ben Nighthorse Campbell now says he was never trapped behind enemy lines during the Korean War. That story appears in some of his campaign literature, in a 1989–1990 account in *Nissan Discovery* magazine and in a 1982 feature article about him in *The Denver Post's* Sunday *Empire* magazine.

The *Nissan Discovery* article appears to be a rewrite of material in *Empire* magazine by Robert Cox who spent three days with Campbell on his ranch doing research. The story in Campbell's media kit says that "within days" of his arrival in Korea, he and a squad of Air Force policemen were caught behind enemy lines and "spent five weeks hiding until they found friendly territory."

Campbell denies he ever told Cox that "for a long time we didn't know where we were, and nobody else did either." He said he fired his rifle only once at something he heard rustling in the bushes. Cox sticks by his story, denying he ever "made up quotes."

Whatever.

Terry Considine, Campbell's Republican opponent in the U.S. Senate campaign, has been busy denying he dodged the draft during the Vietnam War. He has contended all along that he wanted to get in there and fight for his country but was rejected for medical reasons. But it now turns out that he received a student deferment for three years before being classified as 4-F.

Many other high-level Republican sunshine patriots found it almost impossible to be assigned to combat duty in Vietnam. Defense Secretary Dick Cheney, House Republican Whip Newt Gingrich and two of George Bush's sons were among them. All were deferred because of their key roles as college students.

We can only imagine their disappointment at being told by their draft boards that they must go back to school and get a master's degree in basket weaving, and that their fervent pleas to go into combat were denied.

Poor Bill Clinton was never able to get in the service. There was some sort of unfortunate and unintentional misunderstanding about when he registered for the draft and when he tried unsuccessfully to get in the ROTC.

One of the lucky ones was Vice President Dan Quayle who was, in President Bush's words, "in uniform" during the Vietnam War. Indeed, he was as press agent in the Indiana National Guard.

At one point, Quayle's campaign literature identified him as a "Vietnam-era veteran." The reference was later deleted because a number of veterans who actually fought in Vietnam felt they didn't want their service in the war to overshadow his.

Details of Quayle's military service are scant, but it is known that this battle-savvy young GI and his fellow weekend warriors were successful in their stubborn defense of Indianapolis from any possible attack by the Viet Cong.

Perhaps you have noticed, as have I, that wars are much more popular after they are over than at the time they are being fought.

Incidentally, did I ever tell you about the time we were outnumbered by the enemy, 100 to one? Shells were exploding all around us when the chaplain turned to me and said ...

October 1, 1992

Remember the sacrifices of those who died for America

NEW BIRTH.

I get goose bumps when I remember sitting on a curb as a little kid watching the William A. Fiedler Drum and Fife Corps swing by the reviewing stand on Memorial Day, playing "Hell on the Wabash" and "Sergeant O'Leary." There is something about drum and fife music that makes me want to get up and join the parade.

Fiedler was my great-grandfather. He built the house in north Denver where I lived for many years. It was an annual ritual for us to watch him and his Grand Army of the Republic comrades march in the parade. Then we'd sit down for Grandma Lizzie's chicken and dumplings. After dinner, he would let me wear his old blue GAR hat.

There were 17 members of his drum and fife corps. Death took its toll on the old soldiers until there were only four left to march: three drummers and a fife player. That's when they stopped. The next year, Grandpa was named the parade's grand marshal. He was 89 when he died in our old house New Year's Day 1931.

After his death, Grandma would sit each day by the front window, waiting for him to come home. She died of loneliness exactly one year later, to the day, also in our house.

Grandpa had been a drummer boy with the Iowa Volunteers. Grandma was his childhood sweetheart. He never talked much about the war, but I always imagined him trying to drum courage into the troops as the captain commanded, "Form line of skirmishers to left. Ho!"

Sometimes in an early summer evening, he would sit alone on the side porch under the Concord grape arbor and softly sing "Tenting Tonight on the Old Camp Ground."

I had another great-grandfather who fought in the Union Army. He was John Amole, a sergeant with the 76th Company of the 176th Regiment of the Ohio Volunteers. His son, my Grandpa Will Amole, told me his father had been cited for capturing a spy. I never met him, but I have a photograph of Grandpa John in uniform and his honorable-discharge papers from the Army.

Perhaps it's because I still have those personal connections with the Civil War that I resent Memorial Day's being used as just another three-day weekend for picnics and cookouts, or for appliance store red-tag sales, or for automobile dealers to make their month-end quotas.

Memorial Day should be a solemn occasion dedicated to the 620,000 Americans who died in that bloody conflict. That's 10 times more than were killed in the Vietnam War. All Civil War casualties were Americans who fought on both sides.

Is it futile to try to get Americans to reflect on those sacrifices nearly 130 years after the fact? The Civil War was a sacred time, during which our nation was defined. Until the battle was joined, our Bill of Rights was only a scrap of paper.

Ken Burns' superb Civil War television documentary helped us look at the conflict, not just as a historical event but as a human drama. Michael Shaara's Pulitzer Prize-winning novel, *Killer Angels,* describes not only the Battle of Gettysburg but what motivated the men and boys who fought it. *Killer Angels* was made into the film *Gettysburg.*

And so Monday, let us again resolve, as Abraham Lincoln said in his Gettysburg Address, "that these dead shall not have died in vain—that this nation, under God, shall have a new birth of freedom—and that governments of the people, by the people, for the people, shall not perish from the Earth."

May 29, 1994

Death of soldiers nothing to celebrate

WHY?

I have put off writing this until the last minute. Because I am the only World War II combat veteran left around here, I am expected to write the definitive D-Day column. I can't do it. I wasn't there.

Sure, my old 6th Armored Division fought in Normandy and in many battles in the European Theater, but we didn't land on D-Day. When we did roll ashore from LCTs on Normandy beaches and saw the carnage and devastation everywhere, I was glad we didn't. Our first sergeant was killed almost immediately after we landed.

Does it make you uncomfortable that the 50th anniversary of D-Day is being called a "celebration"? A few months ago, a travel agent contacted me and asked if I would lead a tour to Normandy to "celebrate" the 50th anniversary of the invasion. I told her I thought it was inappropriate to celebrate the deaths of 23,000 American boys. And boys they were, too. The burden of combat was borne mostly by kids just out of high school.

I returned to Normandy alone in 1950. I walked the then-peaceful beach and explored old German gun emplacements to see what they saw. I went to the nearby military cemetery to visit the grave of one of our neighborhood kids who died there. I looked across the field of what appeared to be an infinite number of white grave markers.

I was overwhelmed with grief. Why them and not me? Why? I didn't feel lucky. I felt guilty.

Monday, the politicians will speak of those who "gave" their lives so that others could be free. But they didn't give their lives. Their lives were taken from them. They had no choice. Listen across the years to the voice of the dying soldier: "Mamma, Mamma. Jesus, God, Mamma. I am so cold. Oh, Mamma, Mamma … "

Any soldier will tell you the war was sanitized for folks at home. Until it was over, they were spared photographs of dead Americans and of body parts ripped away by savage 88mm gunfire. There were no photographs of soldiers killed and wounded from "friendly fire" around St. Lo where the breakthrough occurred.

Monday, let us honor the infantrymen who stormed ashore and faced almost certain death. We hear a lot about smart bombs, surgical bombing and high-tech warfare, but it always comes down to the poor bastards with the rifles who have to take the high ground. It was that way then. It's that way now.

It is important we remember why they had to die. And we should also take note that the Nazis and the fascists are on the move again, and the evil they spawned still plagues the civilized world.

If you happen to be around an old dog soldier Monday, and his eyes mist and his chin begins to quiver and his hands tremble, turn away. Let him be alone with his memories.

One of my worst memories is of the last week of the war. A soldier in our outfit murdered four members of his section with his rifle while they slept. We never found out why. He had been wounded during the bitter Anzio invasion, and had made the Normandy invasion with the Big Red One. We figured he'd had too much war.

Which is the more tragic, the deaths of those four boys who had survived five campaigns only to be murdered by a buddy? Or was it the instant death of a kid who took a 7.5mm slug in the head the minute he stepped into the water on D-Day?

I leave it to you. You decide. *June 5, 1994*

We long remember the dead young men

FOREVER YOUNG.

What do you say to a high school girl who calls on the phone and wants to know what it is like to kill someone? What do you think about, she wondered, when you look down at the body? Do you feel guilt?

That happened to me the other day when she called for help in writing a report for a history class on World War II. She wanted to know what we had to eat, where we learned how to make war and how we felt about what we did.

It's no use trying to get war out of your system. Just when you think its horror and ugliness have slipped beyond recall, something comes up to make it live again in your consciousness.

We have had the 50th anniversary of D-Day, the Battle of the Bulge and liberation of the death camps. Coming later this month is the 50th anniversary of the invasion of Iwo Jima and other Pacific theater battles.

Then there will be V-E Day and V-J Day, and each time we pass these milestones, familiar feelings are kindled to flame again in old guys who were in the war's original cast.

For a long time, folks stifled their yawns and tried to change the subject when World War II stories were told. We became boring old men. At least we were until this 50th anniversary business came up.

Now, all of a sudden, what we had been trying to forget for 50 years, people want us to remember.

Not all my memories are bad. Unlike some, I liked the Army. It was the first place in life I felt I really belonged. I made lifetime friends as a soldier and am in contact with many of them all these years later.

I still have dreams of when we were young and together in the field. In my dreams, we are laughing and sometimes sitting around a fire, or hearing the first sergeant holler, "March order," or listening to Roy Acuff on the radio singing "The Great Speckled Bird."

The passing of time has diminished somewhat the terror and the fear we once endured. And most of us would admit that we see ourselves today in more heroic terms than we probably deserve. It was my experience that there weren't any atheists in the foxholes, and there weren't any patriots in there, either.

I will probably never get over the anguish I still feel for the dead. And those of us who managed to survive still are haunted with the guilt of living while others died. We will always ask ourselves the question, "Why them and not us?" They did not give their lives. Their lives were taken from them.

My way of coping with these troubling thoughts 50 years later is not to remember them as forever dead, but as forever young. And they were young, many still in their teens. While it is true that the war robbed them of their future, of all they would ever be, or do, or have, or love, it never let them get old, and tired, and sometimes defeated.

They never suffered from arthritis, or prostate cancer, or blindness, or Alzheimer's disease, or any of the other ills that have beset the survivors in their declining years. At the instant of their death, they were young and vital, and I will always try to preserve them that way in my memory.

The history of warfare is usually told from the point of view of the generals. It is often depicted as a giant chess game in which kings and knights and bishops are deposed. Personal tragedies are reduced to soulless statistics.

As we pass each of these 50th anniversary milestones, let us remember the forever young to whom civilization owes so much.

February 9, 1995

An old soldier remembers the great city of London was the place to feel the last of darkness ... and the coming of light as World War II ended in Europe

Tomorrow I will close my eyes and have a rendezvous with a memory.

It really began Feb. 10, 1944, when the 6th Armored Division embarked from Pier 89 in New York. We weren't supposed to know where we were going, but no one needed to tell us we were on our way to fight the Germans in the European Theater of Operations.

My battalion was packed like kippers in the USS Henrico, a relatively small Navy assault ship not designed to carry troops great distances. The convoy was the largest of World War II, a veritable bridge of ships zigzagging across the Atlantic. We weren't even a half-day out when the Henrico began to pitch and roll in an angry storm that followed us all the way across the ocean to the United Kingdom 12 days later.

Just remembering the Henrico summons the taste of bile to my mouth, the first symptom of seasickness. Bilge and vomit sloshed underfoot in the hold where we were bunked four deep and in the galley where we tried to eat. From the first day at sea, everyone was seasick but Gordon Manring from landlocked Albany, Mo. If he tossed his cookies, it was when no one was looking.

Maybe it was because the sun was shining and the land felt so firm underfoot when we arrived at Edinburgh that I fell in love with the United Kingdom. We traveled by rail to tiny Ramsden Heath in Oxfordshire. While we were moving into Quonset huts with potbellied stoves the next morning, apple-cheeked children ran up to us and said, "Got'ny gum, Chum?"

GIs were everywhere. Sure, there was some resentment. It was whispered that there were three things wrong with the Yanks. "They are overpaid, oversexed and over here." Generally, though, we were treated warmly. The Brits knew, if we didn't realize it then, the sacrifices we would make when the invasion finally came.

My first visit to London was on a 36-hour pass in early March. During the daylight hours it was the most exciting city in the world. Supreme Headquarters Allied Expeditionary Forces—SHAEF—was there. Gen. Dwight Eisenhower's staff was planning what would be called his Crusade in Europe. The streets were alive with soldiers wearing uniforms of every nation in the free world. Everyone sensed there was great history in the making and this was the place to be.

GIs hung out at Rainbow Corner, a home away from home where silent movie star Bebe Daniels and Adele Astaire, Fred's sister, wrote letters to servicemen's relatives stateside. We could drink real Cokes at the club and dance with English girls to Glenn Miller recordings.

London after dark was really dark. Blacked out and fogged in, the streets were empty except for lovers standing in doorways and an occasional jeep or staff car hurtling through the gloom, showing only pinpoint blackout lights. But in the dance halls, bars and brasseries, pub crawlers were doing the Lambeth Walk. Raucous GIs were drinking Guinness stout and singing, "Roll me over, Yankee soldier, roll me over, lay me down and do it again."

To make the most of daylight hours and save electricity, clocks were advanced two hours in what was then called "Double British war time." People in their homes were listening to the news on BBC and to Vera Lynn singing "When the Lights Go On Again" and "There'll be Bluebirds Over the White Cliffs of Dover."

When the skies finally darkened, the singing stopped, air raid sirens began to wail, and search lights crisscrossed the sky like giant wheel spokes. Then there was the pom, pom, pom of anti-aircraft fire, followed by sticks of bombs from German Heinkel bombers that hammered the great city until the ground shuddered and flames licked away at the night.

I had never heard a shot fired in anger when I was in my first London air raid. There were a dozen of us staying at a Red Cross hostel near Oxford Circus when the sirens began their singsong warning. We were all sleeping on canvas cots when the bombs started falling.

None of us wanted to be the first chicken to run for the air raid shelter, and so we were all trembling under GI blankets. Finally, an old woman in a nightgown and sleeping cap stepped into the room. She said, quite calmly, "I think it's time for you young gentlemen to go to the shelter." Swallowing our foolish pride, we all jumped up at once and started running, half-dressed, for the shelter. As I was leaving, I looked back to see if she was following us. She wasn't. She stepped back into her bedroom and closed the door.

It was that night I realized people back home had no idea what Londoners endured during the Battle of Britain. Night after night after night, after every goddamm night, German bombs and missiles rained down on them. All these years later, I have never found the language to describe their courage and their nobility under fire.

That was my first view of London. My next would come the following year when the war was finally winding down. The 6th Armored had fought its way through all five European theater campaigns. We were deep in east Germany near Mittweida waiting to link up with the Russian army. Fighting had stopped in our sector. We knew the war was ending.

Then a remarkable thing happened. Somehow, some way, for some reason I never knew, I was one of only 20 GIs out of 10,000 in the 6th to be given a two-week furlough to Paris, the Riviera, Switzerland or London. I chose London because I had enjoyed the city so much a year earlier.

Ten years ago on the 40th anniversary of V-E Day—Victory in Europe Day—I wrote about how disoriented I was as I walked along crowded London streets. I kept bumping into people and apologizing for my clumsiness. I wasn't accustomed to being in a crowd. It's one thing to be sloshing with a few guys in the mud, but quite another to navigate through throngs of hurrying pedestrians along the Strand.

There were times when I had to sit down to get my bearings. Everything seemed to be closing in on me. I was glad to be out of combat, but I was almost sorry I came. It was at this point I met Dorothy Fuller, a pretty young woman who was working in a Piccadilly photo studio.

We had tea after she got off work. I accompanied her home to meet her parents. They invited me to spend the rest of my furlough with them. I had just spent my first night with the Fullers when V-E Day was declared. Dorothy and I didn't want to miss a minute of the celebration.

Most of us were just kid soldiers. There had been nothing in our civilian lives to prepare us for the horrors and the massive destruction we had just experienced. When the last shots were fired, soldiers felt a great sense of relief. Untold millions of people had been killed. Behind us were the savage invasion of Normandy, the Battle of the Bulge, the longest and costliest battle ever fought by an American army, and the liberation of the infamous Nazi death camps.

There were also countless little firefights that history has forgotten, but that old soldiers can never forget. They quietly weep when they remember. The end of it all was difficult to comprehend. I thought of the 6th Armored I had left just a few days ago. It was like a tired and scarred old beast, slumped to the ground, resting and licking its wounds.

But I was in London. Spring was in the air. Buttercups were blooming, and this ancient city was ready at long last to embrace peace. If there was anywhere to be on V-E Day it was London. Hitler had tried and failed to bomb this proud city into submission.

For American and British crews of air bombardment and fighter groups, V-E Day meant they would never again have to fly through murderous flak. And while they were happy it was all over, they remembered that 150,000 Allied airmen had been killed and another 45,000 had been kriegies, or prisoners of war, in Germany. Some were sent to the Buchenwald death camp, others lynched with telephone wire or pitchforked to death by German civilians, or tortured by the Gestapo. Some lost all hope and chose suicide rather than endure life in POW camps.

Dorothy and I were caught up in London's incomparable victory celebration. We went to Windsor Palace and saw King George, Queen Elizabeth and their daughters, the future Queen Elizabeth and her sister, Margaret Rose, appearing on a balcony. We saw Winston Churchill. Irish Guards were brawling in the streets. Drunken journalists were celebrating in front of Fleet Street newspaper plants.

Londoners couldn't wait for the night. At long last, there would be no blackout. "How Londoners loved the light," I wrote 10 years ago. "They wanted to breathe it, bathe in it, cover everything with it." The light became symbolic of their liberation from years of darkness.

We were tossed about by the giddy crowds as though we were flotsam on a wild sea. Dorothy was waving a small British Union Jack, a flag I carefully folded and put away as a souvenir. I still have it.

It was about 3 o'clock in the morning when we started back for Dorothy's home in Balham. As we were walking toward the Underground subway stop, I saw something that misted my eyes: People were blacking out their windows again, just from habit. The lights had gone on again, the air raids had stopped, but the long shadows of the war still clouded the lives of people who had suffered so long.

The *Rocky Mountain News* wanted me to return to London for the 50th anniversary of V-E Day. I thought about it for a while but decided not to go. For one thing, I didn't want to sit in one of those dinky airline seats for 10 hours and eat airline food. Because of my lung disease, I don't have the stamina I once had.

I returned to London for V-E Day five years after the war. I went back to Oxford Circus and revisited Trafalgar Square and Rainbow Corner, but the magic was gone.

That's the real reason I didn't want to go this year. The London I knew and loved 50 years ago has changed, and I suspect not for the better. Like a lot of big cities today, it's been victimized by urban decay. Most of its residents now weren't even alive 50 years ago. They won't really understand what V-E Day meant to my generation.

A few old soldiers will put on their medals and parade around during official ceremonies. I wouldn't want to see that. I want to remember them as forever young, the way they were that magic night all those years ago.

Was it Einstein who said that the past still exists, and that time is like a road on which we are traveling? Is wartime London still out there on that road even though we passed it a half-century ago?

I don't know. I do know it still exists in my memory. I know it is in Dorothy's memory, too. I'll call her tomorrow in Tasmania, where she lives now. We'll talk about that night and remember when the lights went on again.   *May 7, 1995*

War's anniversary brings back the grit

YO YO.

When I came home from the Korean War, it was as though there was no war at all. No student protests. No kids burning draft cards or bugging out to Canada. No pictures of Jane Fonda schmoozing with an enemy gun crew. No TV pictures of body bags.

Folks didn't talk or care much about the war that killed 54,246 Americans, wounded 103,284 and left 5,178 others missing in action. Out of sight, out of mind. An estimated 1 million South Korean civilians were killed and about 1.6 million Chinese and North Korean soldiers were killed.

I had been a soldier in World War II and became a civilian war correspondent shortly after the Korean War broke out 45 years ago today. When those of us who went to Korea remember that time, we are overwhelmed with a montage of memories.

I see white South African pilots doing a Zulu war dance around their F-51 Mustangs before taking off at dawn to support U.N. ground troops. I see 700 wounded U.N. soldiers flowing into one overworked MASH hospital in just 72 hours. I see members of the Greek battalion bayoneting retreating Chinese soldiers.

Were you one of 20,000 Marines who fought your way out from the Changjin Reservoir in bitter winter weather to the port of Hungnam where you were evacuated by sea? Did you wade ashore at Inchon? Were you one of Gen. Bulldog Walker's 8th Army troops who turned back attack after attack on the tiny Pusan Perimeter?

I see F-86 Sabre Jets dueling with Russian-piloted MIG-15s over MIG Alley near the Yalu River. I see a small tank patrol entering Chorwon in the Iron Triangle. I see a refugee camp of 90,000 displaced civilians, and I see people dying as I walk through their masses.

GIs who fought at Bloody Ridge, Finger Ridge, Heartbreak Ridge, Old Baldy and Pork Chop Hill look back and wonder how they survived. Some of that fighting raged while armistice talks were taking place between North Korean and U.N. negotiators. A peace treaty was never signed, only an armistice.

If I stop to listen to my memories, I can hear the song, "China Nights," known to most GIs as "I Ain't Got No Yo Yo." And can you remember singing, "The swivel-chair colonel said pardon me, please, but you got blood on your jacket and mud on your knees"?

I remember eating sweet and sour dog in a Korean "sing-song" house. Do you remember Gen. Matt Ridgeway in his fatigue cap and fragmentation grenades hanging from loops on his haversack belt? Do you remember R&R, rest and recuperation, and S&S, sex and sake?

In your dreams can you still hear the drums, bugles, cymbals and obscenities screamed at you by Chinese soldiers before their "human wave" attacks?

I remember flying a close support spotting mission with an Army pilot in an unarmed, little Ryan two-seater. As he called in Marine Corsairs for a napalm strike on an enemy river crossing, we could hear small arms fire directed at us and see bullet holes appearing in the wings.

When we landed, the pilot's hands shook so much he couldn't hold a cup of coffee. The poor bastard had flown 400 missions just like that one. What happened to him? I never knew.

For him and for thousands of other veterans of what diplomats called a "police action," the Korean War will never end in their memories. It was a war they were never permitted to win, but they accomplished their mission of throwing back the North Korean invasion.

June 25, 1995

FAMILY AND LOVE IN THE LONGER SHADOWS

Mom was a proud, strong woman

MOM.

The three of us had been sitting for what seemed like hours around the small round table in the kitchen. Finally, my mother got up, went to the cupboard and came back with a single can of Campbell's vegetable soup.

My father and I watched as she solemnly placed it in the center of the table. "That's the last of the food," she said as she turned her face away.

It was the first winter of the Great Depression. We were living in Casper, Wyo. Pop had been laid off from his automobile tire sales job. After the last can of soup was gone, we somehow made our way back to Denver in our 1927 Dodge.

It wasn't much better here. Each morning, Mom would cut out cardboard liners for Pop's worn-out shoes so he could walk downtown to look for work. But there were no jobs, and when the rent came due and we couldn't pay, we had to crowd in with Grandpa and Grandma Amole and Aunt Anna in their house on West Maple Avenue.

Pop slept in the attic. He was so discouraged, he sometimes wouldn't come downstairs for days. He would just lie there on that old cast-iron bed and stare at nothing. Once a day, Mom would take me up to the attic, I guess to try to make him feel better about himself.

Things got better when Mom was hired as a substitute schoolteacher for $5 every day she worked. It might be Whittier, or Gilpin, or 24th Street, or sometimes Steele or Smedley, and even Alameda, where I went to school.

Finally Pop got a job selling tires downtown, and we saved enough to move out on our own again. That's the way it was during the Depression. We always had something to eat, though, even if it was a can of soup split three ways, or creamed nothing on toast.

213

All of that replayed in my mind last week as I watched my mother slowly die in her hospital room. She had enough strength for all of us during the hard times those many years ago. As she labored for each breath through the oxygen mask, I wanted desperately to return to her some of that strength so she might live a little longer.

But it was not to be. Mom died early Thursday. She was 87.

It was a remarkable life. At 7, she was herding sheep in eastern Colorado from the back of a mule. At 18, she was teaching eight grades in a one-room schoolhouse on a homestead near Nucla. Somehow she managed to attend Western State College and the University of Denver.

Until she went to the hospital three weeks ago, Mom lived alone in the house my great-grandfather built. She took care of herself until almost the very end.

She was strong, proud, independent and full of love for the world around her. She adored baseball and basketball. One of her last great pleasures came when she read a note Vince Boryla had sent to her in the hospital. It said, "Elizabeth, the Denver Nuggets love you."

And so did I. So very much. As I kissed her forehead for the last time and said goodbye, I wondered if there would ever be anyone like her again. *December 8, 1985*

Almighty Corp. takes its toll

ILLUSIONS.

If you have seen or read Arthur Miller's *Death of a Salesman,* you knew my father. You would have recognized him by his "shoe shine and smile." And when the talk got around to "covering the territory," you would have said Frank E. Amole was a dead ringer for Willy Loman.

Not exactly, though. Willy lost his sense of humor when he lost faith in himself and in the Almighty Corporation for which he worked. Except for a dark time during the Great Depression, Pop could always find something to smile about, something funny to say. I guess it was his way of choking down the bitterness.

But like Willy, Pop stopped believing in the Almighty Corporation. There were a lot of Almighty Corporations in his life: Goodyear,

Goodrich, Permite, General Motors and some others I can't remember. He gave them his body, his spirit and his soul. With Pop, the Almighty Corporation was right up there with God, mother and country.

You know what happens in cases of that kind of misplaced devotion. The Almighty Corporation can chew up a man until all the juices are gone, and then spit him out. As I recall that terrible moment in our lives, Pop was working for General Motors. I have never been able to forgive that Almighty Corporation for what it did him.

As a little boy, I suppose I was jealous. Pop was on the road a lot, and I guess I thought he ought to be home, teaching me how to make a kite or playing catch with me. Years later I realized he didn't know how to do those things because his father didn't teach him. Why is it understanding and wisdom are so late in coming?

Pop and I could never talk easily to each other. It was just too awkward for us. I guess we didn't want to risk revealing our feelings. I received only one letter from him while I was away at war. It was handwritten on one of those yellow, lined, legal-sized pieces of paper. I could tell he had worked on it a long time. It read sort of like a business letter and was signed "Frank E. Amole."

When the road show of *Death of a Salesman* came to Denver, I bought tickets for Mom and Pop. The play had a stunning effect on him. He couldn't talk about it without fury burning in his eyes. As he watched, it wasn't Willy Loman he saw up on the stage. Pop was looking into a mirror and seeing himself.

When his faith in the Almighty Corporation was finally shattered, he found a degree of peace in some of the metaphysical, science-of-mind religions gaining popularity at the time. It always hurt him that I could not share his faith in them. Maybe it was just his way of reaching out to me, and I didn't realize it.

Pop died 10 years ago. The end was swift and painless. I have always regretted that I never found a way to tell him how much I loved him.

Quote: "An era can be said to end when its basic illusions are exhausted."—Arthur Miller.

June 15, 1986

215

Let kids be kids while they can

CONFESSIONS.

It was just a week before Father's Day that the last of our four children moved out, leaving us with what psychologists call an "empty nest." I have mixed feelings about this, since our nest has had from one to four kids in it almost continuously for the past 35 years.

I must confess to you that there are some advantages to the roomier nest. The telephone doesn't ring all the time. We don't run out of hot water during the morning rush hour. I sleep better because I don't awaken each time I hear a tire squeal in the middle of the night, or I don't hear the front door open when I think it ought to.

Trish and I have had to adjust our food-buying habits. For some reason, shopping for two seems more difficult than it was for three, or four, or five or six, when the nest was full. Old habits are difficult to break.

We really miss Susan—the last to leave and try her wings—but we are finding it pleasant to spend more time with each other. Our lives have been focused for so long on the kids. I still call them kids even though they are adults. I suppose the non-sexist, non-age-discriminatory description of them should be *persons,* but I can't bring myself to be that impersonal about those I love.

As I have observed here before, being a parent is the toughest thing I have ever had to do. Wisdom comes so late. As Mignon McLaughlin wrote, "Most of us become parents long before we have stopped being children. By the time you realize what mistakes you have made, it is usually too late to correct them. You and your kids just have to learn to live with the consequences."

I suppose I was really four fathers, not just one. I learned early on that each of my children had different needs and that I couldn't be just an all-purpose, generic dad for all of them. They all looked at me through different eyes, and I learned to look back at them with a different vision for each.

I also confess that my biggest mistake was trying to run interference for them. I didn't want them to fail where I had failed. I kept running in and rescuing them when I should have let them take their lumps when they made mistakes. I somehow never understood that experience was a better teacher than I was. To their credit, they have survived my bad judgment and have done well anyhow.

I see a lot of young, upscale parents rushing their children through childhood. Convinced they are "gifted," or "terribly bright," or "special," they put them in accelerated education programs. I suspect that what the parents are really doing is basking in the reflected glory of their children. Parents of athletically talented children do the same thing.

Childhood is such a precious time, but so many parents deny their kids the opportunity to explore it and learn from it. Instead, they want to make them tiny adults the instant they learn to walk and talk. I believe that in a child's formative years, there must be time to imagine, to fantasize and to just go outdoors and get dirty in the back yard.

June 21, 1987

Nurses make us all look good

PANTYHOSE.

We were eating our ice cream cones at a table in Baskin-Robbins. Trish was having pralines and cream and I was slurping away at baseball nut when a young man came in with his three children. The kids were giggling and dancing around in front of refrigerated cases trying to decide which of the 31 flavors they would choose.

Trish leaned over and whispered, "Their mother is a registered nurse, and she is at work at the hospital."

"Do you know those people?" I asked.

"No. I have never seen any of them before."

"Then how can you possibly know that she is a nurse?"

"She went to work at three o'clock this afternoon. She's in orthopedics. She is supposed to get off at 11, but by the time she gets through with report to the all-night people, she'll be lucky to get home by one o'clock."

Over the years, I have learned to go along with Trish's fantasies about people she sees.

"What about the father?" I asked.

"Nice man. He picked up the kids from day care after he got off work. He took them home and heated a tuna casserole his wife made before she went to work at the hospital. He told them that if they cleaned their plates, he would take them to Baskin-Robbins for ice cream cones after dinner."

One of the things you need to know about my wife is that she is a registered nurse. Once an RN, always an RN. Even though she is now employed at Lutheran Medical Center in another aspect of health care work, Trish's instincts have RN stamped all over them.

Her perceptions of people are usually on target. There is no doubt in my mind that if we could somehow go back and find that woman we didn't see, she would turn out to be an RN.

Trish still keeps in touch with nurses with whom she worked at Presbyterian Medical Center and at University Hospital. She also likes to go back to Chicago for reunions at Grant Hospital where she trained. There is a bonding among nurses that is difficult for the rest of us to understand.

She used to say that when she was getting ready to go to work at the hospital, she felt power flowing into her body when she put on her white pantyhose. You'd have to say, though, that going into nursing is hardly a power trip. There are times when it seems to them as though everyone else has the power. But when you push the button for help, it is the nurse who answers your call.

I liked it when nurses wore starched white uniforms and those little caps that indicated where they learned their profession. Most nurses prefer more casual and comfortable wear these days. It must be that I am old-fashioned because I want my nurses to look like nurses, my nuns to look like nuns and my cops to look like cops. Is this stereotyping?

Make no mistake, nursing is tough, demanding work. Nurses deserve more pay and respect than they get. Distraught families can require more time and care than their loved ones who are the patients. The burnout rate is high.

Beyond the pay and the employee benefits, there are rewards in nursing that are unavailable to most of us. There is the miracle of their healing touch. In so many ways, they bring comfort and care to those who can't help themselves. Nurses can take pride that their compassion and their skills help preserve and enhance the quality of our lives.

So I am a week late. Happy Nurses Day, anyhow.

May 12, 1992

Even a tree must turn over a new leaf

STICKY GREEN.

As near as I can remember, our cottonwood tree sprouted in the back yard about the same time we moved in the front door of our Bear Valley house 27 years ago. There were five of us then; Trish and I and the three kids, Muffy, Brett and Jon. Susan came along three years later.

As we were starting a new life, so was the tree. Just as there were five of us, the little volunteer sprout of a tree had five trunks. Over the years, I've had to remove three of the trunks, leaving two. In a way, the cottonwood remains symbolic of our family because the kids are gone now and only Trish and I are left at home.

In the grand scheme of things, 27 years is not so old for a tree, compared to the giant redwoods. But cottonwoods grow rapidly, and I must say that ours is a majestic tree. It towers over our house, and I suspect it is the tallest tree in the neighborhood.

Maybe the reason I am so sentimental about cottonwoods is because we are both natives. I was born in Denver, and the cottonwoods were here when Grandpa came West in 1870. In *The First Hundred Years,* Bob Perkin's superb history of Denver and the *Rocky Mountain News,* he wrote movingly of the day both were born:

"A late-season snow, heavy and wet, fell on Auraria, Kansas Territory, throughout the day and into the night of April 22, 1859. Big puffs of clustered flakes drifted down on the mud roof of cabins and on the conical tipis pitched among the trees along the river. It wasn't really cold: just chill, sodden and dispiriting, were it not for the hints of laggard spring. The cottonwoods were beginning to leaf out, sticky green."

Only the Lord knows how many birds and squirrels have been sheltered in our cottonwood. We've had jays, finches, robins, red-shafted flickers, Bohemian wax wings, doves, a few grackles and an occasional red-wing blackbird. I sometimes wonder how far afield their progeny have gone. How many squirrels have Oreo, Yazzie and Old Snoop treed in the cottonwood?

Brett and Jon, and their pals, Doug, Howie, Cort, Breck, Richie and Steve, played endless whiffle ball games under the tree when they were growing up. Susan's sandbox, and later her playhouse, were under the tree. I have repaired bicycles and wagons and shampooed dogs under the tree. We celebrated Trish's and Muffy's graduations under the tree. When Trish's parents celebrated their 50th wedding anniversary, it was under the tree.

I love the tree in the autumn when its yellow leaves rattle in the evening breeze, and in the winter when its naked branches are lace against the sky.

But now it's coming down. Our beloved old tree has become a neighborhood nuisance and must go. Its cotton seedlings have fallen impartially on the just and the unjust. We have had anonymous cards complaining of the tree and how it causes allergic reactions in children. This summer has been the worst, and its existence has become intolerable.

The complaints have merit. Trish and I know it must go. We want to be good neighbors. We're having it removed as soon as the tree guys can schedule it. I'm trying to look on the bright side, remembering all the tree has meant to us and how well it has served our family.

However, the irony of George Pope Morris' famous lines haunt me:
Woodman, spare that tree!
Touch not a single bough!
In youth it sheltered me,
And I'll protect it now.

June 23, 1992

Dignified death deserves a choice

HOPELESS.

My mother and I were waiting outside the intensive-care unit at Denver General Hospital. It was 1976. Earlier that day, my father had suffered a massive stroke at home. Neither she nor I had much hope for his recovery. He had lost consciousness suddenly, without warning. We phoned for help, and the paramedics arrived within minutes.

A young physician took us into the room where Dad was being treated. He was connected by tubes and wires to a variety of life-support technologies. We looked at him in silence for a few minutes.

220

Mom's hand was tightly holding mine. The doctor's voice broke the silence.

"I'm sorry, but Mr. Amole is in very critical condition," he said. "We can sustain his life indefinitely, but there is no chance he will ever regain consciousness."

And then he paused without directly asking us what we wanted to do. We knew the question, though, and Mom answered almost immediately, "We don't want him to live like this, and he wouldn't want it, either."

The life-support equipment was removed, and he died a short time later. Neither my mother nor I ever regretted the decision. We were grateful to the young doctor for his honesty and to the hospital for acceding to our wishes.

It doesn't work that way with all doctors and at all hospitals, as I learned 10 years later when my mother was dying in another hospital. Her death was long and painful because of an inaccurate diagnosis about which I learned only after she had died. The hospital had treated her for a thyroid gland condition. She died of salmonella poisoning.

Perhaps she would have lived if the critical-care staff physicians had made a more careful diagnosis, but she didn't. During her last days when my hope for her recovery had faded, and I had expressed my wish that her life not needlessly be prolonged, the hospital staff continued to recommend additional surgery and other life-support means.

Finally, she died. I have never quite been able to conquer my anger over the circumstances of her death. She deserved a more peaceful, dignified passing than the prolonged agony she endured. Physicians are supposed to "do no harm," but harm was done to her.

No, I didn't sue the hospital or the critical-care doctors for malpractice. There is too much of that kind of litigation, and I didn't want to be a party to more. I didn't want money. It would not have returned my mother to life and good health. I had to settle for "mistakes were made."

These troubling memories have resurfaced because of Dr. Jack Kevorkian's lonely battle to legalize suicide for patients who suffer from an incurable ailment that irreparably damages the quality of their lives.

Neither of my parents chose suicide, but before their deaths both had made it clear to me that they did not want their lives prolonged artificially if it meant only a painful and hopeless existence.

I was cheered that Wayne County Circuit Judge Richard Kaufman ruled Tuesday that Michigan's absolute ban on assisting hopelessly ill patients commit suicide violates the 14th Amendment's guarantee of liberty. At last, the law may be ready to recognize that if we have a right to life, we must also have a right to death under these circumstances by choice and without outside interference.

December 16, 1993

Bunny dodges the Jim reaper

RABBIT REDUX.

The quick, brown bunny jumped over the lazy dog's back and escaped with his life.

But let's start at the beginning. When we moved into our new (to us) house in Lakewood, we noticed there were a lot of rabbits in the neighborhood. The little cottontails were everywhere; peeking out from under shrubbery, dashing across the streets, snuggling in the deep grass, digging in our neighbor's garden.

They seemed harmless. Actually, we became fond of the little guys, even though they left rabbit poo pellets all over the back yard. "After all," Trish reasoned, "they were here before we were and must be responding to some sort of primordial territorial imperative."

But sooner or later, I thought, our cat, Jim S. Peterson, would discover the rabbits. In our old neighborhood, he stalked and killed field mice, birds, small snakes and even a squirrel and dragged them into our house.

Trish never handled these incidents too well. As a registered nurse, she has confronted almost every kind of human injury and disfigurement with remarkable detachment. No problem. But when it comes to small animals that are killed or injured, she just goes bonkers.

It happened a couple of weeks ago when she found a dead rabbit in the living room. There wasn't a mark on him. In a highly agitated state, she called me at work. "Do you want me to come home?" I asked.

222

"No," she replied, "I guess I can handle it." And so equipped with rubber gloves, a dust pan and a plastic grocery bag she managed to dispose of the dead rabbit.

She was really steamed at little Jim. "If you ever, ever do that again, it's off to the Dumb Friends League. I'm serious. You leave those rabbits alone!" she said.

Jim is such a small cat. I never understood how he nailed that squirrel, dragged him inside. How could he ever carry it up a tree, onto the roof and into the house through a window? He'll never do it again, I thought.

So let's fast-forward to last Wednesday. I was just getting out of the shower and Trish was ready to leave early for work. There was this shriek, "GENE! I need your help right now!"

I pulled on a pair of pants and came downstairs, fully expecting to find her with a broken leg. But no. There she was, trying to keep Jim away from a terrified, very much alive, rabbit. She had already awakened Oreo, our lazy dog, and escorted him outside.

Then it was tally ho! The chase was on. The bunny scampered into the dining room and under the buffet. I got him out with a broom handle, only to see him head for the back door.

Trish opened the door, but the rabbit ran the other way. "I'll lock Jim in the laundry room and get a shoe box. You get gloves," she ordered. I looked down and noticed my fly was unzipped. I had no shirt or shoes on.

Our terrified prey hopped toward the living room, where the first rabbit died. By then, Trish was back with a shoe box. She tried to coax it into the box, but the rabbit wasn't having any of it.

Finally, we drove him into the corner and I grabbed him with my gloved hand. The rabbit squealed. I think it was the rabbit. Maybe it was Trish. Anyhow, I stuck him in the box, clamped on the lid and headed for the front door.

I hurried into the front yard, opened the box and let the bunny go. By then, I was wheezing, my bare feet were cold, and so I went back into the house and hooked myself back onto oxygen. Trish went to work and then I let Jim out of the laundry room.

Well, we have met Flopsie and Mopsie. I can't wait for Cottontail and Peter.

April 14, 1994

223

Finding guidance in the darndest places

UNFOCUSED.

Taoists in ancient China found spiritual peace by contemplating their navels. I guess that's what they were doing. There's no telling, though, what goes on in the mind of a guy who is studying his belly button.

I rarely look at mine, and then only for lint removal. Mine is off center by a couple of inches as a result of surgery years ago. The physician told me he could have removed it altogether. That wouldn't have been too bad. I could have gone to the south Pacific and passed myself off to superstitious islanders as a sun god.

I used to put on my pants by lining them up with my navel. But after the surgery, this left my belt buckle inclined toward the starboard.

The idea of contemplation attracts me, though. I can remember how my father would silently sit on the edge of the bed in the morning.

He would be fully clothed except for his right foot. Pop would have his legs crossed and one sock would be hanging limply from his hand as he stared, unfocused, into the middle distance. In my memory, I can still hear my mother calling from downstairs in the kitchen: "Frank! Quit sitting there holding your sock. Breakfast is ready."

His state was almost catatonic. You could wave your hand in front of his eyes and he wouldn't respond, as though afflicted by some kind of psychomotor anomaly. It wasn't exactly stupor, but almost.

I wondered what was going on behind those vacant eyes. I asked him once what he was thinking about, but he waved me away without explaining.

Now I understand. In recent years, I have found myself similarly purposeless in the morning. In getting ready for work, I move along pretty well until I get down to that final sock. Then I sit, legs crossed with the empty sock hanging from my hand.

Realizing I was doing precisely what Pop had done years ago, it occurred to me that maybe sock-holding is inherited. Is it in the Amole family genetic coding? Can this be identified from our DNA? When they are older, will my sons sit silently on the edge of their beds in the morning, in a trance, dangling an empty sock from their fingertips?

224

What am I thinking? Is it about Michael Jackson's marriage to Elvis Presley's daughter? Or O.J. Simpson losing his job as an actor in the *Naked Gun* motion picture series? Am I ruminating about the Hillary Clinton health care plan? Is it the baggage system at DIA that occupies my thoughts? Am I stewing about the rain forests?

Actually, I am wondering what I shall do about the day ahead. What shall I write about? Do I have to get gasoline before I drive to work? Is this a no-red-meat day for me and will I have to gag down yet another chicken salad for lunch? Will the temperature stay under 90?

Frankly, I even consider calling in sick. Deb Goeken, our city editor, is my boss. I could feign hoarseness and leave a message on her voice mail: "Deb, this is Gene. (cough, cough) I've picked up some kind of bug. (wheeze, wheeze) I think I better stay home. I wouldn't want anyone in the newsroom to catch this thing from me. (hack, hack) It's terrible. I ache all over. I'll call you tomorrow. (sniff, sniff)

I don't do this, of course. I finally emerge from my meditation and haul my rear end down to the *Rocky*. Later in the day I will look down at my feet and discover I am wearing one blue sock and one brown one. *September 4, 1994*

Sleep in peace, sweet old pup

FROST.

All Saturday morning, our old dog Oreo seemed to be following me everywhere. When I sat down on the couch in the TV room, she snuggled into her favorite corner and put her head on my knee. She looked up with those big brown eyes and licked my hand until I scratched her ear.

She has been doing this for a long while, but it seemed different this time and it was. This was the day veterinarian Ross Deckert would put Oreo to sleep. Trish thinks Oreo somehow knew this and wanted to be with us as long as possible. I don't know.

I met Deckert a year or so ago when he came to our house to take care of Oreo. He has a mobile veterinary clinic that operates in the southwest metro area. He told us that Oreo had cancer and wouldn't

225

live much longer. Trish and I decided, though, to take care of her and try to help her make the most of what quality time she had left.

She had arthritis, and her legs trembled when she stood for any length of time. Sometimes her legs would splay from under her and she would fall helplessly to the floor. Her heart was enlarged and she seemed to be gasping for air. She slept most of the time.

Even so, Oreo always looked forward each evening to a short walk up the street from our house. She would stumble and fall and stop to rest occasionally, but she still enjoyed sniffing where other dogs had walked. Trish took her for her last walk late Friday night. She had to work Saturday and wasn't able to be at home with Oreo and me when Deckert came.

I hardly slept that night. I'd get up and try to watch TV or read, but it didn't work. All I could think of was Oreo and what she had meant to us all those years. She had been a gift to our daughter Susan from some of her friends.

Oreo was an unruly pup, biting and snapping at everyone. One dog trainer advised Susan to have her destroyed because she was a "biter." But we stuck it out and she eventually became a gentle, family pet.

Her best years were when we lived in Bear Valley. Every evening—rain, snow, wind or whatever the weather—we'd go to Bear Creek Park for a walk. She loved that. In winter when the park was empty, I'd take off the leash and let her romp wherever she wanted to go.

She loved to jump into Bear Creek and splash after ducks. When the snow was deep, Oreo would run with abandon, joyously kicking up great clouds of snow behind her. Frost would form on her face and long hair, but she didn't care. She seemed to love the cold and her beloved park.

When Deckert's van pulled into the driveway, my heart almost stopped. What a nice guy he is. You'd never guess he was a Marine who served in Vietnam. He once told me he has never been able to get over being spit on when he came home from the war.

Oreo was curled up in her favorite corner when he injected her with a tranquilizer. Frightened, she scrambled into my little office and slumped down beside my favorite reading chair. I went to her and held her head and scratched her ears until she fell into a deep sleep. Then Deckert gave her another injection that painlessly ended her life.

"I'll be in the next room while you say goodbye to her," he said. I knelt beside her and kissed the top of her head. As I did, I touched her nose and it was still cold.

I held up pretty well until he carried her body to his van and drove away. I was alone. And then I started to cry, and I couldn't stop. OK, so I'm a softy.

Goodbye, old girl, we loved you very much.

October 3, 1995

Letter from Dad to aging boomers

DEAR BOOMER,

Congratulations! You have reached middle age. It doesn't seem so long ago that you didn't trust anyone older than 30. Remember when you shouted, "If you can't lead and you can't follow, get out of the way?"

Even though many of you are now buttoned-down and wing-tipped in the suburbs, your generation's rallying cry was, "If it feels good, man, do it!" Actually, you have since learned that you don't do it all that much anymore.

When World War II ended, your parents came home to make babies. It was fashionable then to have at least three kids. I did four. Why so many? My own private view is that we unconsciously were trying to make up for all the people we had killed in the war.

When you were born, your parents were living in subdivisions, hastily erected to take advantage of the GI Bill. In my case, I paid $1,100 down to buy an $11,000 home in University Hills. The interest was 4 percent and the payments were about $84 a month. Sometimes I drive by my old house at 3384 S. Fairfax St. to see how it looks after all that time. Looks nice.

The day I got out of the Army, I vowed to myself that I would never be cold or hungry or frightened again. That probably affected the kind of parent I would become. Having been a Depression kid and a veteran, I wanted a life for you that was better than mine. I wanted to protect you from some of the ugly realities I had experienced.

There was a real sense of community in the subdivisions then. Most of us were veterans who had just married. Financially, we were pretty much in the same boat.

We were so proud of you when you learned to walk. We watched anxiously as you tried to climb over the backyard redwood basket-weave fence.

There were always playmates your age. You'd form little trains with your tricycles to pedal around the block. How you would dance up and down with your hand out for a quarter when Melody Mac and his ice cream truck stopped in front.

Those were good years. You were loved, protected and nurtured. There wasn't a lot of money to spend, but there was enough so that both parents didn't have to work. The GI bill educated millions of young men who probably would never have gone to college without it.

We all realized that one day you would rebel against us as generations usually do. But we weren't quite prepared for the 1960s revolution. We just didn't understand all the long hair, that ear-splitting music, the marijuana, the flag burning, the contempt for government, war in Vietnam, the whole hippie thing.

Now that you are in your middle years, we are amused at how nostalgic you are for the '60s. It's nice you can get together with friends from your generation to remember how it was at the Exodus and the Family Dog.

I'm sorry about all the debt you are inheriting. Part of it is our fault, but not all of it. Congress has failed you and us by not establishing realistic national priorities instead of spending too much money on defense and political pork and not doing anything about the malignant growth of our underclass.

There is something you should understand, though. Those of us who are still alive love you very much. OK, so maybe we overindulged you a little, but it was only because we wanted the best for you.

Sincerely,

Dad.

December 31, 1995

228

Latest link in a chain of love

DEAR JACOB,

You were less than an hour old when Susan handed you to me in the birthing room at Rose Hospital. You squirmed and fussed until I instinctively started patting you softly on your back and began to sway back and forth. I guess holding a baby is like riding a bicycle; you never forget how.

Your Grandma Trish and your Aunt Muffy (Tustin) and I weren't in the room when you were born. We knew it would be soon, though, when your father, Gary, stuck his head through the door of the family waiting room and said, "I can see his head! His head is starting to come out!"

It had been a long wait, though. Your mother and father came to Rose Hospital at 3 A.M. Sunday. Trish and I came about 10 A.M. I settled in and read almost half of Michael Connelly's new mystery, *The Poet*. You were born about 5:30 P.M. That's when your Grandpa Tom Waters arrived. Your father and mother spent the first few minutes of your life alone with you. It was a very special time for them and for you.

The name Jacob Lindsay Waters suits you. You are a husky little guy—8 pounds, 10 ounces, and 21 inches long. You obviously got that shock of curly, black hair from your father. Actually, you have more hair now than I do. The top of my head looks like the elbow of an old fur coat.

There is no way I can explain now how much you will be loved. Your mother and father cherish family values. Your Uncle Brett and Uncle Jon can't wait to see you. It was love at first sight when your Aunt Muffy saw you while the nurse was putting on your first diaper.

Grandma Trish? She has been haunting baby stores for weeks. I watched her last night as she rocked you to sleep in the room where your mother was moved after you were born. Talk about love!

Me? Frankly, Jacob, I never thought you would get here. I have been longing for grandchildren for the past 20 years. I was beginning to think it would never happen. Listen, little fella, you were worth the wait.

Susan told me Sunday night that she and Gary want three more children. You'll have plenty of company growing up. Having been the father of four I learned a long time ago that the heart expands to embrace each child. There will always be enough love to go around.

I had such a wonderful grandfather. All these years later I have such warm memories of how kind he was to me. He was a big, gruff, blue-collar man with calloused hands, but he was always gentle with me. He helped teach me to read by showing me letters in the *Rocky Mountain News.*

He took me to baseball games, bought me strawberry pop and took me to Archer Park. He watched me grow to manhood and met me at Denver Union Station when I came home from the war.

When he could no longer take care of himself he came to live with us in my great-grandfather's old house in north Denver. One night after dinner, he rolled up his napkin in a napkin ring and said, "I am going upstairs to die." That's what he did. He just stretched out on his bed and died. He was 86.

At my age, Jacob, I won't live long enough to see you grow up to be a man. Grandma Trish will have to do that for both of us. You won't have many memories of me, maybe just faded ones of an old man. That's why I am writing this letter to you so that some day you will read it and know how much I loved you.

Grandpa.

January 23, 1996

Drummers marched to traveling music

PAINTED SHUT.

He is standing alone in front of a little railroad station, maybe Las Animas. His right hand is in his pocket and his left is behind him. He is wearing a a snappy three-piece suit and high-top shoes. His head is cocked, and there is a big grin on his face.

It is a photograph of my father, Frank Amole. I carry it with me because that is the way I want to remember him, even though I never saw him that way. The year was 1921, two years before I was born. He didn't have a care in the world. World War I was over. He was out of the Army, single, and the Great Depression was still eight years down the road.

230

Pop was a traveling salesman, a member of a tight fraternity of guys who "made the territory" by train. They preferred to think of themselves as "agents," a small step up from being peddlers. They not only marketed their products in small towns, but they also brought with them the style of the big city, technological marvels and the humor of their trade.

There's no telling how many bawdy traveling salesman jokes there were. They usually involved a gullible farmer, his nubile daughter and a stack of hay. The agents would gather in the lobby of small hotels at night to swap stories and to make out their "swindle sheet" expense accounts.

There was a lot of truth in Arthur Miller's masterpiece, *Death of a Salesman,* but it wasn't the whole truth. Sure, there was tragedy and hopelessness as Willy Loman tried to maintain his dignity, his job and his family, but there was horseplay and fun in their lives, too.

They spoke in colorful metaphors, often related to trains because that's the way they traveled. The weather would be "hotter than a depot stove." If someone were frugal, he was "tighter than a Pullman window." Anyone who has ever tried to open a painted-shut Pullman window understands that.

If something smelled bad, it would "stink a dog off a gut wagon." If the weather was chilly, it was "colder than a well digger's (heh, heh) lunch." If someone's behavior was strange, he was "crazier than a peach-orchard bull." Pop would often say to me, "I'll knock you for a row of Hungarian succotash bowls." Shooting craps, I can almost hear Pop talking to the dice, "Drive up, Wilbur!"

There was no Damon Runyon or John Steinbeck to write about them, but they were an important part of the great American adventure. Most of them were loyal to their employers, loyal to a fault sometimes.

Pop would almost lie down and die for General Motors, but GM broke his heart. He would have understood the anger and hurt being experienced today by workers who have been "downsized," "restructured" and "outcontracted."

The Depression was a terrible time for him. We had to move in with my grandparents. He walked across town every day, looking for work. He had holes in his shoes, holes my mother would try to patch each morning with cutout cardboard.

When he couldn't face life anymore, he stayed in the attic, coming downstairs only for meals. My mother would take me upstairs every day to see him, hoping I would somehow cheer him up.

I can still see the despair on his face. It will be burned in my memory the rest of my life. But I carry this old picture to remember him when his future seemed bright and promising. I also carry it because I loved him, and I miss him even though he has been dead for 20 years.

June 16, 1996

Happy, uh ... whatever it was

CHUCKHOLES.

Do you want to know what a two-time loser is? I'm a two-time loser. Boy, am I ever! Maybe it's memory loss, hardening of the arteries or the first stage of senility, but I forgot our wedding anniversary for the second year in a row.

Last year it was especially humiliating because it was our 30th. If you forget all other anniversaries, you ought to try to remember the ones that end with a zero. But I didn't. Slipped my mind completely.

I'd vowed never to let it happen again, ever. However, last Sunday Trish said to me, "Well, here it is July 14 and it's Bastille Day."

"So it is," I said and then began to sing, "*Allons enfants de la patrie, le jour de gloire est arrive* ... " I missed the hint entirely. Our wedding anniversary is July 15, the next day.

If you're wondering how I could possibly remember the words to the French national anthem but forget my wedding anniversary, so am I. That night after work, Trish asked me how things went that day.

"OK," I said. "Just the usual Monday stuff. Had to crank out another column. And you?"

"You don't know what the date is, do you?" she said. Then it hit me. I felt awful. Trying to recover my shattered dignity, I said, "You forgot it, too?"

"No," she replied with that little bemused smile on her face.

When you're my age, the first things to go are your knees, followed by other infirmities I'd rather not discuss. The memory is next. You can't remember the name of your best friend. I've lost track of the

232

number of times I've blacked out in front of the ATM machine and couldn't remember my PIN number.

Phone numbers that I used to remember I can't anymore. If I write down a phone number, I forget to write down whose number it is.

I am a victim of what Suzanne Weiss calls Newsheimer's disease, the inability to remember what I wrote yesterday. Heck, there are only 10 columns anyhow and the rest are all variations of the original 10.

Ernest Hemingway once made that observation about plots for novels. Maybe that explains why he blew off his head with a shotgun. As Archie Goodwin once said about boredom, in a Nero Wolfe mystery, "I spent two hours trying to figure out a third way to cross my legs."

So much for my apology. Better late than never, I thought, so I sent flowers the next day, one rose for each of the last 31 years.

Trish deserves more than flowers for putting up with me for that long, but then I didn't promise her a rose garden, just roses a day late, I guess. Still, there ought to be more to her life than watching me watch the Rockies on TV.

There is, of course. We have our little grandson, Jacob, to enjoy. Trish's work is gratifying, too. She is volunteer coordinator for Lutheran Medical Center Hospice. Most families who have had hospice care for loved ones as they approach death know how important that work is.

She doesn't find it depressing, though. As a once-and-always registered nurse (she denies the "always" part), Trish is a sensitive caregiver. The degree she was awarded, *magna cum laude* in behavioral sciences, has been a valued resource for her, particularly in dealing with me.

I'm truly sorry I forgot again this year. I know, the road to you-know-where is paved with good intentions. It's just that there are a lot of chuckholes in mine.

Anyhow, Trish, thanks for everything.

July 21, 1996

233

Delivering baby is the easy part

KITTENS.

Artur Rubinstein played impeccable Chopin well into his 80s. George Burns was a hoot in his 90s. And a 63-year-old California woman gave birth to a healthy child. Why? Did she lack fulfillment in her life? Doesn't she understand there is more to parenting than just conceiving? That's the easy part.

What about older men? Are they procreating just to prove they can? Maybe it's a macho thing. I remember a Ronald Reagan news conference in which he bragged that he was still good in bed.

It's a safe bet that an infant daughter made 65-year-old Clint Eastwood's day. Another member of the SOD (Start-Over-Dads) club is Anthony Quinn, who is 78 and has a new daughter. Author George Plimpton is 69 and the father of infant twins. At 77, Tony Randall, is so pleased with his new daughter that he says he wants more.

What an ego boost for aging celebrities to become fathers late in life. That's always good for a Page 1 photo on the *National Enquirer* and grist for the celebrity tabloid TV shows.

Or maybe they are just trying to revisit their youth. There is an awkward point in an actor's life when he's too old to be a leading man and not old enough to be a character actor.

But wait a minute, what about the babies who did not ask for fathers too old to watch them grow up and play important roles in their lives? Were they conceived only to validate their fathers' fading libido?

Maybe not, though. Of course these old guys genuinely love these little tykes when they are born. It's difficult not to love a baby. But that moment is frozen in time. Surely you remember the old saying "The trouble with kittens is they become cats."

In all of the news coverage about the woman in California who had a baby at the age of 63, the emphasis seemed to be on the woman. Not much was said about the baby, only that it was healthy. In this country and others, the issue seemed to be that having a child is a woman's right regardless of age.

OK, but should she? At some point we have to ask whether it is a baby's right to have parents who can nurture her and care for her until she is an adult. Will Randall, Quinn, Plimpton and that lady in California be around to care for those children in their teen years when enlightened parental guidance is so important?

I was 42 when my younger daughter was born. And I have to tell you that there were more than a few times I was taken for her grandfather. At PTA meetings and father-daughter nights at school, I was always the oldest guy in the room. It all worked out fine. I wondered at the time, though, how it would be if I were 10 years older.

Many people have children for the wrong reasons. Babies are not toys. A baby is not a possession, not someone to fill a void in your life, like a cat or a dog. How often do we hear about people trapped in an unhappy marriage deciding to have a baby to bring them together again?

What a terrible responsibility for a tiny baby. Of course there is a lot of gratification in bringing a child into the world, but the parents don't own the child. They are charged with the awesome responsibility of raising it. Parenting is the world's toughest job.

You don't learn what mistakes you have made until it is too late to change them. *May 1, 1997*

Put water bag on front bumper

FILTHY.

Have frequent-flier miles ended the great American tradition of packing the family in a station wagon for the annual pilgrimage to Disneyland? It is a great test of endurance to separate the men from the boys and the girls from the women.

It is also an opportunity to show the little brats that there is more to America than airports. Really, now, if you have seen one baggage carousel, you have seen them all. There is only one way to see this great nation of ours and that is get down and dirty on the highway.

Remember when you boomers were really baby boomers, and your mom and dad hauled you down Route 66 to Kingman and Barstow and San Bernardino? Don't forget Winona. Does that old Nat "King" Cole melody run through your mind about getting your kicks on Route 66?

Of course the kids get restless after two hours on the road. Can you still hear their little voices asking, "Are we there yet?" Why is it impossible to get them all to go to the bathroom at the same time? Maybe it's because their little bladders are not the same size.

"Dad, I have to go NOW! I can't wait until we get to the next filthy station." And so you look for a bush, a tree, a rock, anywhere a little kid can answer the call of nature with some degree of privacy. And then, out of nowhere, cars start streaming by just as your little girl starts to squat. They honk, point and whistle. You swear and give them the old one-finger salute. Your little girl cries and you give her a candy bar.

I suspect the interstate highway system has taken all the joy out of driving the family to California. You don't really see America on what truckers call "the big slab." It's one big, green sign after another. You could be anywhere. You miss all those little rattlesnake farms, "last chance" gas stations and Stuckey curio stores. And on the car radio you hear "Drop-Kick Me, Jesus, Through the Goal Posts of Life."

Remember to keep a damp washcloth in a plastic baggie on the dashboard. The sun will keep it warm. You'll need it when they splatter their snow cones all over the back seat. Play the old alphabet game with them. Get them to holler out the first letter of something they see along the highway. "Daddy, he's cheating. I saw the 'H' for horse before he did."

Always, ALWAYS check into a motel with a swimming pool by 3 P.M. The pool serves two purposes: It gets them clean and tired at the same time. If they still aren't tired, let them bounce up and down on the beds as though they were trampolines.

Never bring along clothes that can't be washed in a laundromat. Bring along a dirty clothes bag. Be sure you have a roll of paper towels in your car at all times. Same thing with toilet paper. There are never enough paper towels or toilet paper.

Don't be too disappointed if they are bored by Monument Valley, the Petrified Forest and the Pacific Coast Highway near San Simeon. They want to go on the Matterhorn roller coaster at Disneyland over and over and over again until you are ready to pitch your cookies.

If you are traveling alone with your kids, have a rotation system figured out so that each kid gets to sit up front with you for 100 miles. Put him or her in charge of the styrofoam cooler with the pop inside. When I was driving, I referred to the kid up front as the "Coke pilot."

That's about it, folks. This is stuff Dr. Spock won't tell you.

June 24, 1997

REPRISE: FINDING THE
MEANING OF LOVE

After major surgery, News *columnist Gene Amole opens the book on his life*

WHERE AM I? HOW DID I GET HERE?

The room was dark, and yet I could see deep into the past. It was so real I wanted to reach out to touch the brass Tiffany lamp on the dining room table. I could smell Grandpa's honest sweat when he came home from work at the Union Depot. I could hear Galli-Curci's voice from the wind-up Victrola in the living room.

My memories began 70 years ago. There in the dark, they were so sharp, so clear, so vivid. I wondered if somehow the past had become the present. Was I living then, or now?

"Will any aide please come to the nursing station," a woman's distant voice whispered in the night. I opened my eyes and thought I was in Mexico. It must have been something about the ceiling that reminded me of a place I knew in Mexico years ago. A man's face appeared above me. "Are you all right? Can I get you anything?" he asked.

"Some water, please," I mumbled through my dry mouth.

Then I remembered I was at Porter Memorial Hospital. I was admitted early May 9 for reconstructive neck surgery that I hoped would end more than a year of unrelenting, hard pain. Certainly I was no stranger at Porter. Over the years, I had back, knee, stomach, lung, eye and prostate surgery there. I knew many of the nurses by name. "They ought to name a wing after you," they would say.

The past year has been difficult. My neck pain was so severe I was no longer able to drive to work. I had to depend on my wife, Trish, and my son, Brett, to get me there. An X-ray examination last summer indicated that discs separating the fourth and fifth vertebrae and the fifth and sixth had deteriorated and should be surgically replaced with a fusion, utilizing bone from the bone bank.

Neurological surgery was performed in September. I wore a rigid cervical collar of heavy plastic and steel for the next six weeks. I was told it was called a "Philadelphia Collar." This, of course, reminded me of the epitaph W.C. Fields wrote for himself, "I would rather be living in Philadelphia." What a glorious day it was when it finally came off! But my relief from pain was temporary. It became intolerable again.

I was unable to sleep in a bed. I made the rounds of physical, massage and osteopathic therapists with only marginal relief. I went to a pain clinic where I received steroid injections. I was told that a "pain block" procedure was risky and might damage the spinal cord. I was popping pain pills at night but trying to avoid them in the daytime at work.

I reluctantly ordered a recliner chair. Trish and I picked out one we thought didn't look like a recliner, sort of. I didn't like the idea of being an old grouch like Frasier Crain's father in the TV show, gimping around on an aluminum cane and frumping down in a rump-sprung old recliner.

It was March, and spring was here! I began to take notice of grape locusts pushing up through the black earth. Trish loved standing on the back deck with her binoculars, sweeping the horizon in search of "her" blue heron that must have nested in the cottonwoods along Bear Creek. The pain was constant. My chin dropped, and I was no longer able to shave my neck with a blade.

All that seemed unimportant the Sunday morning I awakened to find I couldn't brush my teeth, or button my shirt, or do much of anything with my hands. Before I called the doctor, I sat down at my computer and tried to write my name. I couldn't. My fingers flopped helplessly on the keys. It was an agonizing moment. Those of us who follow the writing craft, whether as journeyman, poet, famous novelist or local newspaper columnist, think through our fingers. I wondered if this was the end of it for me. I knew it was a stroke even before I was admitted (again) at old Porter Hospital.

This time I was on the fourth floor where stroke patients and others with physical disabilities were given rehabilitation therapy. Slowly, control was returning to my hands. People reassured me that even though I might not ever be able to write again, I could "speak" my columns into new voice-recognition computers. I gave up trying to explain that there is no way in the world I could "speak" my column.

Yes, I write for the ear. I want readers to "hear" my voice as they read my words. But the process, for me, is a painstaking one. The words just don't spill out. In his book *PrairyErth,* William Least Heat-Moon likens writing to stone masonry. It's a matter of chipping away at stone/words until they fit with as much precision as possible. Poet Thomas Hornsby Ferril made a similar observation about his work, noting that the ancient Greek word for poetry also means "building." Certainly my modest literary skills are not on a par with his or Heat-Moon's, but I employ their methodology.

And so rambling into voice-recognition computer technology is not even an option. We have come to believe, wrongly in my estimation, that there is a technological solution to every problem. Because of my stroke, I write more slowly now than before, sometimes rewriting a word several times until I get it right.

Regaining manual skills after a stroke involves constant repetition of finger exercises. The smallest tasks can be maddening. At the "stroke table" in Porter's rehabilitation dining room, we laughed at each other trying to open those little cellophane packs of two soda crackers. Same thing with small containers of jelly and margarine. I must say, though, that even under the best of circumstances, getting the cellophane pack open without crumbling the crackers is a daunting task for anyone. Nabisco should find a better way.

For more than a year, I had difficulty swallowing food and liquids. An upper GI (gastrointestinal) examination was ordered to determine why. It involves drinking phosphorescent barium while being examined by X-ray. I had hardly taken a sip of the chalky stuff when the technician rushed out of her protected control booth to ask me a startling question: "Did you ever break your neck?"

When I told her I hadn't, she told me not to move but to remain seated. Other technicians were summoned. I couldn't see them, but I could hear them whispering anxiously about what they had seen.

The hurried conference ended, and I was wheelchaired back to my room. Word of what had happened had already reached the fourth floor, and the nurses and aides were ready for me. I was helped back into bed. The side rails went up and I was told I couldn't leave my bed under any circumstances. Moments later, the physician in charge of Porter's rehabilitation department arrived to tell me the neurosurgeon who had performed the original discectomy fusion procedure had been summoned from her office at the Swedish Medical Center complex.

She arrived about 20 minutes later and informed me that the fusion had failed and that I would have to undergo orthopedic reconstructive surgery on my neck. The hated cervical collar went back around my neck, but I was permitted to get out of bed and move around. After all, I had been walking around for months in this condition, and a little while longer wouldn't matter that much. "I told them your head won't fall off," she said.

Also in attendance was the neurologist in charge of my stroke therapy. "Let's do the surgery now and get it over with. I'm already here," I said to her with only a feeble attempt to conceal my growing impatience with what was happening to me.

I had to keep reminding myself that I am a 74-year-old man and that body parts do wear out. I was shown the X-rays, and my neck was indeed a mess. In doctor talk, the fusion had "spit the plugs," which meant that the two bone implants had just popped out. They were about the size of .38-caliber bullets. It was too risky to leave them there. If bone fragments were to make their way into the spinal canal, I could be in real trouble.

"Surgery is not possible now, not at least for six weeks," my neurologist said. She explained that my blood was being thinned by medication so that clots wouldn't form, causing me to have another stroke, possibly a life-threatening one or one that would leave me severely debilitated. My stroke therapy continued for several more days, and I was released from the hospital.

I went back to work immediately. My son Brett picked me up to take me to work every day. There was no way I was going to sit around the house for six weeks worrying about what was going to happen to me. Even so, I felt badly about missing all the time at work. I offered several times to retire, but the good old *Rocky* stood by me and told me they wanted me to resume my column when I could.

Certainly, my columns are not literature, but they were wonderful therapy for me. "They keep me off the street," I like to say. I can't recall much of what I wrote about during this period, but they got me through what seemed at the time like an endless waiting period. I returned to Porter at 6:30 A.M. May 9, and I entered the operating room at 8:30 A.M.

As consciousness gradually returned that night, I became aware that my neck pain was gone, completely. I cautiously moved my right shoulder. No pain. But there was intense pain in my left hip. Then I remembered. The reconstructive surgery involved removing a large piece of bone from my pelvis and using it to fuse the vertebrae together. I tried feebly to sing to myself: "De hip bone's connected to de neck bone. Dem bones, dem bones, dem dry bones." The bone is being held in place with a titanium plate screwed to the vertebrae. It will always remain there.

The next morning, I was returned to the fourth-floor rehabilitation wing, where I had to learn to walk all over again; how to sit down and stand up; how to use a walker and then a cane; how to get in and out of a car; how to go up and down stairs; how to sit down on a toilet and get in and out of a bathtub; how to do so many little physical things I had always taken for granted.

The pain in my pelvis was nearly as bad as the pain in my neck had been. I was kept under constant medication for pain control. I still am. Several times a day, nurses would ask me to rate my pain on a scale of one to 10. Trying to be a hero, I said, "Eight," but it felt more like a 12. Finally, when they would ask me I would say, "It only hurts when I laugh."

The therapists were patient but firm. Porter, like all other hospitals, is struggling with the challenge of changes in the health-care industry, and an "industry" I am afraid it is becoming. Porter is not out to make money, but it must compete with for-profit hospitals. Insurance companies call the shots, and sometimes their aim is poor. Patient census can vary greatly every day. A wing is full one day, empty the next. Porter's staff is constantly challenged to meet these changing conditions. I marvel at their ability to do so.

A young woman gave me my first bath. I would guess her age at about 22. She wheeled me to the shower room on a chair contraption with an open toilet seat. She managed to get that damnable surgical gown and my undershorts off me. Then she lathered me up and hosed me down as she would a cocker spaniel. Believe me, I have no secrets from her.

Through the long nights, a large woman helped me to the bathroom, measured my urine, took me back to bed and packed my pelvis incision with ice. What humble work that is, and yet she did it with dignity and care.

And then there was the young immigrant from Poland. He had studied medicine there but has been unable to be admitted to medical school in this country. He gave up trying, is now married with two children and plays in a rock band on weekends. Maybe he'll look at a nursing career, he says.

Many of the aides have medical-school aspirations, like the young Korean-American aide who works weekends while he attends the University of Colorado at Boulder. He worries about being admitted to a good school after he gets his B.S. degree.

A Jewish mother at a Seventh-day Adventist hospital? Yes, and what a wonderful nurse she is. I had known her during my previous stays at Porter. Actually, she isn't old enough to be my mother. She is young enough to be my daughter. A little gold Star of David is always around her neck. She has a son and a daughter who are both college students, and she is proud of the literary skills they have developed. "When they were kids," she said, "I would take them to the Tattered Cover and let them choose any books they wanted to read. I didn't care what they were. They both are wonderful readers."

My primary-care doctor is Jeanne Day Seibert. She was a registered nurse before becoming a physician. Dr. Cynthia Norrgran did the original neurological surgery and assisted in the reconstructive orthopedic surgery performed by Dr. George A. Frey. His physician assistant was Mike Murphy. Dr. Jane A. Burnham was the neurologist. Dr. Richard D. Mountain supervised my pulmonary care. I am grateful to all of them.

I'm home now and back in my beloved recliner. I still haven't been able to sleep in a bed, but that will come. I am taking 15 prescription medications, some of them several times a day. I am still being treated for coronary-artery disease, peripheral neuropathy and a bad stomach. My pulmonary fibrosis is still in remission, but I remain partially dependent on oxygen.

Wait a minute, here! What the hell is this, an old man whining about his aches and pains?

No.

This is a celebration. I'm glad it happened. I rejoice that I had the pain, and given the choice, I would endure it again, in a heartbeat. The experience transformed me as nothing else ever has. At the center of it is the love of my family. It wasn't just passive devotion. During those long, stressful days, my daughters, Tustin and Susan, and my sons, Brett and Jon, came to the hospital every day and told me they loved me. Their declaration had a profound effect on me.

In all our years of marriage, I have never felt closer to Trish. It was something in her eyes as she said good night to me. If there is such a thing as a Medal of Honor for wives, she deserves one.

Why now? Much of it had to do with my nightly journeys into the past. I would lie there in the dark, tethered to an IV pole and a urine bag and let my mind find its way through all I could remember from those childhood days on West Maple Avenue to the present. I have had a wonderful life, not always an easy one, but one that has left me with few experiences I would change.

Yes, the Great Depression years were an ordeal for my family. Each time I hear complaints from some young people that they may not have enough money to retire, I remember that cold day in Casper, Wyo., when I was a child. My father had lost his job, and the three of us sat around the kitchen table, looking gravely at a single can of soup, all that we had to eat. We came back to Denver and moved in with Grandpa and Grandma on West Maple. Mom was able to get spot work in the Denver Public Schools as a substitute teacher for $5 a day.

I can still close my eyes and see her every morning cutting out cardboard insoles for my father's shoes. He would walk downtown every day looking for work, but the jobs were not there. He'd come home at night, terribly discouraged. Because there was a shortage of sleeping space, he slept on an old bed in the attic. He wouldn't come down for days. My mother would take me up the back stairs every day to try to cheer him up, but he would just lie there, looking at nothing, saying nothing.

Things got better. We moved from West Maple to South Emerson and then to other houses in south Denver. My mother continued to teach, and Pop found work as a salesman in the wholesale automobile-parts business.

Both had come from blue-collar families and wanted to better themselves for their sake and mine. My mother's father had been a farmer in Ohio until my uncle contracted tuberculosis, forcing the family to come to Colorado for the dry air. Grandpa Wilson worked as a foreman on a sheep ranch and later was town marshal in Montrose and was driver of the express-company horse and wagon.

Grandpa Amole had run away from home in Ohio when he was 15 and made his way to Denver. He worked a lot of jobs in town and eventually set out to try to find gold in Victor and Cripple Creek. He became involved in a labor dispute that almost killed him. Colorado militiamen ambushed him one night, tied him to a tree and whipped him until they thought he was dead. But he lived and carried scars on his back and in his gray eyes until he died in 1948 at the age of 86.

I loved Grandpa and he loved me. He was a tough, honest, profane man, a socialist and an atheist, but he was wonderful to me. I can't recall ever seeing any affection between Grandma and Grandpa, though. They both openly expressed love for me, and in the night there at Porter I wondered if maybe they were devoted to each other through me. I don't know. I never understood what they saw in each other. She was refined, well-educated, a Christian Scientist. My mother said it probably had been a marriage of convenience, common in those days.

My parents often expressed love and affection to each other. There was no lack of that in our house. They were devoted to me and would do without so I could have more. They were selfless, caring parents. Even so, I was never a demonstrative person. I guess I was embarrassed, too shy. During one night at Porter, I realized I had never told either of them that I loved them. Not once. God, how I regret that now. It would have meant so much to them. I loved them, but I never said so as my children had said to me.

Why am I writing this now?

Partly for myself. Certainly for my family. I also had time at Porter for some long-delayed introspection. I needed to confront my mortality. Time is running out, and I realized how important it is for me to take stock of "where I am, and how did I get here."

As a combat soldier during World War II, I learned to live my life one day at a time. The meaning of life was never a great philosophical mystery to me. Life is to live, and that's what I have done. In the process, though, I have taken much for granted, too much. Yes, I have worked hard all my life, and I realize now what a great gift work is. I live to work.

I was always a poor student, finishing high school in the bottom third of my class. My parents scrimped and saved to send me to the University of Colorado. I flunked out after a year. It was a terrible disappointment to my parents. All these years later, I realize what a mistake it was for me not to go back to school under the GI Bill and get a degree. I was afraid I would never get back my old job as a radio announcer.

How fortunate, though, I have been in pursuing my career in radio and television and at the *Rocky Mountain News*! It's not that there wasn't a lot of blind luck involved, too.

The most fortunate thing that ever happened to me was to become a partner with my dear friend Ed Koepke. We began our broadcasting careers at about the same time, he as an engineer and I as an announcer.

We struck out on our own in 1956. We had no money but believed in ourselves. In the 30 years that followed, we built, owned and operated three radio stations and a background-music company. We also published a magazine. Others in the trade were fond of saying, "Koepke's got the brains, Amole's got the mouth." He's retired now, and he and his wife, Cordy, enjoy traveling and watching their grandchildren grow up.

There is a large get-well card on the wall here in my study at home. It was drawn by my old pal Ed Stein, whose cartoon strip, *Denver Square,* is becoming so popular. The card is a drawing of the *Rocky Mountain News* building. It is split right down the middle. One reporter says to another in what is left of the newsroom, "Apparently the whole place is held together by Gene Amole," which, of course, is ridiculous. It is held together by so many talented people. The card is signed by more than 100 of my pals, whom I dearly love.

I have no idea how much, if any, of this will be published. If it is, I hope other older people, who lack my forum, will see something of themselves in it. I hope, too, that their children will think about how important it is to express their love, as my children have to me.

It will be a while before I regain my health. I have lost 40 pounds, but I am determined to get out and around again. I want to take Trish on a nice trip somewhere. I want to walk along Bear Creek with my little grandson, Jacob. I want to experience again my beloved bright, blue October. So many blessings, so much love in my life.

Tomorrow?

Tomorrow, I'm going back to work.

June 15, 1997